Politics and Human Nature

Politics and
Human Nature

Edited by
Ian Forbes and Steve Smith

Frances Pinter (Publishers), London

© Ian Forbes and Steve Smith 1983

First published in Great Britain in 1983 by
Frances Pinter (Publishers) Limited
5 Dryden Street, London WC2E 9NW

British Library Cataloguing in Publication Data

Politics and human nature
   1. Political science
   I. Forbes, Ian   II. Smith, Steve
   320'.01   JA71
   ISBN 0-86187-331-9

Typeset by Joshua Associates, Oxford
Printed by Biddles Ltd., Guildford, Surrey

To
Connie and Chris

Contents

Preface

Rousseau hoped to have found in *Le Contrat Social* a legitimate and stable basis of government, 'taking men as they are and laws as they might be.' He opened by asserting that 'man is born free and everywhere he is in chains.' That is already more than observation could possibly establish. Like others before and since, he was deeply involved with a theory of human nature and his famous conclusions relied on a legitimate and stable basis in metaphysics. In this he was being neither careless nor prescientific. No doubt his particular version can be disputed. But all political and social theorists, I venture to claim, depend on some model of man in explaining what moves people and accounts for institutions. Such models are sometimes hidden but never absent, and the rise of behavioural political science has only enriched the stock. There is no more central or pervasive topic in the study of politics.

So this volume is much to be welcomed. The authors explore the theme, as one might expect, among Utopian thinkers and those with visions of a better political order. But they find it also in works of seemingly neutral analysis and in the study of practical affairs, like work, war or bureaucracy. Hume once remarked rashly, 'mankind are so much the same, in all times and places, that history informs us of nothing new or strange in this particular.' The authors here are not of that opinion, but they insist all the same that there is more to human nature, even in its historically conditioned aspect, than local variations. The editors point up motifs and questions most instructively, and summary is best left to them.

I am pleased to be able to give the book a personal welcome, too. The lively Politics scene at the University of East Anglia owes much to both editors, to Graeme Duncan and John Street and, at an earlier stage, Vincent Geoghegan. Their enthusiasm for the topic of human nature is no trick of the pen and their interest in it is shared by colleagues in other disciplines. That is a local fact but one with wider import and the book will, I am sure, find readers beyond the confines of Politics. The themes, which the editors dissect and all the contributors amply demonstrate, are of general importance for the social sciences. The book is timely and I am very happy to wish it well.

Martin Hollis

School of Economic and Social Studies
University of East Anglia

Acknowledgements

This volume grew out of a panel, convened by Graeme Duncan, for the 1982 Annual Conference of the Political Studies Association. Six of the papers (those by Forbes, Smart, Stafford, Nicholson, Street and Smith) were presented at that conference and the authors would like to thank those who commented on their papers. The remaining chapters were solicited by the editors from those who attended the panel's meetings.

The editors would like to thank June Dunnett and Anne Martin for typing the final manuscript, often under unreasonable deadlines and nearly always from unreadable drafts. Finally, they would like to thank Connie Forbes and Chris Kinrade for so cheerfully putting up with two individuals who clearly exhibited the worst aspects of human nature.

Introduction

STEVE SMITH

The focus of this volume is on the concept of human nature and its role in politics. It is essential, at the start of this volume, to make one assumption explicit, and this is that the concept of human nature is central to political discourse and analysis. Political argument, just as much as political activity, involves a conception of what is involved in being human. However, this assumption does not imply another, although virtually all those who have a notion of human nature would wish that it did; this would be that the conceptions of human nature involved in political argument are coherent. As the contents of this volume make only too clear, such coherence is rare.

Hence the central rationale for the volume is that the concept of human nature underpins political analysis. Whilst this may be made very explicit in some accounts of political behaviour (see, for example, Chapter 5 of this volume), it has to be teased out of many more (see Chapter 2). Thus, even when an explicit theory of human nature is not present, this does not mean that no conception of human nature underpins or is prior to analysis. Furthermore, such conceptions, whether explicit or implicit, are very often internally contradictory. Just as Marx's and Mill's views of human nature are to a large extent incompatible, so are there serious contradictions in the view of human nature put forward by each of them. Many of the chapters in this volume seek to clarify the views of human nature held by individual thinkers.

Essentially there are two uses of the term 'human nature' in this volume, in the sense that the writers analysed tend (often unconsciously) to use the term in two distinct ways: the first refers to human nature as that basic set of intrinsic characteristics revealed by various aspects of our behaviour. Thus it is a commonplace to hear in political argument the claim that people cannot be changed because their human nature is of a certain, and fixed, manner. Although this tends to be a conservative view of society and individuals, it is nevertheless a very common perspective. It is seen as limiting change and as compelling certain, usually restrictive, social arrangements. Liberals and socialists, on the other hand, tend to adopt a rather different usage of human nature, in that they speak of it as a matter of essence or potential. Thus for them political discourse concerns an evaluation of existing or proposed political arrangements in terms of an *a priori* human nature. It is exactly this process that allows Marx to criticize capitalism and propose certain arrangements for the organization of society so as to allow human beings to behave in a manner which does not, for the first time in history, go against their nature.

These two conceptions of human nature are not mutually exclusive, since many writers use aspects of each in various parts of their work. Thus a conservative writer might assert that social change is undesirable since it conflicts with what human nature so obviously is, as revealed by past behaviour, yet at another time he might argue that certain laws (for example, economic ones) prevent human beings from reaching their potential. Such a contrast is clearest in those writers who assert that human nature prevents certain kinds of changes and yet claim that society must allow areas of human nature to flourish. However, this confusion is much more widespread, if less obvious, than this. As many of the chapters in this volume show all too clearly, many thinkers do not adopt a consistent view of human nature, nor is their view necessarily an explicit one.

The reader of this volume may well expect to find a common usage or definition of human nature in the various chapters. As should be clear from the above, this is not possible for the simple reason that those who write about human nature do so with a bewildering variety of definitions, and all too often without any at all. Human nature becomes the untestable bedrock of many theories of politics; its presence can be assumed, its effects can be asserted, and yet it is only rarely made explicit or, in any sense, justified by reference to empirical criteria. In this way, human nature can be a powerful theoretical term, without any prospect of testing against the evidence. Of course, when any attempt is made to subject the concept to any testing, just what the evidence is (as distinct from what is irrelevant evidence) becomes the battleground.

So, if there is not just one definition of the term in this volume, how can the term be usefully employed? Why spend time examining the concept and its role in political argument if it is not possible to agree on one definition? The answer is twofold; on the one hand, we are concerned to see the role that the concept plays in various theories of politics. This is not so that we can take the various uses and arrive at some kind of synthesis; rather, we are concerned to focus on one concept and examine a variety of theories in the light of it, to see just what role it plays, for example, as a theoretical notion. On the other hand, examining an individual thinker's view of human nature, or the writings of specialists in a particular issue-area, allows us to see how consistent is the view of human nature adopted. Exactly because the term is so handy, in that it can be asserted without definition, so it can be used in a variety of ways in different parts of a theory.

If a single definition of human nature is not the goal of this volume, what does it hope to achieve? The major aim is to illustrate, for a variety of individual thinkers and traditions and for a number of specific issue-areas, the way the concept of human nature is used. This does not lead us to a kind of relativism, in that such a focus allows, indeed impels, us to discuss the ways in which we can judge various conceptions of human nature. The most obvious is also the least helpful; that is, to confront the various views of human nature with the 'facts'. Unfortunately, such an enterprise is doomed from the start, since there exists no neutral body of empirical material that lends itself to being divided into facts and irrelevant pieces of information. As has been noted already, what is evidence for one view of human nature is irrelevant for another, especially when one view is based on human nature as revealed by behaviour and the other is based on values. Imagine a conversation between a Skinnerian and a Freudian; not only would they disagree about what human nature was, and what the implications of this were for politics, but they would also not see the same world of facts. Indeed, what would be central to the Freudian would not even be relevant for the Skinnerian. Now, there are ways of comparing the two views, in terms of the explanatory power of rival research frameworks, but this is by no means a straightforward procedure in which the means chosen are in some way neutral.

What can be attempted, though, is to examine each theory of politics to see two things: first, what is the view of human nature adopted in the theory; second, to see what role human nature plays in the theory. At this point, the conception of human nature can be examined in the following manner:

(a) Is the view of human nature logically consistent, or are different (and possibly mutually exclusive) conceptions utilized in various parts of the theory?

(b) Is the conception of human nature explicit or implicit?

(c) If explicit, is the conception of human nature supported by evidence? If so, is this evidence compatible with other (non-utilized) conceptions of human nature?

(d) If the conception of human nature is implicit, is it supported by any evidence or is it merely stated *a priori*?

(e) Does the role played by human nature in the theory follow logically from the way it is defined? Or is its role unrelated to its definition, and perhaps consistent with other definitions?

(f) What are the political implications of the view of human nature contained in the theory? Do those implications necessarily follow from that view?

Such an examination would allow for an analysis of the role played by the concept of human nature in particular theories of politics. In discriminating between theories, the concept is useful since it allows us to examine the extent to which the usage satisfies the above criteria. Quite evidently, many of the views of human nature examined in this volume do not satisfy these criteria: some are simply inaccurate, in that they are based on incorrect evidence; but the majority suffer from more subtle problems, for example the relationship between the role of the concept and its definition.

Above all then, this volume is concerned to examine the role that the concept of human nature plays in accounts of political behaviour. This reflects our initial assumption, that the concept is a central, if often an implicit, one. In teasing out the reliance of various theories on conceptions of human nature, this volume seeks to achieve two further goals: first, to show how important a view of human nature may be in any theory of politics; second, to illustrate how the concept may be used to hide untestable and highly controversial assumptions, which then, by the intervening variable of a concept of human nature, critically affect conclusions and prescriptions.

The organization of this volume reflects the two most obvious areas in which the concept of human nature is used in political argument. First, Chapters 2–6 examine various thinkers and traditions in terms of the role played by, and the nature of their account of, human nature in their theories. The second area of usage concerns the role played by the concept of human nature in the analysis of various issue-areas. Chapters 7–11 examine a selection of such areas. Finally, the various individual chapters are sandwiched between a chapter by Graeme Duncan, which examines the uses of the concept of human nature in political argument, and a concluding chapter by Ian Forbes, which summarizes the major findings of the individual chapters in terms of more general arguments about human nature. What we hope emerges from this volume is not so much a clearer conception of what human nature is as an understanding of the role such conceptions play in accounts of politics, and an ability to commence the lengthy journey of choosing between rival accounts of what our nature entails.

1 Political theory and human nature

GRAEME DUNCAN

Discussion of human nature has a shifting place in the formal discourse of philosophers and political scientists. Sometimes it is popular and overt, at others it is dismissed with contempt, or buried. The dismissive tendency is represented in the views that theories of human nature are a soft segment of both political theory and its less sophisticated half-brother, ordinary political argument, and are irrelevant to political science. Yet ordinary speech and practice contain their own conceptions of human nature. However, according to linguistic analysis, Marxist and other theories of ideology, and empirical political science (especially behavioural), such conceptions belong only to the area of subjectivity, unprovable assumption, wish fulfilment or empty assertiveness. If there are no objective or neutral or value-free criteria in a world of diverse values and selections of fact, one may be tempted by the nihilistic and false conclusion that one man's snarl, shout, whine—or taste or preference—is as good as another. From some other, perhaps overlapping, perspectives, such as anti-communism or anti-extremism, discussion of human nature may seem wild Utopianism, and ultimately madness. From the other side, too, there are characteristic doubts, as 'human nature' seems commonly a politically conservative notion, useful for dismissing schemes of reconstruction.

It is clearly difficult to establish what kind of an object of enquiry human nature is, and the methods and criteria by which a particular account of it might be supported or attacked. But even if some so-called facts of human nature might be expressed bettter as facts about society or about particular human beings, even if there are doubts over what the notion properly comprehends, and even if arguments about human nature remain ultimately indeterminate, the issue remains central in political theory and cannot be simply thrown aside. So, what kind of thing is this human nature, about which there is so much loose talk and so much real disagreement? What part does it play in social and political theories, and how might we discriminate between, and defend and assault, different accounts of it?

At the centre of political theory lies the effort to establish a relationship between human nature, however that is conceived, and the state (or whatever formal authority relationships are deemed necessary), and to recommend specific programmes or courses of action on that basis. The advocacy which is inseparable from political theory rests primarily on assumptions about powers and limits of people in the worlds in which they find, or might find, themselves. Crudely, a view of human nature is a view of what people actually or normally are, as they exist (Burke or Freud); or what they truly, distinctively or ideally are (Aristotle); or what they are potentially (Marx or Marcuse). The first of these is expressed usually in terms of interests, drives or needs (biological as well as cultural and social); the second in terms of standards and definitions (what it is to be rational or human); and the third in terms of capacities or possibilities. Thus men and women need political authority, a power out of themselves, or they are calculating egoists, or naturally aggressive; they are rational animals; they have the power, within appropriate social conditions, to be creative, versatile and communal beings. These are all difficult notions which overlap, and are therefore neither always nor easily separated out: a view of human nature may contain elements of each. Nor does a basic approach necessarily tie neatly with a distinctive political position; for example, needs are associated commonly with conservatives and potentialities with radicals, but some writers discern human needs for a decisively new mode of social existence, and the reformer or radical may see some potentialities as dangerous, nasty and unpleasant, requiring taming. In addition, views of human nature are set, normally, within a particular view of history. For example, the conservative will see human nature as revealed in past history and actual human behaviour (in the interpretation of which there may be a strong element of idealization), whereas the radical will tend to present history as a systematic suppression or violation of human nature. Clearly they identify people, and the contexts in which they are or might be set, in quite different ways.

My own preference is for conceptions of human nature which contain notions of potentialities or powers or capacities. However, these do not float free. It is always 'human nature', or human capacities and incapacities, within or under certain conditions and circumstances. And our differences about men and women are closely related to different views of these conditions and circumstances. The more appropriate general question is not 'What is human nature?', but 'Of what are people capable, and incapable, in such and such circumstances?' Specification of the relevant circumstances is therefore vital. The commonsensical limits or conditions, with which the more Utopian accounts of man must be faced, include physiological or genetic conditions, set by the human constitution itself (and these will normally form part of our conception of human nature, rather than constituting an external limiting factor), the natural or physical environment (economic resources) which is increasingly man-made, and those social and political routines and arrangements which are inseparable from large and complex industrial societies, be they capitalist, state capitalist, socialist or whatever. There is disagreement over the precise weight to be given to these surrounding elements, and their impact —varied, variable and changing—will hinge partly upon the conception of human nature itself.

The dominant model of human nature in Western political thought is a conservative one. It includes the Christian doctrine of original sin, whose political form asserts the necessity of institutions, secular and ecclesiastical, to restrain or repress depraved or fallen man. Earthly Utopianism is rejected. Hobbes, in a secular version of original sin, depicted how life would be if individuals followed their natural or unsocialized drives. Hence, logically, government and the coercion necessary to political order were justified in terms of a view of what social relationships would other-wise be like. Edmund Burke savaged rationalists, revolutionaries and Utopians for their insolence about human nature. They were ignorant that 'the nature of man is intricate: the objects of society are of the greatest possible complexity',[1] and hence were unaware of the limitations of normal people and of their satisfaction with existing arrangements. Burke himself assumed certain more or less fixed human needs and desires, which made some imagined forms of social life literally unrealizable. The corollary was that efforts to establish such new worlds would lead, through the destruction of the traditional signposts which guide and define us, to the widespread loss of personal identity and security.

Such a claim, that people do not have the substance to survive in what is presented as a bare and open world, in which they would float or blow away, or be subordinated to despotic and terroristic rule, is thrown frequently against the champions of authenticity and liberation. 'Liberation' is seen as social dissolution. This critique rests upon assumptions about what civilization and social structures are and require: the counterattack, stressing the strong ideological element in the conservative theory, is that perpetuating one specific civilization or social structure is not to maintain civilization or society itself, but to prefer one form of life to others.

Resting on a particular conception of human nature, this strand of anti-Utopian thought—the 'Utopian' may take the shape of communism, socialism, democracy, international order and amity, or whatever—has had continuing ideological significance and potency. Our contemporary intellectual counter-revolutionaries are engaged in a more weighty task than that of merely debunking irrelevant and amusing social visions, such as those of Fourier. The purpose is, rather, to defend civilization itself against visions of total social change, which are held to be partly responsible for twentieth-century barbarism. Visions of the perfectibility of man, or of substantial human improvement, which underlie Utopian dreams and perhaps, in a more muted form, even reformist hopes, are highly suspect. The simple-minded cultural determinism or environmentalism of the Enlightenment, the easy assumptions about remaking society and the disregard of the complexity of sentient beings have disturbed many twentieth-century thinkers, who are less convinced both of people's power to transform society and of the desirability of attempting to do so.

There may be doubts, of course: we are not faced simply by crass or bland conservativism, challenging change on principle. John Passmore, for example, in offering an erudite account and a firm critique of the quest for perfection,[2] remarks that he grew up in a world marked by the effects of fanaticism, which made him 'very conscious of the fragility of civilization, the relative ease with which fanaticism can destroy it.'[3] That explanation made, however, he remains worried by the criticism that *The Perfectibility of Man* 'encourages complacency, contentment with things as they are, by suggesting that any sort of enthusiasm, any attempt to encourage men to pass beyond the everyday limits of their life, is automatically to be condemned.'[4] Given a strong sense of the fragility of civilization, it is going to be hard both to interpret Utopian or enthusiastic thinkers and to characterize and evaluate 'the everyday limits of their [people's] life' or, in Talmon's phrase, 'the sum total of the existing generation.'[5] Flexibility may be underrated, and positive and constructive impulses wasted.

Such significant recent thinkers as Popper,[6] Polanyi,[7] Talmon,[8] and Berlin[9] are a group of John Waynes of political theory, presenting histories of ideas in which the goodies are sorted out from the baddies, the baddies being identified in large part by their grandiosity about, and their actual ignorance of, human nature. Talmon, for example, discerns competing strands in democratic theory and practice, totalitarian and liberal democracy, which are the product of two deep-rooted instincts in men and women—the yearning for salvation and the love of freedom. Sane, common-sense liberalism, as expressed by Talmon's (though not by my) Mill, incorporates the latter instinct, and treats human beings more or less as they are, whereas the yearning for salvation expresses itself in a closed community. It does not respect people as they are, and it is often the result—especially in its extreme form—of psychological imbalance, for example, Talmon's Rousseau[10] or Feuer's Marx.[11] The radical theorist, rather than the world, becomes the object of criticism and a suitable case for treatment.

Talmon asserts a close connection between the desire for an impossible state of harmony—or, at least, one which could not be achieved by liberal democratic means—and acceptance of violent and totalitarian means to seek its realization. Seeking immediate and fundamental change, and faced by recalcitrant human material, his visionaries refuse to admit defeat and accept brutality and terror as necessary instruments of reconstruction. The logical structure, as he presents it, is of course unacceptable from his viewpoint:

(1) Men are of such and such a character (Talmon).

(2) Utopians demand arrangements which are incompatible with (the preservation of) this character (Utopians).

(3) Hence they necessarily assault human nature (and thus men and women), given their impatience and their insensitivity to actual selves, real people. They reject what to Talmon is a basic limit on political aspiration, 'the sum total of the existing generation.'

Searching for the precursors of recent horrors, Talmon dissolves history into high-quality propaganda.

A similarly cautious view is taken by many of those political scientists —I offer a crude and uncluttered though not a caricatured summary— who present their ideas as an emanation from political realities, or the political realities of so-called affluent Western societies. The resulting prescription is commonly a pragmatic, worldly-wise, unextended liberalism.[12] The essence of this ageing liberal orthodoxy is that in normal conditions the great mass of people are ignorant and apathetic about politics: widespread political apathy just is natural. People's private concerns are generally dominant, and there is a clear but not an imposed distinction between *homo politicus* and *homo civicus*: you have your choice. Freedom and responsiveness are ensured by the pluralist system, specifically by the competition of élites. Apathy is also desirable, as efforts to change this normal, contented, limited, domestic animal into a citizen participator have one of two results: strong coercion for political ends, or the emergence of authoritarian and probably violent movements as the unwilling participants seek to escape the terrible burdens of ambiguity, choice and openness. The explanation is that people are not allowed to live according to their own nature: in its (often disguised) prescriptive form, liberal political science asserts or secretes certain values and certain views of human nature. The valued society—liberal pluralism—is seen as the most compatible or consonant with the dispositions and capacities

our nature. It responds to or reflects what people essentially
certain and most desirable stage of social development. It
y that human nature is the result of contingent economic,
social and political forces, and to present its own vision, not as an interested
and blinkered response to a particular historical form of society, but as
a proper reaction to common human needs and concerns, and to the
arrangements imperative in any complex society.

It should be noted, however, that while the 'empirical' political science
which reached its peak in the 1950s and 1960s has a strong conservative
aspect, there are significant differences between liberal and conservative
accounts of human nature. Their ideal person, their sense of the appropriate constraints upon people, and their desired social contexts all differ.
The liberal values choice, diversity and negative freedom, while the conservative wants more formal restraints, and is suspicious of liberal optimism,
assertiveness and liberty. But neither asserts that everybody is the same,
that human nature is all of a piece. Their social theories generally
recognize and incorporate existing social divisions and principles of stratifi-
cation, usually presented in an idealized light. The bulk of human kind,
the masses, women, the working class, may be deficient in the relevant
political and cultural capacities or gifts, but there are those who are born
to rule (traditional authority justified by special or unusual qualities) or
who are politically competent or expert or impartial (to be discovered
through a pluralist and meritocratic system). In neither case are human
natures identical.

But the radical, who focuses upon potentialities or capacities, need not
claim that the potentialities of everybody are the same and in principle
unlimited, that anybody could be the same as anybody else, that everybody could realize all their potentialities, or that anybody could be
anything. Radicalism need not accept a choice between environment and
genetic inheritance, and opt for the blank sheet. Rather, its essential
claim may be that everybody has significant and unrealized potentialities,
and could be more (or less?) than they are—and perhaps that, given
encouraging circumstances, people would go in very different directions.
Accepting the continuing importance of both luck and diversity is perfectly compatible with saying that certain differences ought to be ironed
out, or that certain resources ought to be made more generally available,
perhaps in the interests of an enriched or fuller diversity.

The radical, then, is not necessarily committed to the assertion that
all people are equal, or could be equal, in respect of physical attributes,
mental capacities, moral achievement, etc. But the actual structure and
political thrust of a radical account of human nature is generally very

different from liberal and conservative ones. In essence it is claimed that people, as they are, are deformed, mutilated or arbitrarily restricted by contingent processes and arrangements. Given this view, history becomes a history of violation rather than a history of moralization. Culture, instruments of socialization, private property, massive institutional conglomerates or ideal types such as capitalism, are seen as the forces which make people what they are, but not as they need or could be, or as they truly are. Given some such explanatory theory, the elaboration of strategies for change, and the depiction of the blossoming of human powers in a new form of society, radical theories may gain an air of realism and solidity. Thus we find Marx, for example, indicting capitalism (specific capitalist institutions) for its frustration of human versatility, creativity and sociality, drawing in broad outline a form of society in which humanity is realized, elaborating strategies and defining the forces which could bring the existing order to an end, and identifying those institutional changes within capitalism which lay foundations for the future. His views may not always be compelling, but his social theory has a model structure.

It is an assumption of this chapter that any prescriptive political theory —and it is hard for social theory to be otherwise—makes assumptions, which may be tacit, about human nature. Of course, this is not all there is to political theory, nor do views of human nature occupy an identical place in each political theory. Accounts of human nature are critical and normative instruments, used to support one kind of regime or series of developmental stages, and to dismiss others as violating or being incompatible with that nature. However, the fit may not be immaculate: on opening up a conception of human nature we may discover that it has hidden possibilities or implications, which enable it to support different recommendations from those of the author. If, in aristocratic theories, possession of land is a source of virtue, why not land for all? If, as in many liberal pluralist theories, the politically active are virtuous—moderate, flexible, thoughtful—why not encourage as many as possible to be like that, rather than closing politics off? We may find that there is some disjuncture between the account of people as they are and the vision of the future splendid, for example, between the weighty, destructive world of many radicals, with its penetrating, all-pervasive socialization and mutilation, and the free, creative people of the new world. Another area of disjuncture may be between the conception of a fully-developed person and the social arrangements deemed compatible with widespread self-development, for example, is self-development compatible with a market system?

One of the points made in my introductory comment was that argument over human nature necessarily involves argument over the external limitations upon and possibilities open to people, and hence concerns directly the feasibility and realism of political programmes, goals and ideals. The limiting factors mentioned earlier may seem peculiarly relevant to optimistic or radical social theory, and certainly any such theory should take account of them, but they cannot be taken to be unequivocally conservative in their bearing and implications.

Work on our physiological, genetic or biological constitution may suggest that some people at least have unchangeable needs or drives—unchangeable, anyhow, as far as acceptable methods and desired ends are concerned. It has been argued that, if it was demonstrated conclusively that there exist 'unchangeable characteristics of human nature postulated by the genetic or biological approach . . . radical thought must change.'[13] This seems logical, but it depends upon exactly what the 'unchangeable characteristics' are and what range of variation of channelling is possible, on what changes radical thought is urging and whether what is to be changed is the unchangeable part and, related to this, the context within which the unchangeable resides. It is certainly the case that sociobiology, whose basic assumption is that biological facts explain social facts, seems commonly to rule out such ideals as equality, and that human emotions and goals are reduced to—or described in terms of—'territoriality', 'agressivity', 'rank–order–drive' and so on. Such theories, for example, those of Lorenz or Wilson, are commonly—and fairly—criticized in terms of their methodology. Genes are invented for which there is no evidence, animal–human equivalences established through the use of metaphor, and an apparently objective science bolsters the status quo by ruling out socialist and similar ideals.

That there are limits set to human self-development by the amount and availability of resources must also be accepted, even though the scientific or empirical basis is disputed. Moreover, the actual point at and way in which any limits are met rests upon political choices (for example, regarding the mode of distribution) and on assumptions about the role of human activity or practice (for example, producing more or differently or better). Finally, political arrangements and routines vary, but in complex societies at least account needs to be taken of the limitations imposed by size, distance, the division of labour, including political labour, and so forth.

What we understand as human nature therefore cannot reside in a vacuum, social or environmental, but must be related to a variety of practical, real-world considerations. The ideal circumstances for human nature to unfold, for people to develop themselves, may not be achievable for any number of reasons, ranging from contingent factors, themselves varying in strength and deep-rootedness, to necessary or unavoidable ones. Particular structures, social arrangements, physical environments, genes, mortality and physical decline will be limiting or destructive conditions as far as some specific view of human nature is concerned. Radically different selves may emerge in new economic and social conditions—conditions which may not be realizable, or realizable only at unacceptable costs, while actual conditions may regularly bring out the wrong propensities. Men and women are determinate beings, subject always to certain constraints, limitations, frameworks, exclusions (which may be the result of previous choices).

Accepting this claim, we will part company with R. D. Laing in his outright denunciation of civilization. Laing may indeed be correct in his view that the child's infinite and diverse potential is sharply restricted in society, and even that potentialities for positive growth and humanity are destroyed or seriously hindered. Children, he writes, 'take up their positions in the space we define. They may then choose to become a fragment of that fragment of their possibilities we indicate they are.'[14] Such social definition, occurring through many institutions and practices, is restricting and thereby mutilating, in Laing's view: it prevents the emergence of full and autonomous selves and the openness and accurate self-images associated with these. But socialization does and must take place in some form or other, and it always involves limitation, definition and structuring of the individual. In social existence a certain person emerges or is made, and though much of the content is accidental or contingent, dependent upon a specific environment which might have been otherwise, it could not be nothing or everything. There is always some definition and some closing-off of options or possibilities. This includes the fact that we do not always get the circumstances or breaks that we need, to become what we may have it in us to be. However, if Laing's free, open and many-sided development floats free of the minimum conceivable conditions of social life, certain possibilities which lie within reach may be unnecessarily or arbitrarily ruled out. Hence a series of reformist observations are in order, noting the significant differences between modes of socialization, the immense variety of human experience and culture, the fact that children do not and need not experience the world just as their elders do, that they are not born with the distinctions which we now make, that dominant conceptualizations of things are neither natural nor universal. It should be clear that these remarks are not intended to support a conservative view of man, but to cut Utopian speculation down to size, by observing in broad terms existing and actual limits, while recognizing them as in many cases open to dispute and to manipulation.

The preceding comments suggest that there are basic disagreements about human potentialities in both general and specific contexts. It goes without saying that disputes in this area are not simple to resolve. The significance of evaluation and judgment, the fact that accounts of human nature, whether expressed in terms of needs or capacities or power or whatever, arise within particular evaluative or ideological frameworks, forces rejection of the apparently uncontroversial claim that prescriptive normative theory must be based upon an accurate empirical assessment of the real world. Well-researched, deeply-considered empirical assessments, offered in good faith, differ. We may be able to make bald and basic statements which are uncontroversial, for example, that people need food and shelter, or such unincisive generalities as that the world has economic limits or that people cannot develop all their potentialities. But as views of human nature (needs, capacities, interests) are morally impregnated, and vital to assessments of the various social orders, their 'factual' or 'descriptive' component cannot be detached and examined in isolation. More specifically, empirical political science or behavioural psychology cannot correct straightforwardly the absurdities of unworldly political philosophers, though some hard-nosed political scientists have thought that they were doing just that.

To say this is not to support an equality of ideas and arguments, as if we should accept all the ingenious and evasive devices, all the immunities to relevant evidence, through which people protect their ideas or belief-systems. Politics often seems a field of conversion rather than of logical and empirical testing of hypotheses. At this point the liberal, properly delighted with moral diversity and intellectual pluralism, may collapse into helplessness, complaining that all we can do is to bang our heads together, agree that everything is ideological and insist that our differences are irresolvable. But, remaining fervent in recognition of and respect for the diversity of beliefs and ideologies—which may give psychological, if not philosophical, support to the strangest believers—a better response for the liberal is to insist upon an area of legitimate disagreement, while pressing for procedures which guarantee what is seen as rational or responsible or reputable argument. The nihilist pit is too deep if it accommodates Nazis and madmen. Certain theories, like irresponsible people, fail to meet their obligations. The practical standard then becomes, not some unworldly objectivity or rationality, but conformity to a liberal intellectual consensus, for example, a model of openness, including responsiveness to evidence and counter-argument and a logical or coordinated structure of argument. Of course, this does not ensure an escape from no man's land.

Given that there are no commonly agreed criteria for appraising political beliefs, including beliefs about human nature, that—as is often said—there are no proofs of political beliefs, but only good and bad defences, what can we say about the means of appraising beliefs and the kind of susceptibility which they should have to criticism and to facts which are hard to accommodate? Theories of human nature can be submitted, appropriately, to critical scrutiny in at least three ways: confrontation by evidence, generally sociological, which is relevant to their basic tenets; logical analysis of their parts and of the theories of which they are part, concerned particularly with internal consistency and precision; and moral and descriptive critique which is concerned with the concrete or practical bearings or meanings of particular views of human nature. The first set of queries asks whether the theory is feasible, or engages the facts where appropriate. The second asks whether it is consistent, whether it hangs together, whether it makes sense. The third concerns what it would actually amount to in practice, whether it is nice or nasty.

Confrontation of political claims by evidence may rest upon over-simple conceptions of identifiability and falsifiability. A weak and vulnerable attack is to confront views of how things should or might be with conceptions of existing political reality. These normally consist of descriptive generalizations about the state of the world, and may utilize a sharp contrast between political science—ostensibly empirical, concerned with things as they are, actual people—and political theory—normative, concerned with goals or ideals, the good society or the good life. Thus, for example, J. S. Mill's account of the democratic citizen may be attacked via evidence from voting surveys, ignoring the radical and idealist character of Mill's claims, and the relevant and assumed conditions. A more far-reaching form of critical attack will hold that the ideal picture differs not only from existing reality, but from how things must be—laws of human nature or of human psychology, or the laws or imperatives governing all (complex) societies may be invoked.

But the implications of voting studies for political theory are not clear-cut and decisive, in either the weaker or the stronger forms. Wrestling with the general question, Runciman suggests that Lazarsfeld provides sociological evidence directly relevant to the tenets of political theory.[15] I would weaken that, or at least deny that the nature of its relevance or its implications are established, and say that it is evidence of which theorists of democracy need to take account, especially regarding questions of feasibility. One must admit the gap between fact and value, between existing and ideal societies, and challenge those normative theorists who maintain a monastic detachment from the world, failing to consult relevant facts. None the less, the impact of the evidence remains to be mediated theoretically. One cannot move straight from existing democracies to democracy as such: what constitutes democracy may itself be disputed, or new and different conditions facilitating self-determination or participation may be envisaged. In any case, 'democracy' cannot be examined directly without preconception or defining framework. Inspection is structured by definitions, selections, judgments and by valuations.

Logical analysis requires, in the first instance, that the object of analysis should be specified, so that we know, as clearly as possible, what we are talking about. It will then be possible to explore the internal consistency of a theory of or about human nature. This is a complex enterprise combining conceptual, moral and empirical analysis. Are the values, for example, the elements of the desired human nature, compatible with each other? Do the valued potentialities hang together? Are liberty or self-determination compatible with virtue or with equality? Is freedom in one area, such as politics, compatible with freedom in another, such as the market? Are the means of realization, or the future institutional structures, compatible with or supportive of the ideal human qualities?

The effort to demonstrate what counts as an embodiment or a concretization of a political ideal, to show what the vision amounts to or might amount to in the flesh, is a difficult one. My assumption is that accounts of human nature—as it is and as it might be—can be expressed in terms of intelligible social visions. Difficulties inevitably arise, in part because visions of ends, imagined worlds, are presented commonly in broad and abstract terms, and because they often presuppose special conditions and radical transformations. It may be deemed impossible in principle and absurd in practice to require down-to-earth elaborations of what a very novel state of affairs would be like. And yet it seems perfectly proper to ask: what would this or that ideal look like in institutional and other practical terms? What would it mean for liberties and choices, coercion, government? Our political preferences will certainly influence interpretations of the ideals and values of others. Accepting—as I do, for example—a natural diversity of human ideals and interests, and consequently a need for authority relationships to order social life and for protections against intrusive or violent authority, visions of single-minded and intense moral communities are rejected. But the assault may go further, imposing such a character arbitrarily on visions that do not fit. Hence answers to proper questions may be crude and unsympathetic, as the interpreter makes different assumptions about human nature and society, and perhaps also accepts the historical use made of a particular thinker's ideas as a confirmation of their character. Thus Talmon bases his history of ideas upon 'the inner logic of political Messianism' and not upon the ideas within their own historical context: 'The continuity of a tradition matters more than the authenticity of the interpretation of the canon.'[16] It may, for certain purposes, but ideas often enter the stream of history in a distorted form, so the 'logical development' of ideas shifts attention from what the writer under consideration actually wrote, and the conditions under which he or she did so. Logical implications may be actual perversions. So-called disciples may be betrayers (for example the fate of Marx's ideas in the Soviet Union), as historical actors are not interested, normally, in the environment and precise meaning of the ideas which they seize.

There are many social visions which arouse the conservative's ire. These include visions of a society of participatory equals, of a dominant 'general will', of barefoot doctors, and of the happy marriage of individual and community in a Gemeinschaft. A common response is to interpret such visions concretely in terms of a conservative theory of human nature and social structure, perhaps using the nastier historical interpretations and supposed implementations of the original doctrine as evidence of what was implicit in it from the very beginning. The resulting simplification normally involves detachment of ideas from their context, social and theoretical, and a testing of the ideal against reality as conceived by others. In this way Marx's so-called 'ideal totalitarianism', the vision of a society in which the dichotomy between individual and society has been eliminated, is on other premises totalitarian, as natural coordination appears inevitably as domination. Yet, on Marx's assumptions, underlying social trends, the steady change of human beings and practical action brought remarkable new possibilities within reach. I am not claiming that Marx's assumptions were in fact realistic, but that it is unfair, given his total social theory, and anachronistic, to present him as a proto-Stalinist, an advocate of engineered unanimity or of a manipulated form of plebiscitary democracy.

This tendency to misrepresent and debase radical political visions is revealed also in an article in which Eugene Kamenka and Alice Ehr-Soon-Tay bring out the communitarian assumptions underlying many of the contemporary attacks upon the liberal contractual state.[17] They are concerned at the continuing appeal of Gemeinschaft as a social type. Claiming that the dreams and fantasies of industrial and post-industrial society 'have always been of a non-industrial, non-specialized and non-fragmented world',[18] the authors conclude: 'But while the fantasies multiply, those who live in actual Gemeinschaften continue to vote with their feet in the opposite direction.'[19] Grand ideals are reduced, *a priori* and ahistorically, into degenerate historical forms, which may in fact have little to do with the ideal as perceived by the original authors, though there may be links via a verbal fetish or an ebullient generality. Imagined societies are reduced to awful and, on the face of it, unrelated historical cases through the super-imposition of rival views of human nature and social imperatives upon them. Ideal Gemeinschaften are reduced to what may be arbitrarily labelled Gemeinschaften in the real world; though we may find somebody else's ideal community, for example, Walden II, stultifying or repressive *as it is actually described.*

I have not attempted to defend one conception of human nature or one set of values against others. Our preferences in this respect will not be decided by the degree to which a particular theory meets the standards which are presented roughly here.[20] My claim is simply that, in defending and elaborating our own preferences, we should take account of the broad range of relevant evidence, seek to tighten the relationship between different parts of the theory (for example, between the view of human nature, the account of obstacles and limits, and the actual political prescriptions), and give some idea of the actual social shape or form of our values. Meanwhile, no doubt, political theorists will continue to construct their complex and ingenious mixtures of facts, selections, evaluations and faiths, sometimes too loosely and with too evasive an eye on the demands of logic and the possible existence and relevance of difficult and potentially challenging material. We can at least ask reasonably for a critical and self-conscious interplay between theories, and between theories and the untidy world to which they relate in various ways. The goal is not the grand one of rational proof but, rejecting privileged appeals and answers, it includes at least a clarification of differences of framework and vision.

Notes

1. Burke, E., *Reflections on the Revolution in France*, London, Dent, 1955, p. 59.
2. Passmore, J., *The Perfectibility of Man*, London, Duckworth, 1970.
3. Ibid., p. viii.
4. Ibid.
5. Talmon, J. L., *The Origins of Totalitarian Democracy*, London, Secker, 1961, p. 232.
6. See Popper, K., *The Poverty of Historicism*, London, Routledge, 1960, *The Open Society and its Enemies*, London, Routledge, 1957 and *Conjectures and Refutations*, London, Routledge, 1963 (especially 'On the Sources of Knowledge and Ignorance' and 'Utopianism and Violence').
7. See Polanyi, M., 'Beyond Nihilism', *Encounter*, No. 78, March 1960.
8. See especially Talmon, J. L., *The Origins of Totalitarian Democracy* op. cit., and *Political Messianism. The Romantic Phase*, London, Secker, 1960.
9. See especially Berlin, I., 'Two Concepts of Liberty', in his *Four Essays on Liberty*, Oxford, Oxford University Press, 1969.
10. Talmon, *The Origins of Totalitarian Democracy*, op. cit.

11. Feuer, L., 'Karl Marx and the Promethean Complex', *Encounter*, December 1968.
12. As examples, see Dahl, R., *A Preface to Democratic Theory*, Chicago, University of Chicago Press, 1956; Milbrath, L., *Political Participation*, Chicago, Rand McNally, 1965; Berelson, B., *et al.*, *Voting*, Chicago, University of Chicago Press, 1954; and Lipset, S. M., *Political Man*, London, Mercury Books, 1963.
13. Sargent, L. T., 'Human Nature and the Radical Vision', in Pennock, J. R., and Chapman, J. W. (eds), *Human Nature in Politics*, New York, New York University Press, 1977, p. 259.
14. Laing, R. D., 'The Politics of the Family', in *The Politics of the Family and Other Essays*, London, Tavistock, 1972, p. 79.
15. Runciman, W. D., *Social Science and Political Theory*, 2nd Edition, Cambridge, Cambridge University Press, 1969, p. 93.
16. Talmon, *Political Messianism*, op. cit., p. 8.
17. 'Participation, "Authenticity" and the Contemporary Vision of Man, Law and Society', in Cohen, R. S., Feyerabend, P. K., and Wartofsky, M. W. (eds), *Essays in Memory of Imre Lakatos*, Dordrecht, Reidel, 1976.
18. Ibid., p. 338.
19. Ibid., p. 339.
20. I have tried to present the form of a radical theory of human nature in 'Human Nature and Radical Democratic Theory', in Duncan, G. (ed.), *Democratic Theory and Practice*, Cambridge, Cambridge University Press, 1983, pp. 187–203.

2 Marx and human nature

IAN FORBES

Marx's views on human nature have to be analysed in the context of his desire for human emancipation through great, yet controlled, social change. These two factors, in combination, mean that Marx's assumptions concerning men and women remain crucial in his analysis of society, whether that analysis be focused on the accumulation of capital, factory legislation, or the preconditions for revolution. However, by no means does the Marxian critique amount to a sustained and articulated approach to the problem of human nature, with important consequences. In particular, it militates against a complete understanding of the processes of change in society, the choices between different kinds of change, and the manner in which those processes are augmented and encouraged, or deflected and inhibited. In considering Marx and human nature, then, three key perspectives will predominate. First, there will be a brief discussion of the role of concepts of human nature in political theory generally, in order to provide the focus necessary for the examination of Marx's contribution, which constitutes the second perspective. The aim here is to construct a framework in which his various statements on human nature can be understood, both for their substance and as an element of Marx's theory of social change. Finally, this developmental model of human nature will be explicated and assessed in terms of its contemporary relevance, in order to highlight those features which deepen an understanding of the kinds and directions of possible social change in advanced capitalist society.

Human nature and political theory

Within political and social theory, it is too often the case that a particular conception of human nature, or a particular characteristic, is inserted simply to resolve an otherwise unworkable set of propositions about society and the people within it. This occurs at all levels of explanation—even the trivial—but the political significance can be paramount. An example of this in its most systematic form is described in the chapter on feminism, but other instances abound. Rioting and looting, both in the United States and more recently in Britain, are cases in point. Instead of a recognition of the effect that exceptionally high rates of unemployment, poor housing, racial discrimination and inflation has on the under class, blame is attached to the individuals and groups concerned, in two ways.

First, as Connolly points out, New York looters have been described as 'those who refuse to take advantage of the real opportunities available to them', which in effect makes them accountable for their own actions as well as their more generalized plight.[1] Such a description, attacking looters as well as alternative explanations, employs a very simple model of free will as the basis of human nature, the illogical conclusion of which lacks even the possibility of avoiding a Hobbesian 'war of all against all'. This view of human nature, then, can be used to construct an explanation of some social events, but is unable to sustain an explanation of the society in which those events took place.

The second way of laying blame is a direct use of statements about human nature. Thus riots and looting in Britain were explained by reference to greed and the natural tendency to imitate. In this case the Hobbesian solution can, and does, win endorsement, even by the Archbishop of Canterbury.

> All human societies are flawed by fundamental human failings; selfishness, aggression, and the lust for power over others. Properly disciplined force is needed to keep those other forces in check. Men and women are not naturally peaceable and law-abiding, and no matter how good the communications, how restrained the police, force is alas sometimes inescapable.[2]

In other words, even a decent liberal state is forced to act against the very nature of its citizens.

Examples such as these indicate how assumptions about human nature are intertwined with political explanation. Some are generated by the method of explanation, while other assumptions actually shape the explanatory model. This is equally true of a fully articulated political theory. Here, three specific structural properties can be identified, all of which involve propositions about, and consequences for, a conception of human nature.[3]

The primary component of every political theory is an evaluation or critique of existing society. Entailed in this are descriptive statements, focusing on what men and women are like in a given society. Second, there is always the vision of the future or proper society, wherein men and women are described as they might be, or ought to be. Finally, there must be an attitude to change in society, and in many cases this results in the development of a theory of change. At issue is the extent to which human nature can change, if at all, and the nature of the role of men and women in shaping, accelerating, or preventing social change. Taken together, the implied statements and propositions constitute the conception of human nature of a particular political theory. In short, they deal with the actual, the ideal or possible, and the agency of change.

However, the mere existence of views and images of human nature does not of itself secure consistency in the derivation and application of those views. Given the relationship between the structure of political theories and conceptions of human nature, it can be seen that human nature is not only a valid focus, but one which can assist in the examination, assessment and improvement of existing theoretical approaches. In each case, therefore, it is necessary to construct or draw out a *theory* of human nature capable of organizing and connecting a particular collection of statements and propositions about men and women, such that analysis and conclusions are generated on a systematic rather than *ad hoc* basis. The practical significance of this is manifold, since it facilitates discourse on key assumptions about men and women, and identifies the claims that are amenable to investigation and substantiation. Moreover, inadequate and insufficiently developed features of a political theory can be highlighted. Certainly, this is true of Marxian and Marxist theories. The failure, on their part, to provide a distinctive and convincing approach to the study of human nature is something of an inconsistency. Methodologically and substantively, their contribution ought to be unique in formulation and application, but this is not the case.

Finally, the gathering and treatment of information about ourselves as individual humans, and not just the social structures within which we exist, must always be a prime concern. While an examination of structures does tell us a great deal about ourselves, the connections between changing structures and changing ourselves are by no means automatic or clearcut. This is a crucial concern, especially if we wish to change society, and if, as Lowenstein argues, only 'an external social and *internal human* transformation can renew society'.[4] In this sense, then, the study of human nature has the potential for a positive contribution to any radical view of the world, and the problem of the possibilities for change.

Perspectives on Marx

One of the claims of this chapter is that Marx, Engels and later Marxists are faced with the theoretical and practical difficulties, outlined above and in the preceding chapter, that the relationship of human nature to theory entails. In short, the question of human nature stubbornly refuses to go away, despite attempts to deny its importance, whereas a firm recognition of the reality of human nature, while readily achieved, is often at the expense of cogency and precision, and may involve undermining central Marxian tenets.

Conceptions of human nature that rely on the notion of alienation, that derive their inspiration from Marx's early works, are the chief targets of these latter accusations. Such an approach is seen to lean heavily on the idea that human nature has a hard core—an 'essence'—against which the impact of social and economic conditions can be counter-posed and assessed. But, as Lucien Sève argues, 'human essence' is an abstract idea in which 'man is seen as the subject of history for whom social relations are phenomena, an exterior manifestation.[5] On the other hand, as Hirst and Woolley point out, an exclusive emphasis on those social relations can amount to a 'denial of nature' altogether.[6]

They are, therefore, two opposing strands that dominate political and social theory with respect to Marx and human nature. Idealism dogs the first approach, where, for Sève, 'that logical monstrosity, the abstract "general individual", is the skeleton in the cupboard of the psychology of personality.'[7] Alternatively, an insistence on the primacy of social relations can slide into a structuralism that precludes any other considerations and inputs. Althusser's 'real humanism', for instance, erases individuals with content, with perception of alternatives.[8] Clearly, a central theoretical difficulty is the status and role of 'the individual', and is a problem to which this chapter addresses itself. As Marx stressed, 'real living human individuals' are not only the first premiss, but a condition which continually presents itself. A genuine interest, therefore, in the individual in advanced industrial society, the way he or she is constituted and can change, is an outright necessity, not a luxury or an irrelevance. Nor is it sufficient to rely on the notion of a 'social individual', which is at worst a semantic detour around, and at best a compromise that glosses over, basic problems. Without an explanation of human nature toward such social individuality, then it is no more than a Utopian assumption, to do with human existence in a largely undefined future society.

The present task, then, is to reclaim the individual from the grip of legalistic, human rights, individual freedoms explanations, and to construct a Marxian theory of individuality. The first and most pressing thing to concede is that there must be a scope for human autonomy beyond the confines of structural determination, without accepting that this is the same thing as free will, or an essence. It means that we cannot, even if we wanted to, provide a full account of human behaviour and motivation in solely materialist terms, even though this understanding is fundamental, and must form the basis of analysis.

On this particular issue, liberal thought is in a relatively strong position —the burdens of proof fall lightly, if at all, on their claims and arguments about men and women. In riposte, it is not enough to argue, with Marcuse, that it is only repressive tolerance that appears to vouchsafe the much-vaunted autonomy and choices available in capitalist society. This may prove a handy argument in the clinches, but fails to explain how, collectively, we are to distinguish between real and unreal choices, or why we should not prefer unreal choices to none at all. A similar problem exists with Habermas's notion of legitimation. It too, is a defensive argument, that explains above all the apparent lack of accuracy of Marx's predictions concerning change, specifically from capitalism to socialism, as well as the failure of working class movements ever since. Notions like repressive tolerance and legitimation certainly aid our understanding, pinpointing the ways in which the ruling class (not necessarily the owning class) functions politically in defence of its objective interests, and even indicating crisis moments and tendencies. However, a concomitant indentification of the active role of progressive—yet non-bourgeois—historical forces is not so forthcoming.

Implicitly, the study of human nature from a Marxist perspective *can* furnish us with the appropriate insights. The objection to this idea is that class analysis is downgraded or, worse still, ignored altogether. It is not suggested here that it has lost its validity, but that it has limited efficacy. Put another way, while Marxists can construct a class analysis, even of Eastern European societies, such an analysis lacks the ability to deal with the individual in society with the same assuredness.[9] As Bahro claims,

> Like the utopian socialists and communists who Marx sought to dispense with, we must once again take the species interest as our fundamental point of reference—only now in a more concrete manner. It might well have been no more than a Hegelian error to have burdened a particular class, and a class in the reproduction process, with the fate of humanity as a whole.[10]

The focus on humanity, and therefore human nature, represents a shift from determined classes to the people that fill and sustain those classes. But, for Althusser, this is a regrettable failure to cleanse the methodology of the last traces of philosophical idealism. However, in the denial that people can undertake revolutionary actions that are not ultimately reducible to class analysis, old problems remain, and new ones are created.

Instead of human nature residing in and springing from 'the ensemble of social relations', this ensemble no longer relates to the reproduction and expression of our nature. That milieu is itself ideology, 'the "lived" relation between men and their world'.[11] Moreover, Althusser argues that ideology 'is profoundly *unconscious*', to be understood in terms of structures that 'impose on the vast majority of men'.[12] Yet this makes even more pressing the questions—what are Althusserian men, and why are not all men and women included? 'Determination in the last instance by the economy' and other 'radically new concepts' provide insufficient answers, except implicitly.[13] It is clear at least that in Althusserian Marxism the 'majority of men' are infinitely plastic. But human nature is not so easily evacuated of substance, since plasticity is a positive attribute, not a precept for determination. In any case, plasticity is an inadequate proposal without close definition of the relevant time scales—in the short term it is patently inaccurate.

The question of time scales is all important. An examination of men and women in capitalist society cannot produce one coherent image of human nature and still avoid irrelevance or the error of a generalized abstract individual. Only in the broadest sense does capitalism create its special expression of human nature, and this formulation is analytically blunt. The capitalist society under scrutiny, and the stage of its historical development, must be established.[14] It must also be recognized that Marxists, when they do go in search of human nature, want to find a solution which not only conforms to a commitment to radical social change, but actually accelerates or advances the possibilities for such change. For some, this approach is so prejudicial as to invalidate the entire exercise as social science: for Marxists, this is the very reason for social science.

A Marxian theory of human nature

Marx was not claiming that human nature did not exist. The vital point is that human nature is a valid tool for analysis only when it is conceived in its real or objective perspective—given social conditions. This means that Marx did have what can be labelled a *conception* of human nature, a series of general characteristics that defined humankind as a separate species with particular needs and powers. At base, these feelings, needs, faculties and capacities *always* have to be expressed and satisfied, in that they 'exist under all conditions and can be changed only in their form and direction they take.'[15] This is another way of saying that 'life involves before anything else, eating, drinking, a habitation, clothing and many other things.'[16] Other things may well include love or creativity, for example, which are also mere attributes, not sharply defined predispositions to behave in particular ways, or behaviour wrought by specific structures within society. Such a conception, however, does not amount to a full description of what it is to be human in this or that society. The ensemble of social relations is itself a dependent variable, according to the state of the development of the productive forces within a given mode.

There are several conclusions to be drawn from these remarks. First, when Marx did refer directly to 'man', he could not have used the term in an abstract sense (except to criticize such a practice). His use of the term in a none the less generic manner always applied to real, living individuals in determinate circumstances, hence 'real, active men'.[17] Second, descriptions of men and women in different social structures (feudal, capitalist, communist) necessarily incorporated distinct impressions of human nature. In each case, it took a particular form—rural stolidity, capitalist selfishness, communist co-operativeness, at least in caricature. As a result, Marx was able to refer to human nature both generically and descriptively, as definition as well as contrast.

From his original *conception* of human nature, then, Marx was also able to derive a number of images of men and women, which are themselves representations of human nature. If we call these second order impressions *notions* of human nature, it becomes possible to differentiate between specific description (a notion), and universalistic abstraction (a conception). It is important to do this, because there are links between conception and notion that need to be explored. For example, how do we account for the discrepancy inherent in Marx's positive regard for humanity and his scorn for non-socialist human nature? How does one kind or expression of human nature give way to another? Since one notion of human nature would be superseded after social transformation by another more advanced notion, how can we assess the stages of transition? Most important of all, if capitalism must tend toward structural break-down, how confident can we be that greedy capitalist human nature can readily be usurped by the required communitarian and co-operative spirit, qualities so essential for the successful construction and continuation of socialist society?

If there are answers, they must reside in Marx's method. Put simply, if there is a developmental path along which society has already travelled, and one of the options for the future is a continued progression toward socialism, then this must also be the case for the development of humanity. As Carol Gould argues in *Marx's Social Ontology*, there is a 'logic of historical development' that connects both the stages of pre-capitalist societies, capitalism, and communal society, and the social relations within those three stages, namely community, individuality and external sociality, and communal individuality.[18] The necessity and connectedness of each of these stages of production establishes the same degree of necessary connection between the human nature that springs from the character of the specific 'ensemble of social relations'. Put another way, the human nature we confront in any given society will always be in the context of the pre-existing nature. For example, elements of a commitment to and need for some kind of community persist, as do more negative features like racism and sexism. As in the economic sphere, there are residual effects of earlier societies that, when not in contradiction to the supplanting mode of production, will continue to be reproduced, even though they are not determined by the economic structure.

In general terms, this means that the notions of human nature relevant to feudalism, capitalism, and communism can be explicated, and especially that an understanding of *capitalist* human nature is fundamental to the notion of human nature in the final, communal stage. Moreover, the *notion* of human nature to be derived from the examination of communal society, i.e. what a fully socialist existence is actually like, will be virtually coincident with the indications provided by Marx's first general considerations of his *conception* of human nature. In part, this is due to the Rousseauian element in Marx's view of human society—that all societies to date have allowed only a restricted, warped and unbalanced expression of humanity to take place, whereas communism, however non-specifically and grandly, promises to draw out an articulated and integrated, certainly wholesome, expression of humanity. Thus Marx's view of human nature is not merely strategic or unreflectively *a prioristic*, because his account of future society seeks the production of the concrete conditions necessary for a fully emancipated, fully human existence, instead of pretending that such a model pre-existed, and therefore justified, those concrete conditions. Human nature is an ally in the effort to change society, it is not its guarantor.

Applying, then, the progression through history Marx attributed to successive societies to corresponding notions of human nature, it can be concluded that feudal nature was subject to a lopsided development into the capitalist individual. In an explosion of egocentrism as selfishness, greed and ambition, early capitalism burst into creative life. The bourgeoisie, enjoying the freedom equally to experiment and exploit, made rapid and dramatic progress. These architects of the new society have their historical role, and Marx applauded their efficacy in the *Communist Manifesto*. At the same time, this class clearly violated his *conception* of human nature, since the proletarian mass is degraded and exploited.

It is at this point that Marx's theory of change begins to look suspect, since these are the very conditions which are to alert the proletariat to *their* historical role. Political action in the context of the economic interests of his class would herald the 'third stage', a new society of 'free individuality, based on the universal development of individuals and on their subordination of their communal, social productivity as their social wealth.'[19] Unfortunately, this account is either wrong, or it is too glib and gross, unable to convey the complexity and conditionality of even imminent social change. Capitalism confronts us as a resilient and adaptable economic and social order. Since it defies predictions based on class, a more considered and probing approach is required, that is able to take account of other factors and other explanations, especially those concerning individualism.

Human nature in capitalism

Leaving the realm of grand historical processes, but accepting its tendency, the initial construction of an explanation would divide capitalism into three internal stages—a classical Hegelian progression—and examine the notions of human nature associated with all three. Each stage could be expected to display a variety of characteristics, ranging from immediate social significance to indications of the future form. This conforms to our earlier statements concerning the relationship of images of human nature to political theory, since critique, vision and theory of change are addressed and embellished.

Early capitalist nature, then, is a vital expression, breaking through the old feudal limitations with considerable vigour. As an expression of human nature, these first capitalists are to be admired, being progressive, innovative and dynamic, using and amplifying a range of creative powers. Crucially, the success of the bourgeoisie, of this kind of human activity in conjunction with the developing forces of production, is to be understood in terms of its delimiting effect on society. As Marx pointed out,

> All fixed, fast-frozen relations, with their train of ancient and venerable prejudices and opinions are swept away, all newformed ones become antiquated before they can ossify. All that is solid melts into air, all that is holy is profaned, and man is at last compelled to face with sober senses, his real conditions of life, and his relations with his kind.[20]

In the first place, this image highlights the emancipatory aspect of a human nature that is not fixed but is flexible within determinate limits. Humans are invested with the ability to break down or through the conditions of their existence, and establish a new comprehension of themselves in the world of their making. Second, Marx was making another claim about the nature of capitalist society—that it was producing, for the first time, the conditions under which men and women were freed from mystifications about themselves as humans.[21] Apart from being adaptable, then, human nature can, under given circumstances, acquire extra powers and needs. Taken together, these factors explain Marx's enthusiasm for the capitalist mode of production. If there are these revolutionary and progressive elements inherent in capitalism, then his major statements concerning the transition to socialism have a historical precedent, and there clearly *is* justification for believing in another radical transformation of people and society. Nor does such a transformation have solely to rely upon economic determination. On the other hand, social change cannot be based on a simplistic assumption about human malleability, which defines the dominant economic and social order as the obstacle of overriding importance, and sees all other problems of transition solved in the wake of its removal.[22]

In the second of these stages of capitalism, the ideology that underpinned the transition from feudalism itself became the dominant ideology, a new role that reflected the change in the ethos of capitalism as well as its practice. Here a number of elements combined to forestall continuing revolution, and produced a second kind of capitalist human nature—less dynamic and more individualist. For Marx, the capitalist order 'resolved personal worth into exchange value', implying that the intrinsic value of human beings was ultimately being debased and suppressed, rather than extended and given occasion for expression.[23] This is consistent with the development of capitalism away from its early conditions of free competition as a sphere for endeavour, experimentation, and radical change, into what Lenin believed to be the last or monopoly stage.[24] However, this proved not to be the case. In this stage, capitalism was materially, politically and psychologically supreme. Consciousness of capitalist exploitation did not increase, nor did class polarization and conflict intensify in the expected manner. Instead of being alienated through emmiseration, workers (especially in the West) became committed to a system that provided material enrichment and variety in relative abundance, and proletarian revolution left Western shores, never to return, at least in the form that Marx and Engels understood. Consequently, class boundaries appear less relevant in the formation of belief and personality structure. There is a general and prepossessing selfishness and desire for material satisfaction, the steady decline of familial and communitarian association, and cohesive social traditions falter under sustained attack and sheer lack of interest.

Human nature under this second phase of capitalism acquires a character consistent with the society within which it is expressed. Unsatisfactory kinds of human beings are produced, in the sense that people are characteristically evoked by the repressive and exploitative, yet seductive, nature of capitalism. The greed inherent in this mode of production is rewarded, and the competitiveness necessary for survival and success becomes increasingly evident. Individualism, which appears as self-sufficiency and egoism in social relations, is given impetus, but in a one-sided fashion. 'Real' human needs and desires are distorted, since their major outlet must be experienced as materialism. Rationality, on one level a welcome attribute of the capitalist mode of production, is also a justification for dishonesty, unscrupulousness and exploitation, at the expense of its integration within a range of human responses.

However, as one might expect of even a 'very general dialectical model', the second stage of capitalism, and the direction of human endeavour associated with it, fulfils a critical function.[25] The generation and satisfaction of contrived and directed wants works to expose the contradictory nature of capitalism and highlight Marx's core beliefs concerning human nature. Satisfaction of material wants does not amount to the material satisfaction of *human* wants and needs. Provision of basic necessities like eating, drinking and habitation may be workable and adequate for the health of a battery hen, but for humans such a mechanistic approach to social life is impossible, for two major reasons. First, humans have the capacity, constantly exercised, to be involved in the decisions surrounding the use and distribution of social resources: hence the ubiquity of politics. Second, and of direct relevance to the phases of capitalism, economic well-being results in the desire to fulfil distinctively human needs. Western capitalism, therefore, has satisfied requirements at one level of our nature, but in so doing, has found itself constitutionally incapable of meeting the demands it engendered at the higher level.

This does not mean, however, that no progress is possible under capitalism. Quite the opposite is the case. Capitalism is, despite itself, achieving things originally reserved for a future socialist order. This is not an unexpected finding, given the contradictory nature of this mode of production, but the focus here is *not* class conflict. The changes to which we here refer will not be squeezed into any such analysis, because class conflict is predicated on the understanding that political action is taken in the context of objective economic interests. Undoubtedly, political involvement in class struggle has a radicalizing impact, but this by no means establishes all the social forms, and people well fitted to sustain them, that will be needed in post-capitalist society. As Lane argues, 'at least two parallel processes are required for change in a socialist direction, economic and psychological. But these may not be in harmony with one another.'[26] The importance of the psychological dimension is by no means a new idea, as the chapters on Critical Theory and Psychoanalysis amply demonstrate, but it remains the case that Marxism has yet to settle on the way to integrate this 'new' information about human social existence, in two key respects. First, the theory of, and approach to, social change is called into serious question, and second, the *positive* aspects of advanced capitalism require greater attention. An understanding of human nature, then, not only undermines the case for swift revolution followed by a dictatorship of the proletariat, but can also highlight and articulate the development of individuals and their relationship with modern society.

Given a developmental model of human nature, and our view of capitalism in terms of dialectical stages, it is therefore possible to construct the third notion of human nature, corresponding to advanced capitalist society. This third notion pinpoints progressive elements within a progressing human nature, on the basis that earlier, unsatisfactory or partial, expressions of human potential give way to more enriched modes of existence. Unreflective greed, competitiveness and egoism are attenuated by a greater awareness of self, of individuality as a determining factor of considerable importance, at least in *personal* social life. There is more likely to be dissatisfaction with, and lack of commitment to, the structures and practices of a society which, although providing substantial material reward, does not conform to strong self-images. 'Self-development', for example, stems from a recognition that the individual's needs and capacities are multiple and varied, and can become a defence against stultification at the workplace. Individualism, in this stage, is even more apparent, but is in the context of the importance of social interrelationships, a fundament of Marx's ontology.

Such psychological changes can have a profound social impact.[27] Indeed, our developmental model would lead us to expect that the third stage of Western capitalism is accompanied of human nature with profound revolutionary potential. Moreover, it means that the impulse to force everything into class terms and to be generally dismissive of the activities of the middle strata must be resisted. For instance, the suspicion of materialist goals in late capitalism is likely to exacerbate the tendency of under-consumption, an economic phenomenon that does not need to be directly related to class analysis. In the same way, the example of the Greens in West Germany demonstrates that effective political action need not conform to either class conflict or parliamentary (bourgeois) models of politics. The Greens are conspicuously unwilling to allow politics to be defined for them, and derive their own meaning and practice. First, the political activity of the movement is in the context of issues that individuals as distinct from interest groups or classes or parties deem important. Yet those issues, were they translated into policy, would secure benefits that are indivisible across society, and relate strongly to *human* values, not the grand requirements of Utopian thought or political theory generally. Second, their political practice reflects the personal experience of involvement in politics at an intimate, participatory level, where non-hierarchical, anti-specialist forms of discourse, decision-making and organization have been developed.[28] Thus they tap and express a consciousness within the community of the inadequacy of contemporary social structure and practices.

The significance of this third notion of human nature under capitalism lies in its ability to embody the characteristics of what Gould calls 'communal individuality', which, for her, is the form of social interaction consonant with a future *socialist* society.[29] That such a form is already beginning to appear is indicative, to use Lane's apt expression, of 'the capitalist genesis of socialist man'.[30] The development of capitalist society, therefore, is accompanied by the development of expressions and capacities of human nature. Furthermore, this particular stage demonstrates the manner in which the expression of human nature can constitute a force against the dominant social formation. Since human nature has content, it can never be entirely defined by and subservient to the economic and social structure in which it is manifested. As such, there is good reason to endorse the belief of Marxists that a future communist society *is* humanly probable, rather than just possible. Consequently, the serious study of human nature, in this third and more complex mode, has a degree of importance usually reserved for the work on working-class consciousness.

Conclusion

This outline of the three notions of human nature within capitalism, and the implications it entails for a theory of change in society, can lead us back to a consideration of Marx's *conception* of human nature. Those features regarded as progressive across the historical epochs of feudalism, capitalism and communism provide the necessary detail to support Marx's claims that the distinguishing feature of humans is the production of their means of subsistence. Apart from the crucial methodological import of this assumption, there are two aspects of this claim that are of interest here. First, it presupposes 'an historically created relation of individuals to nature and to one another'.[31] This clearly implies a progression in the ability of human beings to deal with their environment. Mastery over nature—impossible in any event, given the scarcity of natural resources —is not what Marx envisaged, even though he assumed that capitalism demonstrated the potential for human control. Nevertheless, the fact that humans engage nature, rather than merely exist within it, is telling. Compared to the notion of human nature under feudalism, notions of human nature in capitalist society incorporate a sophisticated capacity to deal with nature. Thus Marx's original conception of human nature, which included the assumption that men and women had the *potential* to control nature, is borne out by an analysis of the kinds of human nature that are produced under different historical conditions.

The second aspect of the production of material life entails the assumption that such a process would ultimately fall under the conscious control and direction of human beings, that they would develop themselves and their understanding and abilities to the point at which this was possible. Again, this implies a potential and a clear pattern of development. The grounds for arguing that *this* segment of Marx's conception of human nature can be endorsed or substantiated are not well established, but there are some favourable indications. Apart from the incidence of new political forms and practices which seem to go beyond class politics, we can add Lane's argument that the greater technical sophistication required by advanced industrial society has led to specific changes in the capacity of humans: namely, an increase in 'cognitive complexity', most definitely a prerequisite for the massive undertaking of conscious control of the productive forces.[32]

On these kinds of grounds, it can be seen that the development of human beings in capitalism is certainly consistent with the progression to human, as distinct from class, control of material life. In general, then, the two levels of dealing with human nature—as a conception and in respect of different notions—can produce both the means to study human nature and behaviour and useful results. And in the specific case of Marx's thought, this approach helps us to see that his original conception of human nature bears close relationship to the model of human existence he envisaged under socialism, at the same time allowing us to assess the validity and strength of those assumptions. Most encouragingly, it makes it possible to broaden our understanding of society, by translating assumptions that refer to vague and unspecified potentialities into human attributes as definite powers with motive and determining force.

Notes

I would like to thank John Street, Martin Hollis, and Graeme Duncan for their comments and assistance.

1. Connolly, W., *Appearance and Reality*, Cambridge, Cambridge University Press, 1981, pp. 157, 159.
2. *Parliamentary Debates, House of Lords Weekly Hansard*, No. 1170 (1–4 February), 1982, p. 1413.
3. It is not suggested that this is the only way to think about human nature and theory. Cf. Graeme Duncan's chapter and the Introduction to Stevenson, L. (ed.), *The Study of Human Nature*, Oxford, Oxford University Press, 1981.
4. Lowenstein, J., *Marx Before Marxism*, London, Routledge & Kegan Paul, 1980, p. 183 (emphasis added).
5. Sève, L., *Marxism and the Theory of Human Personality*, London, Lawrence & Wishart, 1975, p. 24.
6. Hirst, P., and Woolley, P., *Social Relations and Human Attributes*, London, Tavistock, 1982, p. 23.
7. Sève, op. cit., p. 12.
8. Althusser, L., *For Marx*, Brewster, B. (tr.), Harmondsworth, Penguin, 1969, pp. 242 ff.
9. I am thinking particularly of Konrád and Szelényi, who, in the process of writing *The Intellectuals on the Road to Class Power* (Brighton, Harvester, 1979), discover to their surprise 'the explosive critical potential of Marxist theory'. q.v. p. xvi.
10. Bahro, R., *Socialism and Survival*, London, Heretic Books, 1982, p. 65.
11. Marković, M., *The Contemporary Marx*, London, Spokesman Books, 1974, p. 86.
12. Althusser, op. cit., p. 233.
13. Ibid., p. 227.
14. This is not therefore merely an attempt to construct what Marx described as the 'so-called general development of the human mind', in the Preface to 'A Contribution to the Critique of Political Economy' in Marx, K., and Engels, F., *Selected Works*, London, Lawrence & Wishart, 1970, p. 181 (hereafter *MESW*).
15. Marx, K., *The Holy Family*, quoted in Marković, op. cit., p. 86.
16. Marx, K., and Engels, F., in Arthur, C. J. (ed.), *The German Ideology*, London, Lawrence & Wishart, 1970, p. 48.
17. Ibid., p. 47.
18. Gould, C., *Marx's Social Ontology*, London, MIT Press, 1978, pp. 4–5.
19. Marx, K., *Grundrisse*, Harmondsworth, Penguin, 1973, p. 158.
20. Marx, *Communist Manifesto, MESW*, op. cit., p. 38.
21. q.v., his claim that 'all earlier stages appear to be merely *local progress* and idolatry of nature.' Marx, K., *Grundrisse*, McLellan, D. (ed.), 2nd Edition, London, Macmillan, 1980, p. 99.
22. Fromm, E., *Fear of Freedom*, London, Kegan Paul, 1942.
23. Marx, *Communist Manifesto*, op. cit., p. 38.
24. Lenin, V. I., 'Imperialism, the Highest Stage of Capitalism', in *Selected Works*, Vol. I, London, Lawrence & Wishart, 1947.
25. Keat, R., 'Individualism and Community in Socialist Thought', in Mepham, J., and Ruben, D. H. (eds), *Issues in Marxist Philosophy*, Vol. IV, Brighton, Harvester, 1981, p. 148.
26. Lane, R., 'Waiting for Lefty', *Theory and Society*, Vol. VI, No. 1, July 1978, p. 1.
27. For a critical review of contemporary cultural experience of self-development,

see Forbes, I., and Street, J., 'Individual Transitions to Socialism'. Paper presented to the Transition to Socialism Conference at Liverpool University, September 1981.
28. The feminist movement has pioneered many of these new attitudes and forms.
29. Gould, op. cit., p. 5.
30. Lane, op. cit., p. 16.
31. Marx, *German Ideology*, op. cit., p. 59.
32. Lane, op. cit., p. 3.

3 Mill and human nature

PAUL SMART

John Stuart Mill's study of the multifarious human condition should be seen as a direct response to four major stimuli: the bankruptcy of classical utilitarianism, the challenge of conservative German metaphysics, the impoverishment of the majority under burgeoning capitalism, and the continued, irrepressible advance of science. His analysis of human nature and character formation is no exception to these general conditions. With this in mind, this chapter will concern itself with several aspects of Mill's enquiry: the freedom of the individual in a determined world (and the concomitant justification of Free Will), the universal laws of the mind of Mill's utilitarian psychology, the formation of character and his science of ethology and, finally, his ambiguous discussion of human instincts.

Mill's aim was change, the progressive transformation of society at every level. The agents of change were to be free individuals, who, through their freedom, would gain a better understanding both of themselves—their limitations and their potentialities—and of their community. Enlightened legislators, possessing a superior knowledge of Mill's proposed sciences of human nature and society, would provide the general prescriptions for improvement. The inevitable progress of humanity would, for the first time, be harnessed by humanity itself. Mill did not intend to provide the definitive science, he hoped merely to be the guide, 'to point out the way' for future examinations of the human condition.[1] This was the purpose of the *System of Logic*, 'Being a Connected View of the Principles of Evidence and the Methods of Scientific Investigation.'[2] It was also a work of personal clarification, which attempted to reconcile divergent elements of his thought, a process which had begun with the 'crisis in my Mental History',[3] and continued throughout the ten years the work took to complete (inevitably leading to constant revision). The end result was an amalgam of metaphysics, empiricism, utilitarianism and historicism, providing for Mill an exhaustive scientific method, because,

> he who can throw most light on the subject of method will do most to forward that alliance among the most advanced intellects and

characters of the age, which is the only definite object I ever have in literature or philosophy, so far as I have any *general* object at all.[4]

Through forging an alliance between the conflicting ideas of the age and formulating a unifying method, Mill believed that he could bring together individuals of intellect and influence, harnessing their collective genius in pursuance of the progressive reformation of society.

Mill's unifying analytical procedure was the 'inverse deductive, or historical method'. This, he believed, would explain the formation and dynamics of human society, an explanation which relied upon the formulation of sciences of the mind and the formation of character, of social life and of social change.

All phenomena of society are phenomena of human nature, generated by the action of outward circumstances upon masses of human beings: and if therefore, the phenomena of human thought, feeling and action, are subject to fixed laws, the phenomena of society cannot but conform to fixed laws.[5]

The importance of a correct understanding of human nature could not be overestimated, especially at a time when 'the German, or *a priori* view of human knowledge, and of the knowing faculties, is likely for sometime longer to predominate among those who occupy themselves with such enquiries.'[6] Mill was adamant in his opposition to metaphysics, particularly that of the English Romantics, but this did not prevent him from accommodating 'metaphysical' concepts such as Free Will within his materialist science of human character formation. Neither did he reject entirely his adversaries' critique of the Benthamite principle of association, conceding that there were limitations in its analysis of human nature. But, as will be shown below, these modifications were made on firm necessitarian foundations and the *System of Logic* remained 'a text book of the opposite doctrine—that which derives all knowledge from experience, and all moral and intellectual qualities principally from the direction given to the associations.'[7]

Intellectual endeavour, the forming of ideas, was, for Mill, the predominant agent of social change. The potential for maximization of humanity's material needs had been secured by the scientific investigation of the material world. Hence, all that now remained within the sphere of random empirical observation was the study of humanity.[8] Such a study would be subjected to the same processes of enquiry employed in the verification of laws governing simpler phenomena. Once the science of humanity had been substantiated, then the real business of change could begin.

Self-culture, Free Will and Liberty

Free Will, or the desire to change one's character, was, for Mill, central to an analysis of individual human nature. Without a full appreciation of this concept, any contemplation of freedom would be totally inadequate. His examination begins with a question:

> Are the actions of human beings, like all other natural events, subject to invariable law? Does the constancy of causation, which is the foundation of every scientific theory of successive phenomena, really obtain among them?[9]

This, it transpires, is only the preamble to general discussion of the celebrated controversy of Free Will and Determinism, or, as Mill termed it, 'Liberty and Necessity'. This debate reveals Mill as an eclectic at work, employing countervailing systems of thought, and combining 'half truths', in the formulation of new hypotheses. However, far from creating a completely original and unique system of thought which transcended the malaise of half truths, Mill squarely placed himself in the school of necessity. His utilitarian background remained secure after all as a basis for his analysis of humanity: 'I found the fabric of my old and taught opinions giving way in many fresh places, and I never allowed it to fall to pieces, but was incessantly occupied in weaving it anew.'[10]

With regard to the study of human nature, this 'weaving anew' resulted in Mill adopting the concept of Free Will but within a necessitarian methodology. His approach, in reconciling what he saw as conflicting theories, provides the reader with a picture of Mill's perception of human nature (as it appeared in the *Logic*). He begins his Liberty and Necessity investigation by posing the question as to 'whether the law of causality applies in the same strict sense to human actions as to other phenomena.'[11] The doctrine of Necessity, in reply to such a question, would assert that an individual's ability to choose and act for him or herself is necessary and inevitable, that the capacities and characters of all individuals are reducible to causal agencies. This affirmative answer to the original question is opposed by the negative opinion held by metaphysical philosophers, such as Carlyle and Coleridge, who claim that the will is not determined by antecedents, but determines itself, such that our own volitions are not the effects of causes. Mill viewed this approach with a certain degree of sympathy. The doctrine of Necessity was a successor to the materialist, empiricist philosophies of the eighteenth century, and, by the time Mill was writing, had become in the main a dogmatized discipline. The Utopianists, and especially the Owenites, were chargeable with such an offence. Mill saw Bentham as a perpetrator of the crime which condemned humanity to the causal agency of outward circumstances.

Having himself been a temporary victim of Bentham's shallow psychology,[12] Mill understood the response of the metaphysical philosophers, who were reacting against the image created by the necessitarian determinists of a 'manufactured man'. Even though he saw this opinion as essentially misguided, Mill believed that it provided a useful service in exposing many of the crude misinterpretations of the doctrine of Necessity adhered to by most of its supporters and practitioners.

> I [do not] deny that the doctrine, as sometimes held, is open to these imputations; for the misapprehension in which I will be able to show that they originate, unfortunately is not confined to the opponents of the doctrine, but is participated in by many, perhaps we might say by most, of its supporters.[13]

What Mill attempted to do was to answer the criticisms of the metaphysicians by establishing beyond reasonable doubt that Free Will was consistent with a correct reading of the doctrine of necessity. At the same time, he attempted in the *Logic* to rescue necessitarianism from its 'fatalist' assumptions and conclusions in an effort to posit a semi-autonomous individual capable of participating in the processes leading to the formation of character. German idealism, which Mill received through the medium of English Romantic writers, had, early in his life, deposited a seed of doubt in what he had previously believed was the efficacy of the practical application of Benthamism, the most celebrated branch of the school of Necessity. Mill's 'compatabilism' in the *Logic* was his attempt at reconciling the ostensibly irreconcilable:

> The metaphysical theory of free-will, as held by philosophers (for the practical feeling of it, common in greater or less degree to all mankind is in no way inconsistent with the contrary theory) was invented because the supposed alternative of admitting human actions to be necessary was deemed inconsistent with everyone's intuitive consciousness, as well as humiliating to the pride, and even degrading to the moral nature of man.[14]

Apart from the assumption of a moral human nature, both Mill's interpretation of Necessity, and that of it's 'misinterpreters', held in common the general premiss of the doctrine—that if we knew an individual thoroughly, knew the motives that influenced that person's mind, taking into account the character and disposition of the subject—'the manner in which he will act might be unerringly inferred', and that if we knew all the inducements which act upon the individual, 'we could fortell his conduct with as much certainty as we can predict any physical event.'[15] Where Mill departed from his former necessitarian colleagues was in his opposition to their fatalist conclusions. Necessitarians of this persuasion believe that human actions are determined by the human character which itself is conditioned by the current state of social circumstances, education and personal organization. The necessitarian accordingly believes:

> . . . that his nature is such, or that his education and circumstances have so moulded his character, that nothing can now prevent him from feeling and acting in a particular way, or at least that no effort of his own can hinder it . . .[16]

The most extreme exponent of this doctrine is inevitably a fatalist because he is convinced that '. . . his character is formed *for* him, and not *by* him; therefore his wishing that it had been formed differently is of no use, he has no power to alter it.'[17] Mill believed that this 'grand error' should be rectified if we were to obtain a truer depiction of human character and of the processes leading to its formation. His contribution to this cause consisted of postulating a process of character formation which adds to the factors of causation the ability to alter one's own character. Central to his analysis is the concept of 'self-culture', an integral, causal agent of human character which, in conjunction with 'outward circumstances', should be taken into consideration during the course of any enquiry into the formation of human nature. Individuals, therefore, have, to a degree, a power to alter their characters, and only through a free expression of this power can they achieve true individual freedom.

> [Man's] character is formed by his circumstances (including among these his particular organisation), but his own desire to mould it in a particular way is one of those circumstances, and by no means one of the least influential.[18]

However, this desire cannot be used at will. It may be a propensity possessed by all humans, but it is a characteristic that is rarely evident in the process of character formation, because either we are not aware of its existence and potential, or we would deny its very existence:

> We cannot, indeed, directly will to be different from what we are . . . we, when our habits are not too inveterate, can, by willing the requisite means, make ourselves different . . . we can place ourselves under the influence of other circumstances. We are exactly as capable of making our own character, *if we will*, as others are of making it for us.[19]

Therefore, 'if we will', we can change our character. This capacity appears to take on the form of a metaphysical 'Free Will', an innate propensity of human nature. Notwithstanding, Mill retrieves his postulate from the realms of idealism, and replaces it firmly within a materialist framework by explaining that our capability to change our characters is formed for us by experience: 'experience of the painful consequences of the character we previously had, or by some strong feeling of admiration or aspiration accidentally aroused.'[20] This suggests that our desire to change our characters is explicable through an application of the traditional utilitarian principles of pain and pleasure. Either the painful consequences of a previous character, or the pleasurable expectations aroused by an appraisal of alternative examples of individual characters, appear to be the stimuli which form the desire to change. But experience and desire are two separate elements in the process that leads to character formation, and Mill's analysis does not allow for an intermediate process which transforms the raw material of experience into the specialized desire for character change. The mind, for Mill, is a receptacle for experience which is mysteriously transformed into an individual desire to change one's character. Here we see how the thorny problem of Free Will is accommodated within a revised and improved theory of Necessity.

The personal propensity to reform one's character became an integral element of Mill's view of a future liberated age, to the extent that he went on to elevate this capacity to a sentiment of moral freedom of which we are conscious. Moral freedom, therefore, is the achieved desire to modify our character, itself explicable through an understanding of the causal nature of experience. 'A person feels morally free who feels that his habits or his temptations are not his masters but he theirs.'[21] But what is the ultimate master? If the desire to change our character is reliant upon the causal nature of experience, and that desire is our feeling of moral freedom, our moral freedom is, in the last analysis, determined for us.

As such, Mill posited a *semi-autonomous* individual, one who, in the last analysis, is determined by circumstance, education and experience, but one who also possesses a capacity for personal change that is exercised in conditions of complete freedom from restraint:

It is of course necessary, to render our consciousness of Freedom complete, that we should have succeeded in making our character all we have hitherto attempted to make it; for if we have wished and not attained, we have, to that extent not power over our character—we are not free.[22]

Laws of the mind and the science of ethology

Self-culture, Free Will, or the desire to change one's character, is, Mill believed, a capacity which, as with other elements of human nature and character formation, is scientifically explicable, and it is a purpose of Book VI of the *Logic* to provide a secure methodological base for the future scientific investigations of human nature. Mill identifies in the *Logic* two sets of laws, which not only explain the formation of individual human character, but also are necessary in the formation of a 'General Science of Society', itself the prior condition for any effective reform of society:

> The actions and feelings of human beings in the social state, are, no doubt, entirely governed by psychological and ethological laws: whatever influence any cause exercises upon the social phenomena, it exercises through those laws.[23]

To understand social phenomena one has to understand human nature, especially the laws of its formation, the laws of the mind and the laws of ethology. Indeed 'Ethology itself . . . is the immediate foundation of the Social Science.'[24]

For Mill, the science of human nature would be an 'intermediate' science, one which would be capable of establishing general laws of causation, which would provide a complete explanation, if there were no other intervening causes. But observation and experimentation show us that there are a whole number of secondary causes, which on their own appear insignificant, but in combination are in a position to change the effects of the general causal laws. However, as with 'Tidology', Mill believed in the efficacy of general laws of causation 'which affect the phenomenon in all cases, and in a considerable degree'.[25] This could never be an exact science in the sense that the thoughts, feelings and actions of all individuals could be predicted with complete certainty. Any investigation would find it impossible to identify all the circumstances in which each individual might be placed, but for the purpose of general prediction of human behaviour in particular circumstances, approximate truths concerning causation would be sufficient.

Thoughts, emotions, volitions and sensations are all states of mind, all contributing to what is commonly perceived as human nature, but the interpretations as regards their origin differ considerably. Therefore, as with Liberty and Necessity, Mill attempted to steer a course between two extremes, German metaphysics and necessitarianism:

> The majority of those who speculate on human nature prefer dogmatically to assume that the mental differences which they perceive,

or think they perceive, among human beings, are ultimate facts, incapable of being either explained or altered. . . . The German school of metaphysical speculation . . . has had this among many other injurious influences.[26]

Thus, the view of human nature as universal and ahistorical is opposed by an analysis which insists that there are no laws of mind in the sense that Mill employs the term, and all workings of the human mind are reducible to physical, bodily processes over which individuals have no control. Positivists such as Comte regarded mental science as 'a mere branch, though the highest and most recondite branch, of the science of physiology'; Comte went even further and not only 'claims the scientific cognizance of moral and intellectual phenomena exclusively for physiologists,' but also 'denies to psychology, or mental philosophy properly so called, the character of a science.'[27] As with his discussion of a correct understanding of Free Will, Mill, recognizing the dangers of a crude necessitarian analysis—evident both in its view of human nature and the threat to individual liberty apparent in its programmes for the future—tempered the determinism of the traditional utilitarian interpretation by providing an explanation of the formation of states of mind. This, in turn, established general laws of mind which formed the basis of Mill's explanation of the formation of human nature. Mill admitted that each mental state may indeed have an antecedent nervous state, but our knowledge of the latter is so incomplete that for a long time to come we must rely upon the more accurate information concerning the 'uniformities of succession among states of mind' obtained through observation and experiment. Psychology or the science of mind may well be a derivative science, reliant upon physiological laws, and Mill insisted that this must be borne in mind when studying mental states. But, for the present, a science of the mind must be pursued as an independent enquiry. Mill again attempted to encompass within his eclectic analysis divergent interpretations, depositing within each individual mind laws of mental activity, which *may* be the result of physiological laws, but, for the moment at least, exist as independent laws in their own right. These laws rely, in the first instances, upon circumstances which supply the mind with a variety of impressions exciting in us a state of consciousness. Once the impression has been made it can be recalled as a state of consciousness that resembles the original state of consciousness or impression, and can be achieved without the presence of the original cause of the impression. 'This law is expressed by saying, in the language of Hume, that every mental *impression* has its *idea*.'[28] The 'laws of association' were seen by Mill as the other main group of 'simple or elementary Laws of Mind' and he recommended that the reader should refer to James Mill's 'professedly psychological' work, *Analysis of the Phenomena of the Human Mind.*[29] Here, the laws of ideas are examined in some depth, especially the 'principal laws of association, [which] along with many of their applications, are copiously exemplified, and with a masterly hand.'[30]

These simple laws of mind, Mill believed, generate all the complex laws of thought and feeling. They are laws which are universal elements of Mill's philosophy of human nature, serving to explain the workings of the human mind and provide the laws by which mental and physical impressions, whether received simultaneously or successively, are assimilated and processed into mental states, both simple and complex. 'The general laws of association prevail among [the] more intricate states of mind, in the same manner as among the simpler ones.' Therefore,

> A desire, an emotion, an idea of the higher order of abstraction, even our judgements and volitions when they have become habitual, are called up by association, according to precisely the same laws as our simple ideas.[31]

The laws of mind postulated by Mill appear to offer a middle course, steering between the two extremes of German metaphysics and rigid necessitarianism, while at the same time adopting and adapting the half truths of each. What emerges is a view of the workings of the human mind which is still essentially necessitarian in outlook, in that human character is the product of outward causes, but each individual operates according to universal laws of mind. Mental differences, as well as mental similarities, are made explicable by employing these general laws, and all who speculate on the origins of mental states (as well as, no doubt, all those engaged in reform) should 'take the trouble of fitting themselves, by the requisite processes of thought', and before implementing any change, 'referring those mental differences to the outward causes by which they are for the most part produced, and on the removal of which they would cease to exist.'[32]

Although for Mill humankind are not merely biological machines (as envisaged by Comte), they are for the most part conditioned by education, circumstance and the related causal laws of mind, determinants which were held to have direct implications for the vision of society. Therefore, if we understand the roles of each in forming human nature, we can mould education and circumstance into forms which serve the general purpose of encouraging the development of both emancipated individuals and an enlightened society.

However, a knowledge of the laws of the mind alone was insufficient for the purpose of change. Mill insisted that a science of the formation of character was also required. He chose to call this science ethology, and it was to be the link between the universal laws of mind governing individual human character and the science of the 'actions of collective masses of mankind, and the various phenomena which constitute social life.'[33] Empirical laws provided Mill with observations of human affairs within a particular realm of experience. They were illustrations of the consequences of the causal laws of human nature and nothing more. These empirical laws were not to be taken as 'ultimate laws of human action; they are not the principles of human nature, but the results of those principles under the circumstances in which mankind have happened to be placed.'[34] Unfortunately, Mill observed, it was the common practice for metaphysical philosophers, economic theorists and capitalists to adopt transitory, empirical laws of human nature as universal truths, basing their respective analyses on these 'truths'. Mill criticized the economists for 'regarding not any economic doctrine, but their experience of mankind, as of universal validity; mistaking temporary or local phases of human character for human nature itself.'[35] Capitalists also made a misconception, in that they viewed the

> normal state of human beings [as] that of struggling to get on . . . that the trampling, crushing, elbowing, and treading on each others heads, which from the existing type of social life, are the most desirable lot of human kind, or anything but the disagreeable symptoms of one of the phases of industrial progress.[36]

For Mill, ethology goes beyond this circumstantial, historical picture of a transitory human nature, providing us with laws of causation, which explain the formation of the wide variety of human feelings and actions. 'In other words, mankind have not one universal character, but there exist universal laws of the Formation of Character.'[37] Although the laws of ethology are 'derivative laws, resulting from the general Laws of Mind', as a science it remained independent of the science of psychology.[38] Where psychology concerns itself with the elementary laws of mind, ethology is the subsequent science which largely determines the type of character formed by the interaction of the general laws of mind and the specific set of circumstances. But this science of character formation, Mill admitted, can never be an exact one. This, however, is not a failing; as a science, it need only inform us that 'certain means have a *tendency* to produce a given effect, and that others have a tendency to frustrate it.'[39] Ethology is the science of hypothetical laws which affirm tendencies rather than unequivocal facts, tendencies which assert that a given cause will produce a particular reaction as long as the process operates uninterrupted. Mill believed that this limited 'scientific' knowledge would be enough to equip enlightened reformers with the tools to change circumstances:

> When the circumstances of an individual or of a nation are in any considerable degree under our control, we may, by our knowledge of tendencies, be enabled to shape those circumstances in a manner much more favourable to the ends we desire, than the shape which they would of themselves assume. This is the limit of our power; but within this limit the power is a most important one.[40]

Ethology provided Mill with his *axiomata media*, the middle principles, which lie between the laws of common observation and those of the highest generalizations, between the practical knowledge of humanity in a particular circumstance and the science of the laws of mind. The purpose of such a science is to prepare the way for a practical application of the middle principles through the agency of education in its broadest sense. 'According to this definition, Ethology is the science which corresponds to the art of education; in the widest sense of the term. . . .'[41]

Instincts

While discussing the human condition in the *Logic*, Mill paused to consider a number of 'mental facts' that do not appear to conform to those modes of explanation which furnished the laws of mind. These facts are 'the various instincts of animals, and the portion of human nature which corresponds to those instincts.'[42] Mill admitted that these instincts are beyond the realms of an explanation that rests upon psychological causes alone. He appeared to be far more favourably disposed toward a genetic explanation of their existence. 'There is great reason to think that they have as positive, and even as direct and immediate, a connection with physical conditions of the brain and nerves, as any of our mere sensations have.'[43]

Not only, then, are there universal laws of mind, but also, Mill seemed to suggest, there are universal physiological predispositions which partially determine human character. Mill left it at that; humans possess a number of 'animal instincts', and although he added that these instincts may be modified or 'entirely conquered', he failed to identify the nature of those instincts and the extent of their influence in the formation of human character. Mill attempted to formulate physiological laws of mind peculiar to humankind, universal laws that would provide the basis for an understanding of the workings of human nature. However, he appears to have

left a whole area of human activity uncharted, and, maybe more importantly, he chose not to discuss the interrelationship between these
'instincts' and the universal mental laws of causation.

Elsewhere, especially in his later works, Mill's discussion of propensities, desires and impulses and their effect on human character formation
is, perhaps, more enlightening. Innate human sentiments do exist and are
discernible from those elements of character directly ascribable to the laws
of the mind, particularly the principle of association.

Just as the history of humanity provides us with evidence of a transitory human nature, so it also informs us of enduring characteristics,
which, according to Mill, have been of vital importance to human progress.
One such characteristic is the faculty of speculation, which, when all
things are considered, 'is the main determining cause of the social progress.'[44] Although Mill thought it a 'great error' to claim that this faculty
is 'among the more powerful propensities of human nature', he did not
deny that it is a propensity, a natural tendency or disposition.[45] He made
little attempt to establish the origin of this propensity (central to Mill's
belief in progress) but some advances in the investigation of mental states
were being achieved in the field of cerebral physiology. No doubt such
enquiries would eventually provide an explanation for two other propensities which regularly appear in Mill's studies; those related to *self-
interest* and *social sympathy*:

> . . . the strongest propensity of uncultivated or half cultivated human
> nature (being the purely selfish ones, and those of a sympathetic
> character which partake most of the nature of selfishness) evidently
> tend in themselves to disunite mankind; not to unite them—to make
> them rivals, not confederates; social existence is only possible by a
> disciplining of those more powerful propensities, which consists in sub-
> ordinating them to a common system of opinions.[46]

Mill regarded self-interest as a major threat to the general happiness of
the community and the workings of good government.[47] In *On Liberty*,
Mill addressed himself to the problem of uncontrolled desires and impulses
which 'are as much a part of perfect human being as beliefs and restraints',
and concluded that 'strong impulses are only perilous when not properly
balanced', since

> . . . one set of aims and inclinations is developed into strength, while
> others, which ought to co-exist with them, remain weak and inactive.
> It is because men's desires are strong that they act ill; it is not because
> their consciences are weak.[48]

Social conscience is itself attributable to what Mill termed social sympathy, an innate element of human nature, which was also at the root of justice and morality. In *Utilitarianism*, when discussing the ultimate sanction of the principle of Utility, Mill established what he believed to be the 'natural basis of sentiment for utilitarian morality'.

> This firm foundation is that of the social feelings of mankind; the desire to be in unity with our fellow creatures, which is already a powerful principle in human nature, and happily one of those which tend to become stronger, even without express inculcation, from the influences of advancing civilisations.[49]

An individual's own social conscience would be one of the checks and balances limiting the dangerous excesses of the more powerful propensities. Social conscience would need to be supplemented by a system of ethics, itself the embodiment of humanity's natural susceptibility of social feeling.

Therefore, morality itself is not innate, as the intuitionist would have us believe; but, according to Mill, the social feelings, and the accompanying 'social state [are] at once so natural, so necessary, and so habitual to man.'[50] In the same work, in a chapter entitled 'On the Connection Between Justice and Utility', Mill employed both the self-regarding and the sympathetic propensities of human nature in his examination of justice. The sentiment of justice consists of two major elements, 'the desire to punish a person who has done harm, and the knowledge or belief that there is some definite individual or individuals to whom harm has been done.'[51] Mill maintained that both these elements emanate from two sentiments, 'both in the highest degree natural, and which either are or resemble instincts; the impulse of self-defence, and the feeling of sympathy.'[52] Humanity shares with all animals these sentiments, but to a higher degree, in that we are able to sympathize with all human beings and that our more developed intelligence provides us with a wider qualitative range to our innate propensities. It is this more developed intelligence —itself the product of a natural inquisitiveness enhanced by the laws of the mind and the principles of association—which prevents our natural instinct for retribution from becoming indiscriminate. Here the principle of association encourages through education and experience the moralizing potential of our social feelings. It disciplines those natural qualities which threaten the peaceful co-existence of free individuals while cultivating those propensities beneficial to the individual and the community.[53]

For Mill, instincts, or innate sympathies, had a considerable degree of influence in the formation of character. They were also constructive, providing they were harnessed correctly, and only a thorough analysis of these mental states would suffice.

Conclusion

Mill began his systematic investigation of human nature in the *Logic*. The enquiry was partially a response to two distinct yet interrelated dilemmas, one personal, the other philosophical. While under the influence of Bentham, Mill was committed more than most to the philosophy of necessity and the doctrine of Utility. During his formative years, the general happiness principle remained paramount; the determining elements of pain and pleasure, linked with the view of humanity as essentially selfish, conditioned the young Mill's view of human nature. The simple prescription for the attainment of a good and happy society was the enlightened ordering of outward circumstances. His 'mental crisis' put paid to this youthful enthusiasm for a system of thought that had appeared so rational and yet, apparently, was so susceptible to withering attack from social scientists and philosophers alike. Macaulay had perceptively questioned the limited premises employed by Mill's father in his *Essay on Government*, which placed in doubt the efficacy of his philosophical method. For their part, the Coleridgians, especially Maurice and Sterling, challenged the utilitarian assumptions that human nature was solely determined by outward circumstances, reasserting a belief in the individual as an autonomous being, capable of self-culture. Prompted by his own anxiety, Mill began to doubt the efficacy of the pursuit of individual happiness as an end in itself: 'All my happiness was to be found in the continual pursuit of this end. The end had ceased to charm, and how could there ever again be any interest in the means? I seemed to have nothing left to live for.'[54]

The *Logic* became a reasoned attack on the conservative doctrines of German metaphysics, but an attack made from a standpoint which itself was the product of a critical re-evaluation. Mill had noted with despair the development of a popular, yet crude, interpretation of necessitarianism, a doctrine with an admirable eighteenth-century pedigree. Therefore, in conjunction with his critique of idealism, Mill set out to refurbish the premises and methodology of an otherwise sound doctrine, providing it with a progressive historical perspective. The purpose was not only to explain the present nature of individual character and human society, but also to provide a scientific theory of humanity's progress. Inseparable from a theory of history was an exhaustive science of human nature, and Mill elucidated what he believed constituted the causal laws of such a science.

The laws of mind (encompassing those of the formation of original ideas and of association) and the derivative laws of character formation were intended to provide the predominant determinants of human nature. According to this analysis, human nature *per se* is transitory, which, for Mill, served scientifically to disprove the metaphysicians' claim that human nature is universal and ahistorical. But the laws governing the formation of character are not, since they constitute the enduring elements of human nature. Armed with these precepts, the virtuous reformer, spurred on by the *Logic*, could probably agree with Mill's conclusion: 'It is certain that, in human beings at least, differences in education and in outward circumstances are capable of affording an adequate explanation of by far the greatest portion of character.'[55]

However, sixteen years after the publication of the first edition of the *Logic*, he was prepared to admit that

> Human nature is not a machine to be built after a model, and set to do exactly the work prescribed for it, but a tree, which requires to grow and develop itself on all sides, according to the tendency of inward forces which make it a living thing.[56]

He had already attempted to accommodate within his necessitarian framework a concept of Free Will, a provision which sought to explain an individual's ability to choose, the cornerstone of his belief in self-emancipation. By the time he was writing *Utilitarianism* and *Liberty* he had moved on to a view of human nature that incorporated the formative role of instincts and propensities. Some of these dispositions were shared with animals, others were peculiar to humanity (such as the species' distinctive ingenuity and its heightened capacity for self-awareness and self-education). As has been illustrated, these propensities assumed the position of sanctions in Mill's justification of the efficacy of a Utilitarian Morality. This was in direct response to his age-old rivals, the 'institutionists' or metaphysical philosophers, who had challenged the premisses of his adopted and revised doctrine, Necessity. Nevertheless, in the *Logic* Mill assimilated into his own analysis such universal concepts as Free Will, while at the same time insisting on the essential malleability of human nature. Ethology and the Principle of Association were based on the assumption that human nature is malleable, but Mill eventually held a position that appeared to rest upon ultimate universal principles.[57] The possible difficulties resulting from such an alliance seem not to have concerned Mill; suffice to say that any individual engaged in the pursuit of change would require an extensive knowledge of what became a complex phenomenon, namely the science of the human condition.

Notes

1. Mill, J. S., *A System of Logic*, in *Collected Works*, Vol. VIII, Toronto, University of Toronto Press, 1974, p. 835.
2. Ibid., p. i.
3. Mill, J. S., *Autobiography*, London, 1873, pp. 132–53.
4. Mill, J. S., Letter to John Sterling, 20-2 October 1831, in *The Letters of John Stuart Mill*, Vol. I, London, 1910, pp. 8–9.
5. *A System of Logic*, op. cit., p. 877.
6. *Autobiography*, op. cit., pp. 224–5.
7. Ibid., p. 225.
8. *A System of Logic*, op. cit., pp. 833–4.
9. Ibid., p. 835.
10. *Autobiography*, op. cit., p. 156.
11. *A System of Logic*, op. cit., p. 836.
12. *Autobiography*, op. cit., pp. 168–9.
13. *A System of Logic*, op. cit., p. 836.
14. Ibid.
15. Ibid.
16. Ibid., p. 840.
17. Ibid.
18. Ibid.
19. Ibid.
20. Ibid., p. 341.
21. Ibid.
22. Ibid.
23. Ibid., p. 896.
24. Ibid., p. 907.
25. Ibid., p. 846.
26. Ibid., p. 859.
27. Ibid., p. 850.
28. Ibid.
29. Ibid. James Mill's *Analysis of the Phenomena of the Human Mind*, London, 1869, was edited by his son, J. S., who added to the original text a large number of extensive footnotes which include some interesting asides on the editor's views of human nature.
30. Ibid., p. 853. The Laws of Association are three in number: (1) the law that similar ideas tend to excite one another; (2) the law 'that when two impressions have been frequently experienced (or even thought of) either simultaneously or in immediate succession, then whatever one of these impressions, or the idea of it, recurs, it tends to excite the idea of the other'; (3) the law 'that the greater intensity in either or both of the impressions, is equivalent, in rendering them excitable by one another, to a greater frequency of conjunction.' *Logic*, op. cit., p. 852.
31. Ibid., p. 856.
32. Ibid., p. 859.
33. Ibid., p. 875.
34. Ibid., pp. 861–2.
35. Mill, J. S., *Auguste Comte and Positivism*, Ann Arbor, Michigan University Press, 1961, p. 82.
36. Mill, J. S., *Principles of Political Economy*, in *Collected Works*, op. cit., Vol. II, p. 203.
37. *A System of Logic*, op. cit., p. 864.
38. Ibid., p. 689.

39. Ibid., p. 869. The laws of the formation of character are obtainable, Mill points out, by deduction from the general laws of mind; 'by supposing any given set of circumstances, and then considering what, according to the laws of mind, will be the influence of those circumstances on the formation of character.' Ibid.
40. Ibid., pp. 869–70.
41. Ibid., p. 869.
42. Ibid., p. 859.
43. Ibid.
44. Ibid., p. 926.
45. Ibid.
46. Ibid. These pronouncements appear during the course of Mill's enquiry into 'Historical Method', to be employed in an investigation of human progression and *not* in his discussion of human nature.
47. Mill, J. S., *Utilitarianism, Liberty* and *Representative Government*, London, 1910, Mill points out the danger of the 'evil disposition' of 'man's selfish interests' in the operation of good government, pp. 248–56.
48. Mill, J. S., *On Liberty*, London, 1910, p. 118.
49. *Utilitarianism*, op. cit., p. 29.
50. Ibid.
51. Ibid., p. 47.
52. Ibid.
53. Ibid., pp. 47–8.
54. *Autobiography*, op. cit., p. 134.
55. *A System of Logic*, op. cit., p. 859.
56. *On Liberty*, op. cit., p. 117.
57. Of particular interest is Mill's allusion to a universal good, apparent in uncorrupted human nature: 'If you take the average human mind while still young, before the objects it has chosen in life have given it a turn in any bad direction, you will generally find it desiring what is good, right, for the benefit of all; and if that season is properly used to implant the knowledge and give the training which shall render rectitude of judgement more habitual than sophistry, a serious barrier will have been erected against the inroads of selfishness and falsehood.' *Inaugural Address at St. Andrews University*, London, 1867, pp. 75–6.

4 Conservatism and human nature

CHRISTOPHER BERRY

It is a commonplace that all political doctrines assume a view of human nature, but whilst there are many liberal and socialist accounts of it, conservative views of human nature have had less attention. For example, O'Sullivan and Quinton regard the idea of human 'imperfection' as central to conservatism but do not subject the term to extensive analysis; Scruton does refer to a conservative theory of human nature, but this is a rather dogmatic allusion, and Oakeshott, though talking of a conservative 'disposition', explicitly disavows the profitability of speculation about 'human nature'.[1] The aim of this chapter cannot be, within its limits, to 'plug this gap' but rather the aim is to sketch out that reading of human nature that lends itself most distinctively to conservative ends.

Despite the acceptance of the above commonplace, it should not obscure some differences. Conservatism is more directly a theory of human nature than either liberalism or socialism, which are more overtly political doctrines. Of course, liberalism and socialism invoke a supportive picture of men and women as free, equal and independent, or as co-operative workers, and conservatism prescribes some political positions (gradualism) and proscribes others (revolution). Nevertheless, conservatism is better able to handle the universality that the concept of human nature implies: any view of the character and substance of human nature must claim to be a truth about all humans. Superficially, *all* humans are free, *all* humans are social and *all* humans are conservative; yet the favoured readings of 'free' and 'social' provided by liberals and socialists respectively preclude the bulk of societies from being manifestations of this purported universality, if only because, in their favoured usages, 'free' (read open market society) and 'social' (read socialism) are mutually exclusive. Conversely, conservatism can quite happily claim to encompass all. It is this very facility that makes conservatism less directly a political doctrine. Socialists and liberals, whatsoever their theoretical differences, both behave conservatively in practice. Accordingly, rather than it being a weakness of the conservative position to claim that 'Bolsheviks in power are conservative',[2] this claim accurately exhibits the universality implicit in a concept of human nature.

The universality of human nature

Where do conservatives locate the universality of human nature? Most characteristically, this location resides in purported natural processes and it is to the ineluctability of such processes that conservatives appeal. Nature, because it imposes constraints against which it is pointless to jibe, has authoritative status. But humans are, of course, constrained naturally in many ways (as featherless bipeds they cannot fly), so what is further characteristic of conservative thought (at least implicitly) is the importance attached to the physical dependence of the human infant at birth. Of course, this does not encompass conservative thought in its entirety, yet it is that aspect that most directly pertains to the focus of this essay, human nature. Additionally, it is testament to the importance of human nature in conservatism that the centrality of this 'natural fact' of infant dependence can be gauged from its resonance in the key themes of conservatism, such as family, custom, nation, hierarchy, biology and divine purpose. Further, as we shall see, it is in the implications of this natural fact that the most characteristic conservative political doctrine, namely the defence of gradualism, is to be found.

How is it that natural dependence has such resonances? The human infant, in order to achieve its humanity, in order to have an identity, rather than the mere 'being' enjoyed by other animals, requires acculturation, since (in the words of Geertz):

> It is through culture patterns, ordered clusters of significant symbols, that man makes sense of the events through which he lives. The study of culture, the accumulated totality of such patterns, is thus the study of the machinery individuals and groups of individuals employ to orient themselves in a world otherwise opaque.[3]

Other animals are born with their orientation naturally pre-wired, so to speak, but humans, equally naturally, have a prolonged and dependent infancy to enable them to assimilate their culture; they are naturally cultural beings. This assimilation may be said to have two necessary aspects—it is specific and it is temporal.

The most obvious aspect of this specificity is linguistic. The infant, even one reared in a bilingual home, has to learn a language; to speak is to use a specific vocabulary and grammar. Whilst there is no need to endorse fully the Whorfian thesis of linguistically determined 'thought-worlds',[4] the acquisition of a language nevertheless carries with it an orientation, a way of looking at the world. As well as this involving the identification of the world's furniture (240 expressions for the colour of horses' hides are available to the Argentinian gaucho),[5] and its categorizing processes (in Shambala there is only 'today' and 'not-today' and thus no linguistic distinction between yesterday and tomorrow),[6] it also involves the imparting of values (participating in a public world as manifest, for example, in Geertz's description of the 'stage-fright' of the Balinese, who, in their terminology, endeavour to 'de-personalize' relationships).[7] The upshot of this is that a language and a culture form an inextricable whole. This totality lay behind Herder's concept of a *Volk*. In his essay, *Origin of Language*, Herder argued, *inter alia*, against the Enlightenment view of language as the gradual development of meaningful discourse out of automatic meaningless responses. Rather, for Herder, language is indistinguishable from thought; it embodies and expresses what is human. But this embodiment and expression is necessarily specific. A person's language is the bearer of meaning to, and for, him or her; hence the importance of folk-tales, mythologies and the like.[8] Given that language has this intrinsic expressive function, then those who speak the same language share the same experience, and what makes *this* people what they *are* serves to distinguish them radically from other people.

The value of such specificity to conservatives is that it serves both a positive and a negative function. Positively, it is the marriage between conservatism and nationalism. Fichte expresses this when he writes: 'the first original and truly natural boundaries are beyond doubt their internal boundaries. Those who speak the same language are joined to each other by a multitude of invisible bonds.'[9] Nationalism, of course, is not coterminous with conservatism, but in the need of an aspirant nation to achieve identity or sense of self, in order that it can claim to be self-governing, it requires a sense of its own distinctiveness.[10] Conservatives cherish the differences between states, peoples and nations, and the negative aspect to this is the critique of abstract individualism which discounts such differences. This critique was at the forefront of the text most widely regarded as the *locus classicus* of conservatism, namely, Burke's *Reflections on the Revolution in France*. Burke's chief target was the natural rights doctrine of Price and his followers. These rights are 'natural' only in the sense of not being confined to specific societies. Furthermore, because they are abstracted from any specific set of circumstances, these rights are necessarily empty. The basis of these empty rights is a superficial doctrine of human nature. According to this doctrine, human nature is the same at all times and in all places and 'people' possess meaningful attributes independently of the particular culture in which they find themselves. But any such person is a purely fictitious being. Joseph de Maistre states the point emphatically:

There is no such thing as man in the world. During my life, I have seen Frenchmen, Italians, Russians, and so on; thanks to Montesquieu, I even know that one can be Persian; but I must say, as for man, I have never come across him anywhere.[11]

Burke disparagingly traces the source of this specious and superficial doctrine to 'naked reason'.[12] This disparagement of reason is a recurrent motif in conservatism and, again, this assessment can be seen to relate to the infant's lack of independence. Just as the infant is specified through its acquisition of a language, so this acquisition is pre-reflective. When independent reflection is possible, it is already within the paradigm thus acquired. Therefore, the processes whereby the infant acquires its language are significant. The infant learns to speak through its contact with language-users and, necessarily, its relationship to these language-users is submissive: it copies and imitates and it does not question.

The family and acculturation

Who are these language-users? Ideally, they are the infant's parents. The dependence of the infant requires a family. Given that this dependence is an ineluctable natural fact, then the family too partakes of this authoritative naturalness. This naturalness the ancients referred to as natural affection and the moderns refer to as evolutionary stable strategies.[13] The significance of this role of the family to conservatism is twofold. First, the family is not a product of convention. It cannot be abolished and any attempts so to do are foolish, and, as the Soviet experience in the 1920s 'proves', are doomed to fail. Rather, given its ineluctability, the appropriate prescription ought to be to defend the family as an institution. Thus, to give two examples, Darlington uses his scientific analysis, whereby the family is seen as the effect of selective advantage, to explain the insolvency of the Welfare State and to advocate the abandonment of impersonal state control in favour of direct familial and personal responsibility; and second, to the same end, but from the different scientific base of ethology, Eibl-Eibesfeldt also advocates the strengthening of family ties.[14]

This sort of theorizing is typical of the ideological uses to which the concept of human nature can be put. An ideological argument can be identified as one whose function is the presentation of a partial or sectional interest as a general or universal one. The nature of human beings is a universal necessity (like gravity) to which appeal can be made. Just as lifts and stairs are necessary to take me to my fifth-floor office (I cannot fly there), so institutions like the family are necessary thanks to human nature. What this amounts to, in effect, is counselling acceptance of the status quo (the presence of stairs and families), but since any status quo favours some more than others, it is the particular interests of those (males rather than females, for example) thus favoured that stand to benefit from such counselling. Such a differentiation is in tune with the 'nature of things'—the acceptance of which is ineluctable. These are the 'facts of human nature' and they cannot be regarded as a conspiracy to keep some sections of the community in their relatively inferior position because, like gravity, they are neutral in operation through affecting everyone indiscriminately. Since, as argued here, an appeal to human nature has a central place in conservatism, then it also means that conservatism is particularly susceptible to such ideological attack.[15]

The second significant aspect of the family to conservatism is the location of its cohesiveness in instinct, feeling or affection. Positively, this gives to these aspects of human nature a solid status, and, negatively, it means again undercutting the claims made for the self-sufficiency of reason. This claim made on reason's behalf is, of course, identified in the mainstream Christian tradition as the root of Adam's sin. St. Augustine is definitive when he declares that it was humans' 'proud opinion that they were their own beginners' which is the source of that evil will that is sin, so that 'man by desiring more became less, and choosing to be sufficient in himself fell from that all-sufficient God.'[16] It is further the case that, despite their sinful state, humans are not left entirely bereft, because God is good and merciful. Accordingly, His provision of instincts for the most important aspects of human existence—self-preservation, procreation, family care—are testament to this Divine benevolence. Indeed, this point was used by Thomas Reid to confirm the feebleness of reason, since all that most mattered in human life was taken out of its effective scope.[17] It is undoubtedly true that this Christian location of the source of human finitude and imperfection has been important to conservatism (Hooker, Jenyns, Burke, Maistre, Muller, Cortes, etc.), and has been picked up by a number of scholars (Hearnshaw, Hailsham, Kirk)[18] as a constitutive element in conservatism. Yet, as other commentators (Quinton, Scruton) have pointed out, this direct link with a religious doctrine is not necessary. It is this latter view that is subscribed to here. A further consideration against giving religion a defining role is that its most obvious political prescription, namely that, given the axiomatic depravity of human nature, anarchism is impossible, thus making some form of human governance necessary, is scarcely confined to conservatives.

Thus far the specificity of the process of acculturation has been the focus of attention. It is now appropriate to turn this focus on to the second aspect mentioned above—temporality. Here it is sufficient to draw out the implications of what was said about linguistic specificity. Language is learnt, but learning is a temporal process. As we have seen, the learning of a language is synonymous with the learning of a culture. This culture is most immediately embodied in customs or traditions. Customs by definition are creatures of time; they cannot be acquired overnight. The special importance that conservatives attach to customs is derived from their function as maintainers of stability (and hence as confirmers of identity). It is imperative that children ingest their folkways along with their mothers' milk, for

> . . . human society is in perpetual flux, one man every hour going out of the world, another coming into it [so that] it is necessary, in order to preserve stability in government, that the new brood should conform themselves to the established constitution and nearly follow the same path which their fathers, treading in the footsteps of theirs, had marked out to them.[19]

But a culture, like a language, is not the product of an individual. Just as we do not choose what language to speak, so we do not choose which culture to pass on. This is necessary in order that the culture may cohere. Individuals, in their conducts one with another, need to have settled expectations as to how each will act. These expectations are derived from the common ingestation of the same 'cake of custom'.[20] Accordingly, strangers from one's own culture can be distinguished from aliens; a fact with important reinforcing effects on social identity. It is in this way that manners and etiquette (what Burke called the 'decent drapery of life'),[21] which are instilled initially by parents, are not superficial adornments but part of the constitutive fabric of social life. Similarly, that human nature is disposed to maintain conduct through habit is not some regrettable superstition, obscuring the light of (naked) reason, but part of its constitutive complexity.

Parents, therefore, are not free agents; it is their duty to pass on their culture, but, significantly, this is also their natural inclination. It is integral to the love parents bear to their offspring that they transmit to them the means to be 'at home' in the wider setting of their culture. Thus generations are linked one with another in Burke's 'great primeval contract'. The crucial fact about this contract, as a 'partnership not only between those who are living, those who are dead and those who are to be born', is that it is emphatically not the social contract of liberal political theory.[22] This latter contract turned political life into a cost/benefit calculus whereby independent individuals came together to pursue their mutual yet separate interests. This entails that the State is merely a means to the furtherance of the individual's ends (as in Locke's definition that the purpose of government is the protection of property)[23] and, in addition, that these ends themselves can be known, valued and formulated prior to the State.

Conservatives are opposed to such individualism. Again, the comparison with language is felicitous and one shared by conservatives as divergent as von Savigny and Oakeshott.[24] Language is not invented, nor is its usage a matter of individual choice or caprice. The individual is born into an ongoing community—'men are formed by language far more than language is formed by men.'[25] The individual's culture is not some external means for realizing the self independently of it, but is rather the context within which the self (with attendant goals) is conceived of in the first place. This context—language, religion, art, politics—is irreducibly social. Just as language is acquired pre-reflectively and establishes an authoritative paradigm, so too are habits formed pre-reflectively, establishing a basic disposition in terms of which other institutions are to be judged. It is this disposition that Burke terms, quite deliberately, a prejudice, which is

> . . . of ready application in the emergency; it previously engages the mind in a steady course of wisdom and virtue and does not leave the man hesitating in a moment of decision, sceptical, puzzled and unresolved. Prejudice renders a man's virtue his habit; and not a series of unconnected acts. Through just prejudice his duty becomes part of his nature.[26]

Conservatism and continuity

Again, it is superficial rationalist (radical) minds that dismiss such prejudices as superficial. People are not malleable fodder nor are they animate algebraic symbols that can be manipulated at will. It is a characteristic feature of the pretensions of reason that it can pronounce perfectly universal truths regardless of time, place and circumstance. The model for this thinking is mathematics, for two plus two universally equals four, but this is purely because of its abstract formalism. To separate form from content is the rationale of 'sophisters, economists and calculators',[27] but, when applied to human nature, this only separates that nature from any particular culture: such a separation is meaningless for it deprives humanity (form) from that which imparts meaning (content). Conservative thought stresses the concrete (the unity of form and content), not the abstract, and this is because human nature itself is a concrete product derived from the infant's cultural specification through its cumulative constitutive accretion of customs and habits. It is this imperviousness of human nature to abstract formalism that explains, in part, why many commentators see the concept of imperfection as playing such a prominent role in conservatism. But it is rather that the norm of perfection is arithmetic, with its simple clear-cut right answers, and that this norm is inapplicable to human nature, since, 'the nature of man is intricate; the objects of society of the greatest possible complexity.'[28] The conservative political recommendations to be drawn from this are (given that such perfection is not possible): opposition to those schemes which do imply that perfection; and approval of those actions that harmonize with the prevailing prejudices and habits.

Habit is indeed second nature, and just as the first nature of instinct and natural affection is recalcitrant to amendment by human action, so this second nature, too, sets up limits to what individuals can effectively do to each other. Habits which thus bind generations establish a decisive element of continuity which, in the form of traditions, shape the necessarily social identity of individuals by not only transcending their merely bio-logical particularity but also, simultaneously, by giving them an entrée into the cultural and symbolic resources of their community. To follow a tradition is not to surrender one's judgement, but is to adopt a proper sense of one's own humility. We are born into a world not of our choosing, a world that had existence before us and will endure after us. Measured against. that perspective, we are indeed as 'flies of a summer'.[29] Just as an individual's identity is established in large part by memory, so that of a society is established by its authoritative continuity through time.[30] This can be seen, for example, in the emphasis placed in English conservatism on the tradition of legal institutions, from the immemorial ancient con-stitution through Magna Carta and Habeas Corpus to the present day; to similar effect, it can be seen in the emphasis placed in German conserva-tism on the continuity of the German *Volk* from the folk-tales of illiterate peasants to the universal genius of Goethe. This investing of value in temporal continuity (prescription)[31] is alien to rationalists who judge institutions against the timeless principles of reason or utility, which, again like mathematics, are ever valid because they are not contaminated by the contingencies of time and space (witness the lack of interest in history in Bentham and Godwin, for example).

The significance of this continuity in conservatism is more aptly captured in the legalistic fiction of the *incorporation* of the individual into the body politic than in the imagery of organicism, despite the frequent recourse by most commentators to the latter. Organic metaphors do speak usefully to the conservative doctrine that the individual is not independent, but is a 'member' of a larger whole, but it is less able to convey the sense of obligation to posterity. As inheritors of the 'bank and capital' of past generations, we are merely trustees whose solemn duty it is to bequeath this capital to the next generation.[32] Whilst, again, organic language usefully points up the gradualness and intrinsicality of change, it is less able to identify an appropriate role for human agency. Conservatives are not committed to the denial of change; indeed, almost without exception, they would concur with Burke's dictum that a State without the means of some change is without the means of its conservation.[33] This change should be motivated by awareness of tradition, awareness of the warp and woof of the fabric of social life. Accordingly, any particular generation will utilize the 'interest' from the inherited capital to foster and protect the 'principal', thus bequeathing (entrusting) to the next generation its stock.

Given the conservative reading of human nature, this process occurs both ineluctably and ubiquitously. Parents, in acculturating their offspring, are passing on the tested fruits of their wisdom, which is itself, of course, the distillation of their parents' wisdom, and so on. It is the essential stuff of what Oakeshott called 'practical knowledge'—knowledge of concrete activity, analytically distinct from 'technical knowledge', which is formulable into maxims which may be learnt from a book.[34] Although there are innumerable handbooks on how to rear children, no parent needs these in the sense that without them they would not perform this task: acculturating children is not like installing your own central-heating. Acting as a parent means acting as an authority. Values are instilled by virtue of the authority of the parent over the dependent child. It is only because parents themselves were once children and the recipients of such an authorizing process that they can act as authorities in their turn. The family is thus necessarily a hierarchic authority structure, and this, as a natural consequence of the dependence of the human infant, is an integral component of the conservative vision.

Though the family is the prime source for authority and hierarchy, its very naturalness inclines conservatives to translate this model into other institutions. Hierarchy is the order of nature, and as such is ubiquitous. Whilst for Elyot this was part of an overall divine scheme, for the moderns it is Nature in the form of a 'non-egalitarian biological substratum' and an evolutionary adaptive 'pecking-order'.[35] This translation of the family model is perhaps most apparent in politics where, contrary to liberal doctrine, paternalism has a proper place, and where, contrary to an important strand in socialism, leadership has a proper role. Those on the higher rungs of the hierarchy have the responsibility not only to act as custodians of the political traditions but also to act as caring parents for those on lower rungs. It is integral to this care that it provides example and exhibits discipline; like Coleridge's National Church with its clerisy, it guides, guards and instructs.[36]

This necessary acculturation of the individual through time, and its effect, continuity, explain the conservative's most characteristic political doctrine, namely, an antipathy to radical change. A radical break will have to de-nature individuals, that is, will have to strip 'them' of the sources of their identity. Yet, the very plausibility of conservatism would seem to stem from the near impossibility of doing this. Rousseau, for example, when he does talk of the Legislator having to change ('*pour ainsi dire*') human nature, is clear not only that this must occur before customs have been established, that is, before separate individuals have become *un peuple*, but also that the agency required must be *extra-ordinaire* and needs must invoke divine authority.[37] In practice, most purported radical changes have, in fact, not been so; hence, that favoured reading of the Russian Revolution, and subsequent communist regime, as reverting to the principles of autocracy and bureaucracy pursued by the tsars.[38] The paradox of this is that true revolutionaries should be conservatives, for the 'logic' of revolution is liquidation; eliminate *le peuple* because they cannot be changed, start afresh with a new generation, and acculturate them with the new order. Leaving this pure case aside, conservatives might nevertheless still be thought to be caught in a theoretical inconsistency. If radical change is virtually impossible, why inveigh against it? If something is doomed because it runs against Nature, then of itself it will fail. But such quiescence would be to neglect the custodial role that conservatives see each generation (and its leaders) having. Whilst the culture may survive, that is not to say it will not suffer severe damage, which is to say nothing of the misery that will be inflicted meantime on human lives. Moreover, since the conservative is aware that such change will be ineffective in realizing desired ends, then he or she will urge that it should not be embarked upon in the first place.

There are two points here that can be expanded upon with profit. First, conservatives can be consistent humanitarians. Liberals treat individuals precisely as that—discrete independent self-legislators, who have to rely on their own merits (and luck) to make their competitive way in the world. A strict consequence of this is that the inevitable losers are left to the contingent charity of the more successful. But for the conservative, just as parents (simply because of their 'natural' relationship to their children) treat *all* their offspring with equal love and affection regardless of their achievements, or lack thereof, care of the destitute is a social responsibility. Socialists, on the other hand, through their fictitious doctrine of equality, are not only prone to disastrous and inhuman social practices (such as Joseph Stalin's policy toward the kulaks), but also are unable to discriminate and differentiate between individuals. Yet love and friendship are necessarily individuating.[39] Due to the necessary natural bond between parent and child, it is an empty and pointless rhetorical flourish to lay down the maxim 'love humanity'. It is through learning to love specific individuals that this affection may be sympathetically transferred to others (principally those with whom one can identify, that is, fellow-bearers of one's culture).[40]

Secondly, and relatedly, this humanitarianism precludes conservatives from a deep relativism. The natural fact of the dependency of the human infant means that every culture necessarily acculturates its young. Children, as the recipients of love and affection, are a precious resource, and it is contrary to human nature to treat them with indifference. Thus, whilst conservatives do indeed generally eschew criticism of other regimes/ cultures, this does not prevent them from deprecating regimes that flout standards of human decency in general, and effective family life in particular. Since, as we have noted, conservatives have little time for the abstract doctrine of natural rights, then when cultures are criticized this will not be by invoking some empty dogmatic rhetoric about rights but by using the concrete language of suffering; cruelty to children can be condemned unreservedly the world over.

Conclusion

To draw the threads together: the linchpin of this presentation of the connection between conservatism and human nature is that humans are, in a mutually reciprocal fashion, inescapably naturally dependent and cultural beings. Individuals are a product of their times. What they are is a consequence of their cultural conditioning, and, since this constitutes their very identity, whatever they do manifests this conditioning. This is a necessary process. It is the nature of the human animal that it requires a constitutive cultural 'finish'.[41] The human infant is unable to fend for itself until it has been thus finished. The fact that an individual's sense of identity is, as a consequence of this finishing, inextricably bound up with the acquisition of a culture, means that this cultural context is not perceived by him or her as an independent 'object'; it is, as it were, the lens through which one sees rather than what is seen. This constitutive finish is, accordingly, the definition of the ordinary, the norm, the natural.[42] Simply by doing what 'comes naturally' the individual is affirming conservatism, an attachment to the pre-existent order of things. The fact that this takes place without deliberation explains the frequent association of conservatism with lack of self-consciousness, and inarticulateness.[43] This unreflective naturalness accounts for the substance of the conservative disposition as expressed, for example, in Oakeshott's litany:

> . . . to prefer the familiar to the unknown, to prefer the tried to the untried, fact to mystery, the actual to the possible, the limited to the unbounded, the near to the distant, the sufficient to the super-abundant, the convenient to the perfect, present laughter to utopian bliss.[44]

Conservatism is thus an articulate theory which claims that, although individuals may not articulate it, their behaviour reveals the conservatism of human nature. But this cannot be the whole story. Any description of human nature is also a prescription.[45] The essence of the conservative pre-scription, implicated in the description of human nature as conservative, is that 'you can't kick against the pricks'. This, in its turn, explains the strong negativism in conservatism as a political doctrine. It is at its most articulate when voicing its opposition to policies which require that indivi-duals do re-create themselves; that they do discard that which has made them what they are. The advocates of such policies, and those who might be persuaded by them, need to be told that there are realities of human nature which cannot be ignored, even if their very profundity is exhibited as the inconspicuousness of second nature so that ignorance of them is all too possible. Any contempt bred by this familiarity is ill-judged and ill-advised. It is this relative theoretical articulateness of conservative doctrine, when faced with such ignorance and contempt, that has led some scholars to see conservatism as a 'positional ideology', only generated in certain circumstances.[46]

It can still be asked why we should value, let alone cherish, these cus-toms, traditions and the like which have made 'us' what we are. The con-servative would answer—and this is the nub—that we should value them in so far as we value ourselves. Should this self-valuation prompt us towards change, then it cannot be change *ab ovo* but the 'pursuit of an intima-tion',[47] a perception of anomaly itself generated out of our cultural resources. Such change is, as Burke said of the Glorious Revolution of 1688, properly a preservation.[48] The standards we bring to bear in order to preserve are not to be grafted on externally, but are those that are inherent in the 'capital' of the culture. These standards, though analyti-cally extractable from the *moeurs* of a people, should never be hypostasized into formulae. To apply formulae in order to effect change is to neglect the temporality of social existence.[49] Change must be gradual if it is not

to threaten identity.[50] Like the life of an individual, like the constitution
of a family, the past, present and future of a society should form a whole:
'we were then alive in our predecessors and they in their successors do live
still.'[51] Conservatives imbue this whole with value. It is the whole, by
virtue of its continuity, its supra-individualism and its specific character,
which gives the individual something to identify with and thus have an
identity (only the pathological would reject all that they are). It is human
nature to conserve that which is our own, but that which is most profoundly our own is that which we share with our ancestors, contemporaries
and heirs. It is in this identification of authentic social change with continuity that the intersections between politics, human nature and conservatism are to be found.

Notes

1. O'Sullivan, N., *Conservatism*, London, Dent, 1976, chapter 1; Quinton, A., *The Politics of Imperfection*, London, Faber & Faber, 1978, chapter 1; Scruton, R., *The Meaning of Conservatism*, Harmondsworth, Penguin, 1980, p. 68, cf. p. 119; Oakeshott, M., 'On Being Conservative', in his *Rationalism in Politics*, London, Methuen, 1962, pp. 173–4.

2. That this is a weakness is implied by Livingston, D., 'Hume's Conservatism', in Runte, R. (ed.), *Studies in Eighteenth Century Culture*, vol. 7, Madison, University of Wisconsin Press, 1978, p. 214; Lewis, G., 'The Metaphysics of Conservatism', *Western Political Quarterly*, 6, 1953, p. 730.

3. Geertz, C., 'Person, Time, and Conduct in Bali', in his *The Interpretation of Culture*, New York, Basic Books, 1972, p. 363; cf. Cassirer, E.; 'Man cannot escape from his own achievement. He cannot but adopt the conditions of his own life. No longer in a merely physical universe, man lives in a symbolic universe. Language, myth, art and religion are parts of this universe.' *An Essay on Man*, New Haven, Yale University Press, 1944, p. 25.

4. Whorf, B. L., in Carrol, J. (ed.), *Language, Thought, and Reality*, Cambridge, Mass., MIT, 1956, esp. pp. 134–59.

5. Cf. Steiner, G., *After Babel*, London, Oxford University Press, 1975, p. 87.

6. Cf. Cassirer, E., *The Philosophy of Symbolic Forms*, Mannheim, R. (tr.), New Haven, Yale University Press, 1953, vol. 1, p. 221.

7. Geertz, op. cit., p. 402 ff.

8. See, for example, 'The Origin of Language', in Barnard, F. (ed. & tr.), *Herder on Social and Political Culture*, Cambridge, The University Press, 1969, p. 165. For fuller discussion, see my *Hume Hegel and Human Nature*, The Hague, M. Nijhoff, forthcoming, chapter 2.

9. Kelly, G. (ed.), Jones and Turnbull (trs.), *Addresses to the German Nation*, 1808, New York, Harper, 1968, p. 190.

10. Cf. my 'Nations and Norms', *The Review of Politics*, 43, 1981, 75–87.

11. 'Considerations on France', 1796, in Lively, J. (ed. & tr.), *The Works of Joseph de Maistre*, London, Allen & Unwin, 1965, p. 80.

12. Burke, E., *Reflections on the Revolution in France*, in *Works*, London, 1882, vol. 2, p. 359. Cf. Wordsworth, W., '. . . the dream/Flattered the young, pleased with extremes, nor least/With that which makes our Reason's naked self/The object of its fervour.' *The Prelude*, 1805, Book XI, 11.232–5. Note by way of

contrast Godwin, W. 'By this scheme of naked truth virtue will every day be a gainer,' in Kramnick, I. (ed.), *Enquiry concerning Political Justice*, 1798, Book 5, chapter 12, Harmondsworth, Penguin, 1976, p. 478.

13. Cf. Plutarch, *Moralia*, London, Loeb Library, 1967, vol. 14. pp. 107, 285; Dawkins, R., *The Selfish Gene*, London, Paladin, 1978, p. 177.

14. Darlington, C. D., *The Little Universe of Man*, London, Allen & Unwin, 1978, pp. 259–60; Eibl-Eibesfeldt, I., *Love and Hate*, Strachan, G. (tr.), New York, Holt, Rinehart & Winston, 1972, p. 245.

15. Cf. Young, R. M., 'The Human Limits of Nature', in Benthall, J. (ed.), *The Limits of Human Nature*, London, Allen Lane, 1973, pp. 235–74; Eccleshall, R., 'English Conservatism as an Ideology', *Political Studies*, 25, 1977, 62–83.

16. *The City of God*, Healey, J. (tr.), London, Everyman Library, 1945, Book 14, chapter 13 (vol. 2, p. 44).

17. *Essays on the Active Powers of Man*, 1788, Essay III, pt. 2, chapter 3, in Hamilton, W. (ed.), *Works*, Edinburgh, 1846, p. 558.

18. Hearnshaw, F. J. C., *Conservatism in England*, London, Macmillan, 1933, pp. 27–9, 300; Hailsham (Hogg, Q.), *The Conservative Case*, Harmondsworth, Penguin, 1959, chapter 2; Kirk, R., *The Conservative Mind*, Revised Edition, Chicago, Gateway, 1960, chapter 1.

19. Hume, D., 'Of the Original Contract', 1748, in *Essays: Moral, Political and Literary*, London, Oxford University Press, 1963, p. 463.

20. Bagehot, W., *Physics and Politics*, 1872, New Edition, London, Kegan Paul, n.d., p. 27.

21. Burke, op. cit., p. 349.

22. Burke, op. cit., p. 368.

23. Laslett, P. (ed.), *Two Treatises of Government*, 1690, New York, Mentor, 1965, paras. 85, 94, 95, etc.

24. von Savigny, J., *Geschichte des Römischen Rechts im Mittelalter*, 2nd Edition, Heidelberg, 1834, Vol. 1, p. 21; Oakeshott, M., *On Human Conduct*, Oxford, Clarendon Press, 1975, p. 120.

25. Fichte, op. cit., p. 48.

26. Burke, op. cit., p. 359.

27. Burke, op. cit., p. 348.

28. Burke, op. cit., p. 334.

29. Burke, op. cit., p. 367.

30. Cf. Hale, M. '[The Common Law] is singularly accommodated to the Frame of the English Government, and to the Disposition of the English Nation, and such as by a long Experience and Use is as it were incorporated into their very Temperament, and, in a Manner, become the Complection and Constitution of the English Commonwealth.' Gray, C. (ed.), *History of the Common Law of England*, 1713, Chicago, The University Press, 1971, p. 30.

31. Cf. Burke: 'prescription gives right and title . . . that which might be wrong in the beginning is consecrated by time and becomes lawful.' Letter to Captain Mercer, 26 February 1790, in Cobban, A., and Smith, R. (eds), *Correspondence*, Cambridge, The University Press, 1967, Vol. 6, p. 95.

32. Burke, *Reflections*, edit. cit., p. 359.

33. Ibid., p. 295.

34. Oakeshott, 'Rationalism in Politics', in *Rationalism in Politics*, op. cit., pp. 7–13.

35. Elyot, T., *The Book named the Governor* , 1531, Lehmberg, S. (ed.), London, Everyman, 1962, chapter 1; Eysenck, H., *The Inequality of Man*, London, Fontana, 1975, p. 23; Lorenz, K., *On Aggression*, Latzke, M. (tr.), London, Methuen, 1966, p. 35.

36. Coleridge, S., *On the Constitution of the Church and State*, 1830, Barrell, J. (ed.), London, Everyman, 1972, p. 34.

37. Rousseau, J. J., *Du Contrat Social*, 1762, Book 2, chapter 7.
38. Cf. Conquest, R., *We and They: Civic and Despotic Cultures*, London, Temple Smith, 1980, p. 67, for a partisan expression of this view.
39. Cf. Hegel, G., *The Philosophy of Mind*, 1817/30, Wallace, W., and Miller, A. (eds), Oxford, Clarendon Press, 1971, p. 110.
40. Cf. Burke: 'To be attached to the subdivision, to love the little platoon we belong to in society, is the first principle (the germ as it were) of public affections. It is the first link in the series by which we proceed towards a love to our country, and to mankind.' *Reflections*, op. cit., p. 320.
41. Cf. Midgley, M., *Beast and Man*, Hassocks, Harvester, 1979, p. 286; Bishop Butler, *Analogy of Religion*, 1736, Part I, chapter 5, paras. 15, 16; Geertz, 'The Impact of the Concept of Culture on the Concept of Man', in *The Interpretation of Culture*, op. cit., p. 49.
42. Cf. Benedict, R., *Patterns of Culture*, London, Routledge, 1968, p. 5. Benedict uses the metaphor of the lens on p. 7.
43. Cf. Viereck, P., *Conservatism from John Adams to Churchill*, Princeton, Van Nostrand, 1956, p. 16.
44. Oakeshott, 'On Being Conservative', op. cit., p. 169.
45. I have developed this point more fully in the opening chapter of my forthcoming book entitled (provisionally) *Concepts of Man*.
46. Cf. Huntingdon, S. P., 'Conservatism as an Ideology', *American Political Science Review*, 51, 1957, 454–73; Mannheim, K., 'Conservative Thought', in Kecskemeti, P. (ed.), *Essays on Sociology and Social Psychology*, London, Routledge, 1953, chapter 2.
47. Oakeshott, 'Political Education', in *Rationalism in Politics*, op. cit., p. 133.
48. Burke, *Reflections*, op. cit., p. 304.
49. Cf. Burke: 'Political arrangement, as it is a work for social ends, is to be wrought by social means. There mind must conspire with mind. Time is required to produce that union of minds which alone can produce all the good we aim at.' Ibid., p. 439.
50. Cf. Oakeshott, 'On Being Conservative', op. cit., p. 170.
51. Hooker, R., *The Laws of Ecclesiastical Polity*, 1593, Book 1, chapter 10, *Works*, Oxford, 1820, Vol. 1, p. 248.

5 Utopianism and human nature

WILLIAM STAFFORD

An enduring claim in Utopian speculation has been that the attitudes and behaviour of men and women can be transformed to permit a society of harmony and happiness; for human nature is malleable. Godwin, Owen and B. F. Skinner are examples of this kind of Utopianism. But are these thinkers saying there is no stable human nature? If so, how can we judge a society good or bad? Surely, 'good' in this context must mean good for humanity—arranged to satisfy our nature. But, if there *is* no human nature, then there is no measure of 'good', and Utopianisms of this pattern collapse into incoherence.[1] This oft-repeated criticism is too hasty. Conceptions of good do not require a belief in human nature. Standards can be transcendent—commands of God, or Kantian rational principles. Or they can be derived from a 'necessary' pattern of social evolution; those societies are good which can survive because they accord with the stage whose time has come. Or societies can be judged on internal consistency; do their economic, social and political arrangements conform to the 'human nature' they have created?

Perhaps the search for such solutions is itself too hasty. Do Godwin, Owen and Skinner actually believe in total human malleability? Where are they on a spectrum running from Hobbes's account of an enduring human nature to the relativism of anthropologists such as Margaret Mead or Clifford Geertz? Before tackling this in the texts, some preliminary clarification is advisable. The discussion must employ finer discriminations than the crude antinomy of fixed essence versus malleability. For the extreme positions have few defenders: few advocates of human nature deny entirely the power of education; few relativists shut their eyes to the obvious universals —need for food and warmth, ability to use tools and language, etc.

Among those who assert malleability, a distinction of capital importance is between those whose main theoretical endeavour in this connection is directed towards minimizing unchangeable traits or native characteristics, and those who are primarily concerned to study and understand cultural diversity.[2] The former strategy, associated with behaviourism, has ancestors going back to the late seventeenth century. Locke, Hartley, Condillac,

Helvetius, James Mill and Watson, however much they differ, all aspire to a scientific theory having a small number of premises.[3] The second strategy originates effectively with Herder and its paradigmatic modern advocates are those anthropologists—neither functionalists nor structuralists—concerned with the patterns of meaning which constitute a culture. The former strategy is psychology-oriented, explaining the conditioning, development and behaviour of individuals. The second is sociology-oriented, focusing on social and cultural wholes. This latter approach may go with a rejection of cultural or temporal chauvinism, denying that we are superior to our ancestors or to allegedly primitive societies. Behaviourists often draw exactly the reverse conclusions. For them, the variety of humanity is not to be praised, but overcome; for variety is a falling-short of excellence, or a deplorable departure from equality. For example, Locke recognizes that norms differ; some societies practice infanticide, some cannibalism. What this shows is that they have been corrupted by false associations and bad customs. They ought rather to conform to universal reason. Mary Wollstonecraft deplores the differing attitudes and attainments of men and women, arguing that the differences result from education, and that boys and girls should be trained to common standards. Environmentalism of this stamp asserts the fundamental identity and equality of humanity, playing down genetic differences, noting malleability and conditioning to show how things have gone wrong, and how they might be improved. For behaviourists, therefore, malleability does not necessarily imply relativism: for the defenders of cultural diversity, malleability and relativism usually go hand in hand.

Sometimes the dispute is not about whether there are enduring human characteristics at all. Both sides may admit a few perdurables; the issue is how important these are.[4] Advocates of a malleability thesis may insist that these fixed traits are unimportant or uninteresting. On the other hand, substantial theoretical and moral structures may be built on simple foundations. Hobbes's model of man is not rich; yet H. L. A. Hart has extracted a vital core of natural laws from a handful of truisms about human nature,[5] and Bernard Williams has built a well-known case for equality upon an unambitious assertion of common humanity.[6] Minimizing universals can thus have different effects: *either* it may be concluded that there is no human nature of significance, *or* the few remaining characteristics may gain importance from their lonely eminence.

Bearing these distinctions in mind, the problems identified at the outset can now be confronted in the writings of Godwin, Owen and Skinner, to determine whether theories of human nature in this kind of Utopianism exhibit a common pattern.

Owen and the malleability thesis

For Owen, 'This knowledge will new-form the human race, regenerate man, . . . and open a new world to the human faculties; a new world, which shall change their thoughts, feelings, and conduct . . .'[7] Owen appears to favour a radical doctrine of malleability; and when he says of the terms good and bad that '. . . both . . . have never been the creation of the prejudices and imaginations of the human mind, according to the education it has received . . .', malleability seems to involve relativism. But other passages are ambiguous:

> The future superiority or inferiority of the whole character and conduct of the child will depend upon the right or wrong direction which shall be given from birth to his capacity for feeling, and his power for receiving convictions.
>
> The first may be made so humane, and be so directed, that the matured man may be compelled to feel considerable horror at acciden-tally injuring the limb of the smallest insect, or be made to experience the greatest pleasure and delight in first killing, afterwards roasting, and then eating, one of his fellow-men.[8]

The apparent relativism of the latter part conflicts with the earlier evaluations of superior versus inferior, right versus wrong. Indeed, Owen continually writes as a confident absolutist in his judgements. He offers a list of the thirteen means of happiness for all humankind,[9] and a code of twenty-five laws 'which are alone wise laws for the government of humanity'.[10] Is he confused, or even disingenuously trying to have it both ways, arguing for malleability and relativism when confronted by charac-ter traits (pride, competitiveness, greed) and social customs (e.g. the sanctity of monogamous marriage) which he dislikes, while insisting that his plans for society are eternally right and that love of truth, co-operativeness and delight in others' happiness are permanent, if sometimes obscured, ingredients of human nature? I believe a sympathetic reading can elicit a coherent doctrine, assembled from commonplaces of the radical Enlightenment. Major inconsistencies appear only if, anachronisti-cally, we search in his writings for modern cultural relativism.

He applies the malleability thesis not to *human nature* but to *character*. Tediously he reiterates a conception of 'the never-changing nature of humanity'.[11] First, original instincts fall into three classes—physical, mental and moral.[12] The physical instincts are desires for food, exercise, sleep, rest and sex.[13] His attitude to these is untainted by asceticism; recognizing that we have much in common with other animals, he finds no shame in this resemblance. The mental instincts are a love of truth and a desire to exercise intellectual faculties; these faculties are the power of gaining new ideas, comparing them with ideas already possessed, and hence arriving at general principles. The mind can grasp eternal truth: 'it being certain that truth can never be opposed to itself, or any two facts in discordance. The universe according to our limited notions of universality must be *ONE GREAT TRUTH*, composed of all facts, past, present, and future.'[14] Owen, typical of an unsophisticated thinker of this period, regards truth as a copy of reality, a plain and simple record of facts; facts are unproblematic to unprejudiced minds. Human faculties of perception are receiving instruments which need contribute no colouring, no structure of their own. Moreover, mind can discover the general laws by which the universe is regulated; triumphant science looms large for Owen. Hitherto, the race has been in its infancy, and imagination is strong and unregulated in infants; hence the ascendancy of erroneous and superstitious ideas. Now the age of facts and reason has dawned. Reason has but one tale to tell; in future rational society there will be no disagreement.[15]

The moral instinct causes pleasure or pain in accordance with whether or not the agent has added to the happiness of the species. Happiness is the balanced, temperate fulfilment of all instincts—temperate because excessive indulgence leads to fatigue and ultimately pain.[16] Happiness requires a combination of pleasures of consumption and activity; but the active pleasures do not include competitive striving, or dominating others.

Another vital aspect of human nature is that men and women do not form their own characters. What is the range within which character can vary? Owen employs a threefold classification of superior, bad and medium characters, exhibiting respectively beneficial habits, injurious ones and a mixture. In one passage he suggests that habits are good at court, vicious in the slums, and mixed in middle-class environments.[17] Here is no relativism, no awareness of humanity achieving different expressions in different cultures. For all his sturdy radicalism—his assaults upon religion, marriage and property—Owen ranks his fellows as good, bad and indifferent in accordance with current valuations, assuming these valuations to be absolute and eternal. He recognizes that religion, manners, habits, beliefs, likings and dislikings, even ideas of good and evil, vary with place and time. But he does not conclude that happiness and truth are problematic, or that different conceptions are a natural and desirable part of our being. It is simply that in the past we have been localized, prejudiced animals who have failed to perceive truth and the way to happiness.[18]

Owen embraces the religion of progress, and his conception of it is clear, thin and poor. Progress is measured by the unvarying standards of truth and happiness. It means the fuller satisfaction of human nature as it is now and has always been; there is no suggestion that humanity will change in essence. What causes diversity? Clearly, in the light of the preceding analysis, this formulation of the question is too modern, too implicity relativist. More accurately, then, what causes bad characters and how can they be improved? Owen has a diverse and eccentric list of factors. In language reminiscent of the French Enlightenment he attributes much blame to religion and priests. Religion has disseminated error and declared war on instincts, penning them in the unnatural institution of marriage. Owen waxes eloquent about the way in which religion and marriage have driven countless individuals insane; creatures so disturbed have been poor procreators and so the physical character of the race has deteriorated.[19] Above all, religion has been responsible for a principal mistake in emphasizing sin and blame, holding that individuals form their own characters and are therefore responsible for the evil they do. This has engendered anger, resentment and vengeance. Private property is another source of corruption, a fount of selfishness, vanity, injustice and oppression.[20] The characters of the upper classes have been vitiated by learning from Latin and Greek authors to admire 'the . . . customs, habits and ideas of barbarians'.[21] Underpinning the whole is a standard Rousseauian contrast between nature and artifice. Bad characters have proliferated because human law has defied nature's law:

> As nature gives the organization to man, so will nature best direct when any of the functions of that organization should be exercised . . . and in proportion as human laws and customs have interfered with the dictates of nature, in the same proportion has man been forced to become a vicious and miserable animal.[22]

Nothing could indicate more clearly his limited conception of malleability. Always, human nature remains the stable bedrock; a bad environment can warp it, to fulfil it is the achievement of a favourable one. How is melioration to be set in train? Education is vital; but as Owen recognizes, who will educate the educators? If society corrupts its members, how is a fresh start possible? His answers, as Marx insists, are implausible: extraordinary minds will function as a *deus ex machina*;[23] the mere recognition that we do not make our own characters will diffuse charity and understanding. Owen has no convincing technology for the formation of character. His account of conditioning invites comparison with Marx's; the most profound difference is that, whereas Marx is concerned with the specific configuration of the social whole, resulting from the interaction of its economic, social, political and ideological elements, Owen's gaze focuses upon the parts, the individuals who are moulded for good or ill by their upbringing. Marx's thought is sociological, Owen's psychological. This is evidenced by the variety Owen expects and desires in future society. He does not anticipate cultural diversity—humankind will have one law code, language and religion. Variety will be individual. All are made of the same building blocks—the physical, moral and intellectual instincts or powers. But the exact dimensions and arrangements of these blocks vary from person to person, hence—given education which fulfils nature instead of thwarting it—humankind will be excitingly diversified.[24] Credit for this manifold excellence will be due, not to individuals themselves, but to favourable environments. For Owen's men and women are anything but autonomous; they are made, not self-makers.

What are the social and political implications of this account of human nature and malleability? Owen aspires to refute the case for the legitimacy of social inequality. How different, he remarks, are the habits, manners, feelings, thoughts, actions and appearance of a chimney sweep, dustman or scavenger from those of an archbishop, lord chancellor or commander-in-chief. But if a child born to poverty and one born to privilege were exchanged in their cradles, the reversal of environments would cause a reversal of character.[25] It is not so much that malleability *explains* differences and inequalities, as that it *explains them away*, showing them to be factitious, unjust and eliminable. Moreover, Owen is out to explode ideas of sin, blame and guilt. If no one is responsible for his or her character, blame is out of place, and so is punishment. By our badly arranged societies, by false teachings, by unnatural laws, we make vicious citizens and then punish them for it. Finally, his account of human nature sustains a vision of a future without politics. For, when human beings are made rational, all will think alike; there will be no differences to resolve. Rebels or misfits in the new moral world will be regarded as diseased and put into a mental hospital. Owen is not anticipating the modern Soviet way with dissidents; his mental patients would be smothered with love and kindness until they see the error of their ways.[26] Politics will yield to administration. There will be no democracy: all citizens will take a turn at ruling when they reach an appropriate age.[27] The inhabitants of the New Moral World will have no lust for power—a character malformation produced in bad environments—but will undertake their spell of responsibility as a duty.

Godwin and the science of mind

Godwin, well-educated and well-read in contemporary British and French philosophy, has more interest for political theory than Owen. For he makes a thorough attempt to cut the elements of original human nature to a minimum. This is no novelty; he explicitly continues the associationist arguments of Locke, Gay, Hartley, Helvetius and Priestley. These reject the gloomy view of humanity of Hobbes and Mandeville; but, on the other hand, they are to be distinguished from the optimistic or benevolist theories of Shaftesbury, Hutcheson, Butler, Hume and Adam Smith. The associationists, in whose company Godwin belongs, argue that humanity is neither good nor bad, but malleable.[28] One influence, then, is a philosophical debate; another is science. Godwin, like his predecessors in this tradition, regards himself as engaged in the elaboration of a science of mind. For his conception of science, which is regulative, supposes that a complex phenomenon like the human mind is to be explained by a minimum of general principles. To suppose a human nature having numerous instincts is to multiply entities, a proceeding contrary to science and in imminent danger from Occam's razor.[29] He claims that all the diversity of mind and behaviour stems from one simple, original characteristic: 'The human mind is a principle of the simplest nature, a mere faculty of sensation or perception.'[30] So the only 'nature' we have at birth is five senses, plus an ability to feel bodily states such as hunger or fatigue. Subsequently, as a chapter heading announces, 'The Characters of Men Originate in Their External Circumstances'. This is significant; what is at issue is not whether we have a *nature* (in the minimal sense just outlined he believes we do), but whether we have fixed, genetically-determined *characters*. He discusses three objections to environmentalism: first, the doctrine of innate ideas; second, the theory of inborn instincts; third, the argument that physiological differences cause character traits. His standard Lockeian argument against innate ideas need not detain us; but what he says under the other headings illuminates his theory of human nature. He ruthlessly prunes away original instincts; even grasping and flinching are acquired, explicable in terms of circumstances acting upon faculties of sensation. Self-love, a complex idea requiring awareness of selfhood, cannot be innate, nor the alleged 'instinct of self-preservation', which cannot develop until the child acquires the concept of death.[31] The newborn child has no instinct of pity; following Hartley, he argues that sympathy develops by association. The sufferings of others—their cries and writhings—affect our senses disagreeably, therefore we lend succour. Our original desire is for pleasant sensations; but, by association, in due course the desire for the welfare of others becomes habitual and self-standing.[32] This gives cause for thought. Evidently, the nature of a newborn mind is *not* merely to be a faculty of sensation or perception. There are in addition the tendencies to associate ideas and form habits.

When he turns to consider the argument that characters are determined by physiological differences at birth, Godwin denies that all minds are born alike. Strengths and weaknesses are inherited and conditioning has already occurred in the womb. The main point, however, is that these original differences and intra-uterine experiences have negligible effects on final character by comparison with subsequent conditioning. Here is another trait which, like the ability to associate ideas and form habits, is implied by malleability itself—an overwhelming *impressionability*.[33] Most striking of all, he suggests that some of the supposed physiological givens may be susceptible to conditioning—for example, the size of the brain, or the allotted span of life.[34] Godwin's aims should not be mistaken. He is not claiming that there is no human nature at all; rather he wants to demonstrate that some widespread characteristics, such as piety or patriotism, are not innate.[35] Also, he wishes to assert the potential equality of humankind, hence the unjustifiability of monarchy, aristocracy and all hereditary distinctions.[36] From Helvetius he borrows the argument that genius is produced, not genetically but by a happy coincidence of environmental factors. Dissect a genius, he suggests (post mortem, one assumes), and you will find nothing extraordinary in his organic structure. And in one of his best passages he laments the manner in which the abounding potential of peasant children is systematically destroyed by lives of poverty and toil.[37]

Let us draw together Godwin's account of the characteristics of human nature. We have noted the faculty of sensation and perception, the tendency to associate ideas and form habits, and impressionability. There are yet more; the most important additional element of the 'nature or constitution of man' is 'the capacity of combining ideas and inferring conclusions'.[38] Perhaps the capacity of combining ideas is the principle of association under another name; but the capacity of inferring conclusions is something else, and it is not explained how it evolves out of sensation and association. It is in fact what Godwin means by *reason*: is reason an original power, or acquired? Just as there are pleasures and pains attached to the faculty of sensation, so are there pleasures and pains of intellect; indeed, the exercise of mind gives purer and more lasting delights than sensuality.[39] Finally, in unguarded moments, he refers to other propensities as if they were inherent: the love of society, 'Man is a social animal'; and the love of distinction 'which is characteristic of every mind',[40] which is the cause of excellence and progress. So, in spite of his ambition to reduce native and therefore common traits to a minimum, he ends up with a fair number. How about the other side of the coin? Does he allow that humanity can express itself in many varied forms? Like Owen, he has no sense of desirable cultural diversity. As with Owen, the litmus papers are truth and happiness.

We possess truth when the propositions we entertain correspond to our sensations and to real relations between objects revealed by those sensations. 'Taken in this sense, truth is immutable.'[41] Truth can, and ultimately must, prevail over error; sophistry is powerless against sound argument. This formulation is significant: *either* there is truth, *or* there is error; Godwin ignores the possibility that there may be no absolutes, that our predicament may be to reside forever with half-truths and partial, shifting interpretations. For reason gives clear answers:

> If there be any man who is incapable of making inferences for himself, or of understanding, when stated in the most explicit terms, the inferences of another, him we consider as an abortive production, and not in strictness belonging to the human species.[42]

Happiness is as immutable and universal as truth.[43] At present, each pursues pleasure in his or her own way, but this is unsatisfactory; there is one pattern of life to maximize happiness. The pleasures, in ascending order of delightfulness, are of sense, intellect, sympathy, and self-approbation. This account of happiness or the good for men and women is based not so much upon their sensual nature as upon their nature as rational beings. He appears to believe that the bare fact of rationality implies delight in truth, virtue and independence, and so he erects a massive edifice of moral and social ideals upon a narrow and shaky foundation.[44] 'Reason' is a notoriously obscure and controversial subject; it is far from evident how the values of independence, energy and benevolence can be derived from it. Like Owen he believes the happiness or human good he recommends is of universal application; but because he is more explicit and precise, less bland than Owen, the culture-specific nature of his evaluations is even more strikingly in evidence. When he writes of '. . . the delicious transports of self-complacence . . .' or remarks that the two most regrettable moral defects are '. . . insincerity, and a temper abject and servile . . .',[45] we hear the authentic voice of eighteenth-century dissent. His description of the pleasures of intellect stands poised between an eighteenth-century wonderment at the laws of the universe revealed by science, and a pre-romantic enthusiasm for nature:

> The beauties of nature are all his own. He admires the overhanging cliff, the wide-extended prospect, the vast expanse of the ocean, the foliage of the woods, the sloping lawn and the waving grass. He knows the pleasure of solitude, when man holds commerce alone with the

tranquil solitude of nature. He has traced the structure of the universe; the substances which compose the globe we inhabit, and are the materials of human industry; and the laws which hold the planets in their course amidst the trackless fields of space.[46]

Since truth and happiness are universals, it follows that variations in habits and tastes are signs of 'deviation and error; a disease to be cured, not to be encouraged.'[47] One social and political order is good for all humankind. As men and women become rational, they will move closer to unanimity. Nor is reason a late fruit of time. Men and women are *always* capable of reason; it is false to maintain that 'primitives' are inferior, to be held in pupillage.[48]

So far, despite greater philosophical sophistication, Godwin's theory of human nature has exhibited the same pattern as Owen's; the main difference has lain in Godwin's more thorough attempt to minimize enduring traits—but since he infers more moral conclusions from fewer traits, this makes little difference. There are two important divergences. The first lies in Godwin's attitude to nature in general. He does not recommend obedience to nature's laws. The rhetorical function performed by 'nature' in Owen's discourse—serving as an ultimate, though undefined, court of appeal—is fulfilled, in *Political Justice*, by 'reason'. Godwin, unlike Owen, distrusts nature in the sense of animality.[49] This accords with his preference for intellectual pleasures, and belittling of sensual enjoyments. The most striking example is his attitude to sex; overpopulation may be no problem in future society because, as men and women become more rational, they will delight less in sensuality and procreation may virtually cease.[50] The second major difference is about whether men and women are passive or autonomous.[51] At first sight, Godwin agrees with Owen; characters are determined by circumstances, but Godwin adds a statement of hard determinism. All things in the universe are connected by causal relationships, and human action is not free from these chains; the murderer is no more responsible than the knife he employs, and 'Man is in reality a passive, and not an active being.'[52] But there is a sense in which he affirms autonomy, though without claiming any emancipation from causality. He rejects the distinction between free and determined actions, but insists upon distinguishing voluntary, imperfectly voluntary and involuntary ones.[53] An involuntary action is determined or caused by impulse so as to elude rational control—e.g. blinking, bursting into tears, shaking with fright. An imperfectly voluntary action results from habit. A voluntary action stems from rational decision; the agent transcends passion, prejudice or apathetic conventionality to make an informed choice, and '. . . the perfection of human character consists in approaching as nearly as possible to the perfectly voluntary state.'[54] We are always determined, but our dignity requires that we be determined by reasons, not by impulse, habit or coercion. And here a kind of autonomy is to be found. 'Beware of reducing men to the state of machines.'[55] Owen, by contrast, likens men and women to machines, and is perfectly willing to manipulate them.

Godwin's account of how human nature is corrupted, and his remedies, are richer than Owen's but scarcely more convincing. Political tyranny and corruption, and societies organized on the principles of ascribed status and inequality of property have produced men and women who are either pampered and vicious, or servile and miserable. Turning from disease to cure, there is a curious tension. Sometimes we find Godwin optimistic; vicious and foolish men and women can become wise and virtuous through free inquiry and discussion; 'The road to the improvement of mankind is in the utmost degree simple, to speak and act the truth.' Enormous weight is placed upon sincerity, '. . . the most powerful engine of human improvement . . .'.[56] If men and women would frankly voice their sentiments, freely admonishing bad conduct, general improvement would be rapid. But in Book I, Chapter IV there is a more gloomy doctrine. Godwin discusses education, and he concludes by insisting that the best is powerless against the influence of bad institutions. The world's practices contradict the teacher's precepts, and the pupil is seduced by the alluring follies of the former. Moreover, how can good teachers emerge under bad governments? 'Like the barbarous directors of the Eastern seraglios, they deprive us of our virility, and fit us for their despicable employment from the cradle.'[57]

Godwin's account of the relationship between human nature and environment is, like Owen's, cast in individualistic, psychological terms: '. . . individuals are everything, and society, abstracted from the individuals of which it is composed, nothing.'[58] This can be elucidated by what he says about error. Reared in the culture of Calvinist dissent, he is deeply interested in errors resulting from self-deception. He knows the cunning and crooked ways in which the heart corrupts the understanding, rendering it resistant to good arguments, interpreting the world through the distorting lenses of selfishness.[59] What is striking is that this partiality of vision is essentially *individual*, and is a blindness to 'eternal truth'. Godwin has no sense of how classes or groups develop collective representations, no awareness of the social construction of reality, i.e. of different 'truths'. For he is innocent of any conception of culture, and of the relativism this might imply. It is this innocence which protects his limited but absolute description of human nature.

The political implications of a theory of human nature composed of a few fixed traits coupled with malleability of character are worked out in the most radical fashion. He argues that aggression, greed and lust for power are eliminable; he believes that the love of distinction could be channelled into a desire to excel in beneficence. If social and political reforms can go hand in hand with enlightenment, it will be possible to improve men and women so as to permit the abolition of all coercive restraint. Then will come the euthanasia of government. Like Owen, he believes that, truth being eternal and immutable, rational men and women will resolve their disputes by free inquiry rather than through democracy and parliaments.

Skinner and behavioural engineering

There are important differences between the earlier Utopians and B. F. Skinner. Godwin and Owen argue for the malleability of *character* rather than of human nature itself; Skinner really does believe that human *nature* is malleable.[60] Unlike Godwin, Skinner does not base his claim for the power of conditioning upon a conception of human nature having few original traits. He believes the new-born child possesses many genetically-programmed tendencies; the behavioural engineer reinforces some and eliminates the rest.[61]

As critics have argued, and as perhaps Skinner himself implies, these original traits constrain behavioural engineering. Behaviour can be changed, and desires suppressed, but only by employing other desires which are preserved. Aggression and competitiveness are overcome by bringing them into conflict with desires for food, rest or friendship and ensuring that the useful characteristics prevail. This does not imply that *new* instincts are acquired, nor that behavioural engineering can extinguish all original dispositions. Original traits include reflexes such as rage and fear;[62] beneficial motives include curiosity, desires for diversion, society and affection, sexual and nesting instincts, urges to dominate and control nature, and a tendency to rebel against restraint.[63] These characteristics have evolved because of their survival value.[64] Skinner also thinks that inequality may have a genetic foundation. He does not, like Godwin and Owen, emphasize malleability to attack social inequality. But he also believes that environment plays a major part here, and wishes to organize education to make the most of each child's potential.[65]

There are, then, differences between the conceptions of human nature of Godwin and Owen, and Skinner. But Skinner shares their confident absolutism—there is a good for humanity, and a form of society to correspond accordingly. Like them, he does not relativize truth, but radiates a glad confidence in science.[66] He recognizes that the behavioural scientist is affected by his or her culture, from the prejudices of which he or she can never entirely be free; but 'Within these practical limits, however, it should be possible to minimise the effect of accidental features of prevailing cultures and to turn to the ultimate source of the things people call good.'[67] This implies that a distinction can be drawn between truth and the errors deeply rooted in a culture, and that it is possible largely to emancipate oneself from the latter by embracing the former.

Skinner is not altogether clear or consistent about happiness. He notes that religious cultures may violate every human instinct, thus proving the potency of behavioural engineering. He condemns them, but not mainly because they produce less happiness. They are condemned by social evolution; locked into a social pattern now superseded, in the long term they cannot survive.[68] He also suggests a distinction between human traits which are inessential, pernicious and removeable, and those which are basic, desirable and to be thwarted at peril. In religious cultures 'The basic needs are sublimated. False needs are created to absorb the energies.'[69] This distinction underpins his rejection of punishment. Behaviour can be changed aversively (punishment) or non-aversively (reward). However, it is a fundamental human characteristic to resent and resist force; punishment, therefore, is massively counter-productive.[70] The whole argument is based upon judgement of good and bad for human-kind, these judgements resting upon conceptions of human nature and happiness:

> We all know what is good, until we stop to think about it. For example, is there any doubt that health is better than sickness . . . Secondly, can anyone doubt that an absolute minimum of unpleasant labour is part of the Good Life? . . .
>
> The Good Life also means a chance to exercise talents and abilities . . . And we need intimate and satisfying personal contacts. This *is* the Good Life . . . It is a fact, not a theory.[71]

Skinner can hardly fail to be aware of the anthropologist's conception of culture, and of the relativism it may imply. It is therefore surprising how limited a part this conception plays in his own theories. Differing behaviour patterns in other cultures are used to prove the potentialities of behavioural engineering, but this perception does not affect the psychological and individualistic structure of this thought. A chapter of *Beyond Freedom and Dignity* discusses 'The Design of a Culture', but there is no hint of a culture as a mode of expression, a system of meanings, or a unique way of understanding and ordering a world. The discussion is about how efficient a cultural 'design' is in training humans for group survival. It is as if the behavioural engineer were an outsider, and the culture his or her artefact; goals and standards are not themselves culturally determined, but anchored in an external standard—the demands of survival. The poverty of this understanding of culture is reflected in passages of historical explanation whose superficiality and anachronism is reminiscent of the radical Enlightenment frame of mind of Godwin and Owen.[72] As such, the psychological and individualistic, rather than the sociological character of his thought, dominates:

> Happiness may be taken to represent the personal reinforcers which can be attributed to survival value, and esteem some of the conditioned reinforcers used to induce a person to behave for the good of others, but all conditioned reinforcers derive their power from personal reinforcers and hence from the evolutionary history of the species.[73]

This assumes a process of biological evolution that produces a human species having certain characteristics; it then discusses a technology for conditioning individual behaviour, eluding the intermediate field of culture and society. If anything, this department is more of a blank in Skinner than in Godwin or Owen. They, at least, had interesting ideas about the influence of religion, modes of government, economic and social arrangements, professional habits, customs; they were, after all, pre-Marxians. Skinner merely draws a grand contrast between the unplanned (and therefore irrational and ineffective) conditioning of today, and the planned conditioning of tomorrow. So, for example, the family is rejected as an educational institution paying no attention to properly accredited expertise and is replaced by the scientifically-organized nursery.[74]

It is also interesting to compare Godwin and Skinner on moral freedom. At first sight they have much in common. Both are determinists, and not all kinds of determination are acceptable. Both reject coercion and indoctrination. The techniques of the advertiser and subliminal manipulation are ruled out; men and women must be told the truth.[75] But at a deeper level they are worlds apart. Godwin believes that to be determined by one's independent reasoning is the only mode of action compatible with dignity: Skinner wants behaviour determined ultimately by the behavioural engineer.[76] Similarly, the difference between Godwin and Skinner on punishment is illuminating. Both reject it: Skinner, because he believes it cannot be as effective as non-aversive conditioning; Godwin, because he dislikes all control of one person by another. And if, until people can be made fully rational, some control is required, he prefers punishment. For one who is controlled by force at least knows that he or she is not acting in accordance with his or her own judgement; he or she can be free in mind if not in body. Other forms of control—techniques of non-rational persuasion—enslave the mind also.[77]

Skinner's political ideas follow from his conceptions of human nature and behavioural engineering. There is a truth, which experimental science can establish. There is a good, rooted in human nature; the discordant passions can be eliminated. Consequently, politics is unnecessary. Politics can be replaced by administration, but plenty of that is required. It need not be administration of large units. Since the key task is training individuals, the essential unit is the community within which they are conditioned. Administration must be in the hands of experts; hence democracy would be out of place.[78] 'When we ask what Man can make of Man, we don't mean the same thing by "Man" in both instances. We mean to ask what a few men can make of mankind.'[79] Dissenters—there will be a few—will be regarded as sick.[80] To suppose that such a system would engender no tyranny entails a massive faith in disinterested expertise; there can be little doubt that Skinner has it.[81] Finally, it is instructive to compare Skinner with Owen on Nature and Nature's laws. Skinner does the job for us; he argues that community experiments of the past failed precisely because their founders simply abolished human laws and trusted nature.[82] Nature, whether human or in the non-human environment, is not to be liberated; it is to be controlled and dominated. This is the structural ethic of Skinner's Utopian behaviourism. Correspondingly, whereas Owen was sympathetic towards 'animal' aspects of human nature, Skinner exhibits more than a hint of disdain for the 'feral'.[83]

Conclusions

There are evident differences between the theories of human malleability of Godwin, Owen and Skinner; but the common features are equally evident, and more important. The most fundamental agreement lies in that they do not belong to the tradition of cultural relativism beginning with Herder. They do not glorify diversity, and they draw back from a conception of the person as, *in toto*, a cultural product. All three specify or imply an enduring human nature, a level of reality more basic than the cultural. And if, as with Godwin and Skinner, the original traits, or traits which cannot safely be modified, are few, the absence of competition simply makes these constants more important. All three believe that there is an objective and universal happiness or good for humanity; all admire science, and think that truth can be discovered. These areas of agreement are necessary to their type of Utopianism. If on these issues they embraced the opposite convictions, it would be impossible for them to specify a universally good society and to believe in progress. The three are alike in presenting a theory of humanity which is psychological and individualist rather than sociological. Finally, though they differ over the amount and kind of *administration* required, they agree that *politics* is unnecessary. As Skinner writes in *Walden Two*, 'In some strange way Frazier had undercut all the standard issues in political science, and they seemed scarcely worth debating.'[84]

Notes

1. Hollis, M., *Models of Man*, Cambridge, Cambridge University Press, 1977, p. 6; Goodwin, B., *Social Science and Utopia*, Hassocks, Harvester Press, 1978, p. 61; Keim, D. W., 'To make all things new—the counterculture vision of man and politics', in Pennock, J. R., and Chapman, J. W. (eds), *Human Nature in Politics: Nomos XVII*, New York, New York University Press, 1977, pp. 206-7.
2. Mandelbaum, M., *History, Man and Reason: A Study in Nineteenth Century Thought*, Baltimore, Johns Hopkins Press, 1971, p. 141.
3. Passmore, J. A., 'The Malleability of Man in Eighteenth-Century Thought', in Wasserman, E. A. (ed.), *Aspects of the Eighteenth Century*, Baltimore, Johns Hopkins Press, 1965.
4. Midgley, M., *Beast and Man: The Roots of Human Nature*, Hassocks, Harvester Press, 1979, p. 66.
5. Hart, H. L. A., *The Concept of Law*, Oxford, The Clarendon Press, 1961, pp. 181-95.
6. Williams, B., 'The Idea of Equality', in (e.g.) Feinberg, J. (ed.), *Moral Concepts*, Oxford, Oxford University Press, 1969, p. 155. See also Casey, J., 'Human Virtue and Human Nature' in Benthall, J. (ed.), *The Limits of Human Nature*, London, Allen Lane, 1973, pp. 74-90.
7. Owen, R., *The Book of the New Moral World*, London, 1842, Part 4, p. 12.
8. Ibid., 1, pp. 57, 47.
9. Ibid., 3, p. 5.
10. Ibid., 6, p. 82.
11. Ibid., 2, p. 6.
12. Ibid., 1, pp. 21, 22.
13. Ibid., 3, p. 23.
14. Ibid., 4, pp. 27, 35.
15. Ibid., 1, p. 69; 3, p. 77.
16. Ibid., 1, pp. 22, 46, 51-4.
17. Ibid., 1, pp. 3, 38.
18. Ibid., 3, p. 2; 6, p. 5.
19. Ibid., 3, pp. 32, 7.
20. Ibid., 6, pp. 40, 41.
21. Ibid., 2, p. 33.
22. Ibid., 1, p. 56.
23. Ibid., 7, p. 42.
24. Ibid., 2, p. 6; 1, p. 23.
25. Ibid., 1, p. 32.
26. Ibid., 6, p. 76.
27. Ibid., 4, p. 41.
28 Passmore, op. cit, pp. 22, 34

29. Godwin, W., *Enquiry concerning Political Justice*, Kramnick, I. (ed.), Harmondsworth, Penguin, 1976 (reprint of Third Edition 1798: hereafter referred to as *PJ*), p. 101.
30. Ibid., p. 398.
31. Ibid., pp. 102, 103.
32. Ibid., p. 380.
33. Ibid., pp. 104–8.
34. Ibid., pp. 105, 776.
35. Ibid., p. 138.
36. Ibid., p. 467.
37. Godwin, *The Enquirer. Reflections on Education, Manners, and Literature. In a Series of Essays*, London, 1797, pp. 13, 16.
38. *PJ*, op. cit., p. 139.
39. Ibid., p. 75.
40. Ibid., pp. 676, 705.
41. Ibid., p. 117n.
42. Ibid., p. 141.
43. Ibid., p. 392.
44. Ibid., pp. 139, 176, 674.
45. Godwin, *The Enquirer*, op. cit., pp. 89, 191.
46. *PJ*, op. cit., p. 394.
47. Ibid., p. 249.
48. Ibid., p. 152.
49. Godwin, *The Enquirer*, op. cit., pp. 241; 10.
50. *PJ*, op. cit., p. 776.
51. C. f. Goodwin, op. cit., p. 60.
52. *PJ*, op. cit., pp. 353, 354.
53. Ibid., p. 188 ff.
54. Ibid., p. 127.
55. Ibid., p. 135; see also Godwin, *The Enquirer*, op. cit., pp. 66, 70, 71, 82, 144, 189, 240.
56. *PJ*, op. cit., pp. 490, 317.
57. Ibid., p. 114.
58. Ibid., p. 529; see also p. 221.
59. Ibid., p. 188; also Godwin, *The Enquirer*, pp. 145, 229–30, 301, 306, 311. C.f. Lovejoy, A. O., *Reflections of Human Nature*, Baltimore, Johns Hopkins Press, 1961, p. 24.
60. Skinner, B. F., *Walden Two*, London, Macmillan, 1976 (originally published 1948), p. 182.
61. Ibid., p. 114; see also pp. 92, 93, 162 and Skinner, B. F., *Beyond Freedom and Dignity*, London, Cape, 1972 (originally published 1971), p. 101.
62. Skinner, *Beyond Freedom and Dignity*, op. cit., p. 26.
63. Skinner, *Walden Two*, op. cit., pp. 69, 114, 115; 32; 35, 148; 121; 74; 116; 76; Skinner, *Beyond Freedom and Dignity*, op. cit., p. 29.
64. Skinner, *Beyond Freedom and Dignity*, op. cit., p. 26.
65. Skinner, *Walden Two*, op. cit., p. 83; see also p. 117.
66. Skinner, *Beyond Freedom and Dignity*, op. cit., p. 5.
67. Ibid., p. 164.
68. Skinner, *Walden Two*, op. cit., pp. 192–4.
69. Ibid., p. 194.
70. Skinner, *Beyond Freedom and Dignity*, op. cit., p. 42.
71. Skinner, *Walden Two*, op. cit., pp. 146–9.
72. Skinner, *Beyond Freedom and Dignity*, op. cit., pp. 130, 168.
73. Ibid., p. 110.

74. Skinner, *Walden Two*, op. cit., pp. 104, 105; 121.
75. Ibid., pp. 46, 191.
76. Ibid., pp. 279, 96.
77. *PJ*, op. cit., p. 241.
78. Skinner, *Walden Two*, op. cit., p. 218.
79. Ibid., p. 279.
80. Ibid., p. 159.
81. Ibid., p. 261.
82. Ibid., p. 145.
83. Skinner, *Beyond Freedom and Dignity*, op. cit., pp. 118, 123.
84. Skinner, *Walden Two*, op. cit., p. 261.

6 Critical Theory and human nature

VINCENT GEOGHEGAN

The Frankfurt School, and its distinctive Critical Theory, began to emerge in the 1930s, initially in Germany and subsequently, with the triumph of the Third Reich, in America. In an attempt to generate a Marxism capable of coping with the extraordinary theoretical, political and socio-economic developments of the twentieth century, the most celebrated members of the School, Max Horkheimer, Theodor Adorno and Herbert Marcuse, constructed sophisticated analyses of human nature. If events like the nationalist upsurge of the First World War, the problems of the Soviet Union and the growth of fascism were to be explained adequately, then some theory of human behaviour was required; yet the predominant Marxisms of the day were patently deficient in this area. The theory which they developed in the ensuing decades was both critical and healthily eclectic. Sacred cows of Marxist orthodoxy were ruthlessly slaughtered and infusions from non-Marxist traditions welcomed; these qualities were apparent in the treatment of human nature where, in the case of Marcuse, for example, the residual element of domination in Marx's concept of labour is excised and the psychology of Freud assimilated. The discussion in this chapter focuses on three essays, each separated by approximately two decades: Horkheimer's 'Authority of the Family' (1936); Adorno's 'Sociology and Psychology' (1955); and Marcuse's 'Marxism and Feminism' (1974). It not only seeks to show the similarities and dissimilarites between the conceptions of human nature developed by these men but also to examine the strengths and some of the weaknesses of these conceptions.

Horkheimer and the material world

'Materialism', a term Horkheimer used to characterize his theory in his 1936 essay, indicated both his debt to Marxism and the starting-point for his analysis of human nature. For him, the fundamental fact of having to exist in a material world is the ultimate determinant of human nature. 'Materialism . . . tries to comprehend the historical transformations of human nature in terms of the ever-varying shape of the material life-process in each society.'[1] In the relationship between human nature and its objective determinants, determination does not flow in one direction only but in both directions, through a complex process of interaction. In this respect, and *contra* the crude determinism of vulgar Marxism, Hork-heimer was clearly writing in the spirit of Engels' well-known letter to Mehring: 'Once an historic element has been brought into the world by other, ultimately economic causes, it reacts, and can react on its environ-ment and even on the causes that have given rise to it.'[2]

From the perspective of the process of production, human nature is determined by both its contemporary and historic forms; the individual is shaped by recent economic events and by institutions (the family, church, school, etc.), which reflect earlier such events. Nor has this process generated a unitary human nature either historically or sociologically—earlier modes of production had distinct forms and, similarly, there are group forms within capitalism. Horkheimer's point, 'that particular groups react according to the special character of their members and that this character has been formed in the course of earlier no less than of present social development',[3] clearly echoes Marx in *The Eighteenth Brumaire of Louis Bonaparte*:

> Men make their own history, but they do not make it just as they please; they do not make it under circumstances chosen by themselves, but under circumstances directly encountered, given and transmitted from the past. The tradition of all the dead generations weighs like a nightmare on the brain of the living.[4]

From the perspective of the individual, human nature can be both supportive and disruptive of the social whole. Horkheimer is at pains to point out the complex origins of the supportive function in capitalist society. The capacity of the bulk of the population to sustain a mode of production that deprives them of true existence cannot be explained simply in terms of irrational false-consciousness; rather, the role played by the very rational emotions of fear and hope have to be acknowledged. The memory of coercion, be it violence or hunger, and the fear of its recur-rence, is an important component of the 'social nature' of humanity, like-wise the anticipated benefits from knuckling under; the processes of internalization, intellectualization, rationalization, and ultimately identi-fication, are grounded in these hard facts. Horkheimer used the examples of ancestor-belief in China and the caste system in India to show how the interaction of the rational and the irrational, the understanding and the emotions, the sociological and the psychological, can produce a mentality

derived from a previous mode of production that is resistant to the introduction of a new mode.

Human nature can also be disruptive or subversive of the existing order
as critical quasi-autonomous qualities emerge in the historical process.
Morality may have emerged as an accommodation to a brutal reality, 'as
interiorized force', but it can develop an independence within the psyche
and act as a force in opposition to the status quo. Similarly, despite the
historically coercive regulation of sexuality, 'the romantic love which arose
in the course of such regulation is a social phenomenon which can drive
the individual into opposition to or even a break with society.'[5]

In his analysis of human nature, Horkheimer can be seen to be trying to
avoid the contrary positions found in the works of the early Utopian socialists, Charles Fourier and Robert Owen. For Fourier, human nature is a constant, an immutable collection of passions: 'the nature of the passions has
been and will remain invariable amongst all nations of men';[6] human activity can only adjust to human nature, it can in no way alter or modify it.
However, in the work of Owen, as is discussed in Chapter 5, the emphasis
is on the almost infinite plasticity and malleability of human nature: 'Any
character, from the best to the worst, from the most ignorant to the most
enlightened, may be given to any community, even to the world at large, by
applying certain means. . . .'[7] Human activity can readily and radically
transform human nature. Horkheimer, in contrast, wished to emphasize the
intense resistances of human nature *and* its capacity for change.

The family figures prominently in the 1936 essay. 'The family has a
very special place among the relationships which through conscious and
unconscious mechanisms influence the psychic character of the vast
majority of men.'[8] In short, this institution has been able, through its
control of the earliest environment, to mould the child into an individual
capable of existing in harmony with capitalist society. In the 'golden age'
of the bourgeois family, where the father's pre-eminent economic position plus his physical strength are perceived as a natural power, 'growing
up in the restricted family is a first-rate schooling in the authority behavior
specific to this society.'[9] Paradoxically, Horkheimer also wishes to argue
that this type of family could also nurture a spirit of resistance, since
relationships between members of the family were, unlike most extra-
familial relations, 'not mediated through the market', thus giving individuals the chance to exist as human beings. In particular, sexual love and
maternal care promote a common and oppositional relationship to the
external world. The unusual conclusion is not evaded: 'To this extent the
family not only educates for authority in bourgeois society: it also culti-
vates the dream of a better condition for mankind.'[10]

Class introduces an important qualification to this argument. The proleteriat, according to Horkheimer, tended to derive its image of the family from the bourgeoisie, particularly when economic conditions were not too appalling. In fact, the concept of the strong paterfamilias exercised a particular appeal to the (male) working-class heads of families—who could obtain the authority which society both exalted and yet denied them in their working lives. From this, Horkheimer believes, stems greater cruelty in the working-class family and a masochistic attraction to powerful leaders. However, the proletarian family has often had its bourgeois form rudely smashed as economic pressures forced not only the father but some or all of its other members out to work. No safe haven in which critical humanity might emerge was possible under these circumstances: 'There can no longer be any question of a private existence with its own satisfaction and values. In the extreme case, the family becomes the available form of sexual satisfaction and, for the rest, a source of multiplied anxieties.'[11] But there is some hope here, for Horkheimer speculates that a new communal existence beyond the old bourgeois family might emerge from this wreckage.

The formative role of the family has, in any case, declined, according to Horkheimer, as liberal capitalism has lost its liberal dimension. He argued, in what continued to be a highly dubious commonplace of Frankfurt School thinking, that with the diminution of the father's economic position in late capitalism a weakening of the socialization function of the family has ensued (with the proviso, of course, that archaic authority patterns can linger after their material basis has disappeared). The direct determination of human nature will tend to pass, in this view, to the conscious and unconscious care of extra-familial institutions. Nevertheless, almost half a century after this analysis, the family's social role appears to be as central as ever. David Cooper refers to 'the most basic problem in psycho-therapy—the problem of the progressive depopulation of the room', for when therapy begins 'the room may hold hundreds of people, principally all the person's family, over several generations . . .'—plus the therapist's own internalized family.[12] The task is therefore to identify the members of these vast family groups (and others), and systematically ask them to leave the room until there are only two individuals left—testimony indeed to the continuing tenacity of the family and the difficulty of satisfactorily drawing conclusions as to the fundaments of human nature.

Adorno and the individual

Adorno's 1955 essay commences thus:

> For more than 30 years, the tendency has been emerging among the masses of the advanced industrial countries to surrender themselves to the politics of disaster instead of pursuing their rational interests and, chief of all, that of their own survival.[13]

The element of consent in this process, whereby 'much of this is so obvious to its victims', prompts Adorno to use analytical psychology, 'the only one seriously to go into the subjective conditions of objective irrationality.'[14] This recourse to psychology has been a distinctive and valuable dimension of the critical theorists' analyses of human nature.

With Max Horkheimer's accession to the directorship of the Institute of Social Research in 1930, psychology became an important component of the work of the Frankfurt School. Horkheimer considered that the absence of a theory of the human pscyhe was an unacceptable lacuna in any social theory, and he was aware of the deficiences of Marxism in this respect. Erich Fromm, the Institute's psychological 'expert', pointed out in the first issue of the ISR's journal (1932) Engels' own admission that Marx and he had neglected the psychological dimension of ideology—an admission which occurs earlier in the letter to Mehring quoted above:

> Otherwise only one more point is lacking, which, however, Marx and I always failed to stress enough in our writings and in regard to which we are all equally guilty. That is to say, in the first instance, we all laid, and were bound to lay, the main emphasis on the derivation of political, juridicial and other ideological notions, and of actions arising through the medium of these notions, from basic economic facts. But at the same time we have on account of the content neglected the formal side—the manner in which these notions, etc., come about.[16]

In his 1936 essay, Horkheimer briefly included a psychological approach to try to deepen his analysis of the development of the authority-oriented character in the family and referred to recent work in depth-psychology showing how familial relations, as experienced by the child, lay at the root of the heteronomy and inferiority feelings of the adult. Crucial was the paternal pressure which deflected the child's critical energy away from legitimate social targets and back on to the child itself, thereby transmuting it into guilt:

> The outcome of such paternal education is men who seek the fault in themselves. . . . In the present age . . . a compulsive sense of guilt, taking the form of a continual readiness to be sacrificed, renders fruitless any criticisms of the real causes of trouble.[17]

The book in which Horkheimer's essay appeared, *Studien über Autorität und Familie*, also contained an essay by Fromm devoted to the social pscyhological aspects of authority and the family. Adorno's interest in psychology predated his membership of the Institute and continued subsequently. In the 1940s he participated in an extensive study on authoritarianism and was one of the authors of *The Authoritarian Personality*, a fruit of this project. In short, by the time Adorno came to write his 1955 essay, 'Sociology and Psychology', the Frankfurt School could look back on more than two decades of work on psychological topics.[18]

In his analysis of the psychological dimension, Adorno, like Horkheimer and Marcuse, was predominantly influenced by the work of Freud. All three were at pains to defend Freud's work against what they saw as misguided criticisms and revisions, and they would even rap over the knuckles Freud himself when they considered he was undermining his own achievements. However, the three men did not share a common perspective on Freud. Whereas Marcuse detected a 'hidden trend in psycho-analysis',[19] which both indicated the contemporary world *and* pointed towards possible liberation, Horkheimer (after the 1930s) and Adorno used Freud's work in a more limited and less optimistic sense to indicate the fragmentation of the individual under capitalism. As Adorno wrote in 1946:

> The greatness of Freud consists in that, like all great bourgeois thinkers, he left standing undissolved such contradictions and disdained the assertion of pretended harmony where the thing itself is contradictory. He revealed the antagonistic character of the social reality.[20]

For Adorno, the value of analytic psychology in helping to explain the peculiarities of contemporary human behaviour raises the question of the explanatory status of sociology, which involves asking what the relation-ship is between the psyche and society. In what is essentially a hostile stance *vis-à-vis* Talcott Parsons, Adorno approves of this sociologist's stress on 'the irreducible autonomy of the social system'[21] and his rejection of a number of attempts to explain social events in psychological terms. How-ever, Parsons's failing is that 'he does not suspect behind this incompata-bility any real clash between the universal and the particular, any incom-mensurability between the objective life-process, the "in itself" and the individual that is merely "for himself".'[22] In other words, Parsons failed to grasp that the difference between the realm of the psychological and the realm of the sociological was a difference in reality, an actual and malig-nant difference within the object of study. (Such a failure is evident in

Parsons's 'dove-tailing of the individual and the social system'[23] in a discussion of the superego.)

Parsons is engaged in a bogus holism. The impulse to grasp the totality is sound; it represents an attack on the ideological function of the academic division of labour. However, this same division of labour also illustrates the split that has occurred in reality, a split obscured by untimely, inadequate theoretical syntheses:

> The separation of sociology and psychology is both correct and false. False because it encourages the specialists to relinquish the attempt to know the totality which even the separation of the two demands; and correct insofar as it registers more intransigently the split that has actually taken place in reality than does the premature unification at the level of the theory.[24]

Or put another way: 'An ideal of conceptual unification taken from the natural sciences cannot be indiscriminately applied to a society whose unity resides in its not being unified.'[25]

Knowledge of the whole is therefore to be gained via the specific: 'The only totality the student of society can presume to know is the antagonistic whole, and if he is to attain the totality at all, then only in and through contradiction.'[26]

Clearly, the locus, and victim, of the difference between the realms is the individual. 'In an antagonistic society each individual is non-identical with himself, both social and psychological character at once, and, because of the split, maimed from the outset.'[27] The difference inheres in the individual through a complex and historically changing process of interaction. There is no direct, immediate linkage between the sphere of the instincts and social experience; rather, the demands of society, of 'reality', are 'translated' into the 'language of the id', i.e. they are transformed into elements of a very different world. 'If there is any truth in Freud's notion of the archaic and indeed possibly "timeless" nature of the unconscious, then concrete social circumstances and motivations cannot enter it without being altered and "reduced".'[28] Or again: '. . . all reality undergoes modification upon entering the unconscious.'[29] Thus it is the contemporary role of the ego in the process that spells disaster for the individual. The ego is 'both psychic and extra-psychic, a quantum of libido and the representative of outside reality',[30] and in an irrational, repressive society the strain of trying to reconcile 'the irreconcilable claims both of the libido and of actual self-preservation'[31] becomes just too great for the ego, which consequently regresses toward the unconscious. This regression, which can range from a mingling of conscious and unconscious functions to narcissism, opens up the individual to the influence of baleful social forces, such as fascist political parties, which effectively respond to and manipulate the weak ego and exposed unconscious.

Therefore the contemporary individual is, for Adorno, a fragmented, internally divided creature, a fact the concept of 'personality' obscures. As he wrote in 1946:

> The stress on totality as against the unique, fragmentary impulse, always implies the harmonistic belief in what might be called the unity of the personality and what is never realised in our society. It is one of the greatest merits of Freud that he has debunked the myth of this unity.[32]

He is scathing about attempts by psychiatrists to develop the 'well-integrated personality', the 'well-balanced person', and 'the all-round development of the whole man'. The 'balanced person' in an unbalanced world

> would be confusing his psychic state—his personal good fortune—with objective reality. His integration would be false reconciliation with an unreconciled world, and would presumably amount in the last analysis to an 'identification with the aggressor', a mere character-mask of subordination.[33]

To this Adorno adds Walter Benjamin's satirical characterization of the psychoanalytical 'ideal man' of the 1930s—the 'blond Siegfried'—and concludes that all such attempts comprehensively to project authentic human existence betray their ideological nature. Like Marcuse, he accepts that it is possible to point to elements in current reality that genuinely anticipate a liberated human existence, but, unlike Marcuse, firmly sets his face against any attempt to assemble a composite future existence from them. One can only say what such an existence will not be, and no more. 'Every "image of man" is ideology except the negative one.'[34]

A pessimistic sense of the helplessness of humanity in the contemporary world pervades Adorno's work. The stress of German Idealism on the concealed power of the whole over the parts is favourably compared with the modern 'cult of personality' and its myth of the independent part—the autonomous individual. Whereas in the 1930s the Frankfurt School looked to the revolutionary proletariat for redemption, to Adorno, in the 1950s, such a view was no longer possible. The mode of production was reinforcing the sad state of humanity, not undermining it.

Marcuse and liberation

Marcuse's *One-Dimensional Man* shares a number of the gloomy pre-occupations of Adorno's work. In particular, it paints a highly unflattering portrait of the modern individual in uncritical subservience to the repressive whole. And yet, even in this most pessimistic study, Marcuse characteristically wished to point to tendencies that anticipate liberation:

> One-Dimensional Man will vacillate throughout between two contradictory theses: (1) that advanced industrial society is capable of containing qualitative change for the foreseeable future; (2) that forces and tendencies exist which may break this containment and explode the society.[35]

In *Eros and Civilization* (1955), he had indicated the explosive power of the instincts and developed a theory of instinctual liberation. It is this theory that lies at the core of his 1974 essay, 'Marxism and Feminism'.

Back in 1936, Horkheimer had discussed the role of women in history and referred to a number of thinkers who linked fundamental values and qualities with the woman: Hegel's identification of the principle of 'the whole person' with 'womanliness' and that of 'civic subordination' with 'manliness'; Morgan's portrayal of the positive dimensions of ancient matriarchy, and Engels' view that the transition from matriarchy to patriarchy ushered in class conflict, a split between public and family, and authoritarianism in the family itself. The woman, Horkheimer concluded, could provide a counter to the domination generated in the family:

> To the extent that any principle beside that of subordination prevails in the modern family the woman's maternal and sisterly love is keeping alive a social principle dating from before historical antiquity, a principle which Hegel conceives 'as the law of the ancient gods, "the gods of the underworld" ', that is, of prehistory.[36]

and:

> Because it still fosters human relationships which are determined by the woman, the present-day family is a source of strength to resist the total dehumanization of the world and contains an element of anti-authoritarianism.[37]

Horkheimer is, however, aware that women have not been able to abstract themselves from the inherent authoritarianism of modern society —male domination inside and outside the family has very effectively restricted woman's development. In two important respects the woman can be seen as reinforcing the status quo. The economic dependence of herself and her children on the male breadwinner infects the woman with a conservative fear of any change that might undermine the family economy —a fear communicated in turn to her offspring. Second, the idealized asexual mother and sister act as suppressors to the young male's sensuality, which can resurface in the form of a 'fanciful and sentimental susceptibility to all symbols of the dark, maternal, and protective powers.'[38]

Adorno argues in his *Minima Moralia* (1951) that greater (if still subordinate) employment prospects for women have not improved their lot. 'The admittance of women to every conceivable supervised activity conceals continuing dehumanization. In big business they remain what they were in the family, objects.'[39] Like Horkheimer, he believed that women 'reflect and identify themselves with domination',[40] and sketches a malicious picture of the modern woman locked into the false values of the age:

> Provided only a certain abundance of commodities are granted them, they enthusiastically assent to their fate, leave thinking to the men, defame all reflection as an offence against the feminine ideal propagated by the culture industry, and are altogether at their ease in the unfreedom they take as the fulfilment of their sex. The defects with which they pay for it, neurotic stupidity heading the list, help to perpetuate this state of affairs.[41]

He contrasts the contemporary 'integrated' woman with nineteenth-century female hysterics 'who undertook . . . the hopeless attempt to break out of the social prison which so emphatically turned its four walls to them all',[42] and concludes: 'The hysteric who wanted the miraculous has thus given way to the furiously efficient imbecile who cannot wait for the triumph of doom.'[43]

These contributions by Horkheimer and Adorno predate the flowering of the Women's Liberation Movement in the late 1960s and reflect a male-oriented and (particularly in Adorno's case) patronizing approach to women's issues. The two men were not particularly sensitive (with good reason, in a number of respects) to the lifestyle and student activist politics that emerged at the end of the sixties. Horkheimer maintained that he identified with many of the impulses behind such politics but perceived a violence in practice which he found unacceptable. Adorno's much-reported personal experience of direct action—when a number of women bared their breasts at one of his lectures—particularly upset him and is said to have contributed to his death shortly afterwards. Nevertheless, their analyses of the role of women did anticipate many of the themes present in the essay by Herbert Marcuse—a man much more attuned to the radical political developments of which Women's Liberation was a part.

Marcuse saw in these events the return of a fugitive humanity long distanced by an inhuman, one-dimensional society. Just as in *Eros and Civilization*, where the 'perversions'—homosexuality, paedophilia, etc.— were held to be upholding the creative, life-giving forces of Eros, so too, in *An Essay on Liberation* (1969) and in other works of this period, the triumphant ingress of this force was seen in the activities of the black/student/hippie movements. Although the wild party of the late sixties gave way to the massive hangover of the early seventies, Marcuse saw in the Women's Liberation Movement a continuing source of hope—apparent in the credo which opens his 1974 essay: 'I believe the Women's Liberation Movement today is, perhaps, the most important and potentially the most radical political movement that we have. . . .'[44]

Women, Marcuse argued, have developed a number of social, mental and physiological characteristics that differ qualitatively from those of men and which could become the basis for genuine human emancipation. In terms of the old nature/nurture debate, these characteristics are socially conditioned but over the centuries have become stabilized into a 'second nature'. Such qualities—'receptivity, sensitivity, non-violence, tenderness and so on'[45]—are produced and sustained by the marginality of women, which also generates the desire for economic, social and cultural equality. Marcuse was acutely aware of the possible conflict between these two levels, where greater integration might lead to the destruction of the qualitative dimension of the female, and this leads to some strategic and tactical ambiguity in this work. For example, in an interview in 1973 he used a news item to infer that women should avoid the dehumanization of integration:

> A women's organisation, I forgot the name, wrote a letter to President Nixon complaining that he did not appoint any women to the Cabinet. Now, if I were in the Women's Liberation Movement, I would have written exactly the opposite letter. Namely, I would have expressed my gratitude to Nixon that he did not include any women in his cabinet.[46]

However, elsewhere, in what appears to be his predominant, mature view on the question, it is argued that the two levels are equally valid and necessary:

> . . . the movement becomes radical to the degree to which it aims, not only at equality *within* the job and value structure of the *established* society

(which would be the equality of dehumanization) but rather at a change in the structure itself (the basic demands of equal opportunity, equal pay, and release from full-time household and child care are a prerequisite).[47]

Nevertheless, one still detects a certain unease about the possibility of combining the two levels.

The problem haunts his discussion of the transition to socialism. Are not political struggles harsh climates for humanist values? How can agression, even violence, coexist with tenderness and non-violence? In an essay of the early seventies, he refers to art for an image of this paradox:

> It is the woman who, in Delacroix' painting, holding the flag of the revolution, leads the people on the barricades. She wears no uniform; her breasts are bare, and her beautiful face shows no trace of violence. But she has a rifle in her hand—for the end of violence is still to be fought for . . . [48]

In psychological terms, Marcuse seems to think that it is possible to activate aggressive energy that is free from exploitation and domination. The leaders of the two major revolutions in this century—Mao and Lenin—were very conscious of this problem, and both concluded that an irreconcilable conflict existed between certain humanist values and the necessities of revolution, whereby the success of the latter depended on the suspension of the former. Their words are well known. For Mao:

> A revolution is not a dinner party, or writing an essay, or painting a picture, or doing embroidery; it cannot be so refined, so leisurely and gentle, so temperate, kind, courteous, restrained and magnanimous. A revolution is an insurrection, an act of violence . . . [49]

Lenin wrote:

> I can't listen often to music, it affects my nerves, makes me want to say kind stupidities and pat the heads of people who living in this dirty hell, can create such beauty. But now one must not pat anyone's little head —they would bite off your hand, and one has to beat their little heads, beat mercilessly, although ideally we're against any sort of force against people. Hmm—it's a devilishly difficult task.[50]

Such views can also be found in Marcuse's work—for example, in his 1965 essay, 'Repressive Tolerance', in which he agrees that although violence is inhuman it can be, and may have to be, used by revolutionaries. In short, Marcuse never fully resolved this very real problem.

Marcuse speaks of the goal of 'feminine socialism', not simply because it enshrines the principle of complete female emancipation, but also because it embodies universal values, located amongst women, which previous socialist thinkers have only imperfectly perceived. Marx for example, is upbraided for the residual elements of domination in his socialism—over-concern with developing the productive forces, an exploitative view of nature and an unacceptable distinction between work and freedom (Fourier and Schiller are considered greater visionaries in these areas). The term 'feminine socialism' indicates the qualitative difference between this conception and earlier, less adequate notions. It is definitely not meant to imply an exclusion of males, for its central vision is the transformation of male/female antithesis into synthesis—'the legendary idea of *androgynism*'.[51]

A classic treatment of androgynism is to be found in Plato's *Symposium*. The scene is a dinner/drinking party—love is being discussed. The poet Aristophanes maintains that originally there were three sexes, male, female and hermaphrodite (male and female) and that each human being was a united pair with four legs, four hands, two faces and so on. To punish them for their proud actions, Zeus bisected them into the form humans have exhibited subsequently, thus populating the world with halves who longed for reunion with one another. The female whole split into women who are attracted to other women 'and pay little attention to men; Lesbians belong to this category.'[52] Likewise, male wholes generate men who 'love men throughout their boyhood, and take pleasure in physical contact with men.'[53] Aristophanes, reflecting influential conceptions of the times, particularly favours this group in marked contrast to the judgement on the halves of hermaphrodites (who pursue members of the opposite sex): 'most adulterers come from this class, as do women who are mad about men and sexually promiscuous.'[54] The import of the speech is that individuals feel inadequate and fragmented and desire, through a love (Eros) which is often obscure to them, to be whole once more: 'love is simply the name for the desire and pursuit of the whole.'[55]

For Marcuse, men and women as currently constituted are inadequate units. Although women uphold universal values, millenia of male domination have generated the poisonous deposits which Horkheimer and Adorno described, and which Marcuse, in a 1972 essay, referred to as 'surplus-passivity'.[56] Men, on the other hand, can point to the real achievements of patriarchal civilization, achieved, though, at the price of domination and exploitation of 'surplus-aggression'.[57] Androgynism would therefore mean the synthesis of the valid dimensions of men and women (Hegel's dialectical sublation or *aufhebung*—the simultaneous ending of a form and the preservation of its truth at a higher level):

No other rational meaning can possibly be attributed to the idea of androgynism than the fusion, in the individual, of the mental and somatic characteristics, which in patriarchal civilization were unequally developed in men and women, a fusion in which feminine characteristics, in cancellation of male dominance, would prevail over their repression.[58]

None the less, the emphasis is very clearly on the predominant female input to this process—the 'male principle' has been historically such a repressive one that the units are not Plato's equal halves. As in the *Symposium*, Eros (in Marcuse, Freud's life instinct) is the road to truth, goodness and happiness, but for Marcuse, Eros' deadly partner Thanatos, the death instinct, has so triumphed in the male world that women have a disproportionate role to play.

After defining androgynism in *Marxism and Feminism*, Marcuse adds:

But, no degree of androgynous fusion could ever abolish the natural differences between male and female as individuals. All joy and all sorrow are rooted in this relation to the other, of whom you want to become a part, and who you want to become a part of yourself, and who never can and never will become such a part of yourself.[59]

These words are ambiguous. If Marcuse means that even in socialism there will be both positive and negative individual differentiation, then this is a commendable antidote to the homogeneous 'paradises' of some socialist conceptions. If, however, he is suggesting that the fundamental form of interaction will be between men and women, then such romantic heterosexual triumphalism is as unacceptable as the priority Aristophanes grants to male homosexuality. It would be particularly remiss in Marcuse's case. Horkheimer's 1936 essay is oblivious of all but heterosexual relations, and connoisseurs of nonsense on stilts are referred to Adorno's remark in 'Sociology and Psychology':

In reducing everything it calls unconscious, and ultimately all individuality, to the same thing, psychoanalysis seems to be the victim of a familiar homosexual mechanism, the inability to perceive differences. Homosexuals exhibit a certain experimental colour-blindness, an incapacity to apprehend individuality; women are, in the double sense, 'all the same' to them.[60]

Marcuse, however, had long been a champion of erotic pluralism, and in *Eros and Civilization* in particular, had looked forward to a blossoming of forms of interaction far beyond the male/female dualism. It would be most uncharacteristic of him to have regressed to the sterilities of Adorno and Horkheimer in this respect.

Conclusion

It is difficult to draw together in a brief conclusion the main elements of the rich and varied analysis of human nature offered by the Frankfurt School. On Marxist foundations they built an imposing edifice using materials from many sources—most notably, perhaps, from the works of Sigmund Freud. At the heart of this analysis is a sensitivity to both the enduring and the transitory elements in human nature, and an awareness of the great complexity of its emergence and development. This is apparent in Horkheimer's words of 1936:

> The term 'human nature' here does not refer to an original or an eternal or a uniform essence. Every philosophical doctrine which sees the movement of society or the life of the individual as emerging out of a fundamental, a historical unity is open to justified criticism. Such theories with their undialectical method have special difficulty in coming to grips with the fact that new individual and social qualities arise in the historical process . . . These . . . theories fail to do justice to the methodological principle that vital processes are marked by structural change no less than by continuous development.[61]

Horkheimer's essay revealed the Frankfurt School's general perspective on human nature and the specific role of the modern family in the formation of the individual. Adorno sought in his piece to define the relationship between the complexities of society and those of the psyche in an attempt to explain the irrationality of contemporary behaviour. In Marcuse's contribution, the possibility of a liberated humanity is explored with special reference to the role of women. Clear differences between the three thinkers emerge, particularly between Horkheimer and Adorno on the one hand (in Horkheimer's case, after the 1930s when he came much more under Adorno's influence), and Marcuse on the other—a difference that could crudely be characterized as pessimism versus optimism.

As is inevitable in all bold speculation the underlying assumptions are exposed and invite attack. The three most obvious avenues of attack are: first, to attack the historical materialist underpinnings of the theory—that human nature is ultimately determined by modes of production; second, to deny the validity of their Freudian model of the individual; and third, to object to their particular formulation of the relationship between Marx and Freud. A number of other objections have been adumbrated in the chapter—the role of the family, humanism and revolution, male and heterosexual chauvinism.

However, the main purpose of this chapter has not been criticism but rather an attempt to show that the Frankfurt School has made a valuable and interesting contribution to the study of human nature. At the very least, their work displays very great insight, challenges conventional wisdom, and points the direction for future research.

Notes

I would like to thank the following for their helpful comments: Bob Eccleshall, Margaret Ward, the editors of this volume and, as ever, John le Juen.

1. Horkheimer, M., *Critical Theory*, New York, The Seaburg Press, 1972, pp. 50–1.
2. Marx, K., and Engels, F., *Selected Correspondence*, Moscow, Progress Publishers, 1975, p. 435.
3. Horkheimer, op. cit., pp. 53–4.
4. Marx, K., and Engels, F., *Collected Works*, Vol. 11, London, Lawrence & Wishart, 1979, p. 103.
5. Horkheimer, op. cit., p. 58.
6. Fourier, C., *Design for Utopia*, New York, Schocken Books, 1971, p. 55.
7. Owen, R., *A New View of Society*, London, Dent, 1972, p. 14.
8. Horkheimer, op. cit., p. 98.
9. Ibid., p. 107.
10. Ibid., p. 114.
11. Ibid., p. 124.
12. Cooper, D., *The Death of the Family*, Harmondsworth, Penguin Books, 1972, p. 7.
13. Adorno, T., 'Sociology and Psychology', Part 1, *New Left Review*, Vol. 46, 1967, 67.
14. Ibid.
15. Ibid., p. 68.
16. Marx and Engels, *Selected Correspondence*, op. cit., pp. 433–4. This is pointed out in Slater, P., *Origin and Significance of the Frankfurt School*, London, Routledge & Kegan Paul, 1977, pp. 9 and 95.
17. Horkheimer, op. cit., p. 109.
18. See Jay, M., *The Dialectical Imagination*, London, Heinemann, 1973, and Held, D., *Introduction to Critical Theory*, London, Hutchinson, 1980.
19. Marcuse, H., *Eros and Civilisation*, London, Sphere Books, 1972, p. 29.
20. Cited in Jacoby, R., *Social Amnesia*, Hassocks, Harvester, 1977, pp. 27–8.
21. Adorno, op. cit., p. 68.
22. Ibid., p. 69.
23. Ibid., p. 70.
24. Ibid., p. 78.
25. Ibid., p. 69.
26. Ibid., p. 74.
27. Adorno, T., 'Sociology and Psychology', Part 2, *New Left Review*, Vol. 47, 1968, 85.
28. Ibid., p. 80.
29. Ibid.
30. Ibid., p. 86.

31. Ibid., p. 87.
32. Cited in Jay, M., 'The Frankfurt School's Critique of Marxist Humanism', *Social Research*, Vol. 39, No. 2, 1972, 302.
33. Adorno, op. cit., Part 2, p. 83.
34. Ibid., p. 84.
35. Marcuse, H., *One-Dimensional Man*, London, Sphere Books, 1972, p. 13.
36. Horkheimer, op. cit., p. 118.
37. Ibid.
38. Ibid., p. 121.
39. Adorno, T., *Minima Moralia*, London, New Left Books, 1974, p. 92.
40. Ibid.
41. Ibid., pp. 92–3.
42. Ibid., p. 93.
43. Ibid.
44. Marcuse, H., 'Marxism and Feminism', *Women's Studies*, 2, 1974, 279.
45. Ibid., p. 283.
46. Marcuse, H., 'Interview with Marcel Rioux', *Forces*, 22, 1973, 78.
47. Marcuse, H., *Counterrevolution and Revolt*, London, Allen Lane, 1972, p. 75.
48. Ibid., p. 78.
49. Mao Tse-Tung, *Quotations*, Peking, Foreign Language Press, 1967, pp. 11–12.
50. Cited in Conquest, R., *Lenin*, Glasgow, Fontana, 1972, pp. 31–2.
51. Marcuse, 'Marxism and Feminism', op cit., p. 287 (Marcuse's emphasis).
52. Plato, *The Symposium*, Harmondsworth, Penguin Books, 1972, p. 62.
53. Ibid.
54. Ibid.
55. Ibid., p. 64.
56. Marcuse, *Counterrevolution and Revolt*, op. cit., p. 77.
57. Ibid.
58. Marcuse, 'Marxism and Feminism', op. cit., p. 287.
59. Ibid.
60. Adorno, op. cit., Part 2, p. 96.
61. Horkheimer, op. cit., p. 66.

7 Psychoanalysis and human nature

MICHAEL NICHOLSON

A psychoanalytic view of human nature could briefly be regarded as one in which unconscious motivations and attitudes are deemed to be of great, perhaps overriding, significance. It follows plausibly, if not necessarily, that an understanding of social and political behaviour also requires the recognition and analysis of some of these unconscious factors.

Psychoanalysis, strictly interpreted, is a form of psychotherapy based on the theory of the mind, first developed by Sigmund Freud. While Freudian theory is that to which I shall mainly refer, this is not the exclusive emphasis of this chapter, and only in part depends upon it.

There are basically two issues. The first is to what extent it is correct to assert that unconscious factors are the prime determinants of our attitudes to major social issues such as war and violence. Secondly, is it possible to have theories of these unconscious processes, and if so, then do such theories exist and, in particular, is Freudian theory such a theory of the unconscious mind?

There are, of course, many sceptics on the subject of Freudian theory, though it is not always clear whether doubt surrounds this particular theory, or whether it is believed that even in principle there can be no theory of the unconscious. Both proponents and opponents of psychoanalytic thought conduct the debate with venom and passion, often making the limits of the argument difficult to discern. Psychoanalysts are variously regarded as fools, rogues or the saviours of mankind. Those who have been influenced by psychoanalytic thought are regarded as weakened versions of the above. I have been influenced by psychoanalytic thought, but self-regard prohibits me from putting myself in the first of the two categories, whilst modesty prohibits the third. I shall confine myself in this chapter to a discussion of why, and roughly how, psychoanalytic accounts of behaviour are not merely useful but critical if we are to understand political behaviour at all.

Some comments on psychoanalytic thought

This is not an account of Freud's views on politics. Freud did write on politics, at least in a generalized sense (e.g. in *Civilization and its Discontents*),[1] and on political leaders (e.g. President Wilson) from a psychoanalytic perspective.[2] However, as a political thinker he is not very important, being superficial and ill-informed. Nevertheless, his basic views have very critical social and political implications, some of which it is my purpose to draw out.

His comments on social affairs are profound only in the eyes of the truly faithful. He was perturbed, for example, in *Thoughts for the Times on War and Death*,[3] by the hitherto unexpected enthusiasm with which human beings went in for mutual slaughter—a habit which, prior to 1914, many people thought the human race was slowly abandoning. Later, it led him to the view that mass destructiveness is an aspect of the death instinct (*thanatos*), and he rather reluctantly admitted the existence of an aggressive instinct which was, he thought, another aspect or rather a perversion of the death instinct. He gloomily remarked that mankind was clearly closer to animals than we would like to think, but none of this really adds up to any particularly original view of human nature. The monograph's temperate tone, however, is impressive, given the virulence of people's attitudes at the time.

While Freud's social views in themselves are not of very great interest, the general theory of human behaviour and motivation from which they sprang have profound political relevance, particularly in a world as committed to self-destruction as is ours. On the whole, Freudian theory somewhat underplays the aggressive drives, in contrast to the sexual drives, of human beings. Indeed, the critics of psychoanalytic theory might do better to look at the important aspects of human behaviour which are less well explained in the theory, despite their manifest importance, rather than to attack the more reasonably well-attested parts of the theory. As far as social behaviour is concerned, it is the aggressive drives which are both the most puzzling and important.

Basically, I shall regard psychoanalysis to mean simply a theory of the unconscious and, in particular, *not* view the Freudian theory as being sacrosanct. I make three assertions. First, a theory of unconscious motivations and attitudes is possible, where 'theory' is used in a sense which is related to its common usage in empiricist or neo-empiricist philosophies of science. Second, Freudian theory is the best developed of these theories, which is not to claim that it is not imperfect in many significant respects. Third, childhood experiences are critical in the formation of adult attitudes, emotions and passions. The first of the propositions is necessary to my argument; the second two are contingent, but desirable. Clearly, the third follows from the second, but other theories of the unconscious exist which are not Freudian. I also draw attention to the two components of psychoanalysis. First, it is a theory of the unconscious mind; second, it is a therapy which is used (controversially) to relieve and 'cure' neurotic conditions and (even more controversially) psychotic conditions. It is psychoanalysis as a theory and not as a therapy with which I shall be concerned in this chapter.

It must be noted that Freud, and doubtless many other analysts, would not have been very happy with this distinction. In the introduction to one of his more detailed case studies, that of 'Little Hans', Freud states that psychoanalysis is not an impartial scientific investigation, but a thera-peutic measure. Its essence is not to prove anything, but merely to alter something.[4] This is the clinician speaking. Nevertheless, I think a failure to make a distinction between theory and therapy is misguided. The purpose for which psychoanalysis was conceived was clinical, and the evidence on which it was formulated is derived from clinical experience. These, how-ever, are totally separate issues from the nature of the statements made about the mind. Further, these statements about the mind can be, and of course, have been, applied to interpretations of human behaviour that have no connection whatever with therapeutic situations, and indeed it is mainly non-therapeutic situations which are the prime concern here.

There is a wide variety of views about the nature of psychoanalysis that I believe to be mistaken. Karl Popper[5] holds it to be insightful but un-scientific; Peter Medawar[6] holds it to be nonsense; Paul Johnson[7] holds it to be wicked. If Medawar is right, then this exercise is worthless from the start; if Popper is right it is probably, though not necessarily, trivial. Consequently, in the next section, there will be a brief outline of the argu-ment against Popper and Medawar. Paul Johnson can be left to the experts on Sin. First, however, a little more on psychoanalysis as such.

Psychoanalysis originated primarily with Freud; he was basically responsible for developing the essential theory. The notion of an un-conscious mind, at least in some intuitive sense, was not novel. But an explicit theory of it, its relation to the conscious mind, and the possibility of bringing out of the unconscious things we wished to defend ourselves from (even at some heavy cost in other ways) were much more clearly articulated by Freud than in any other previous work. Freud's theories enabled whole sets of psychological phenomena such as phobias, depres-sion and hysteria (specially defined) to be related to the whole psycho-logical portrait of the individual and his or her past experiences which

otherwise appear, with little coherence, in purely an *ad hoc* guise. Because
of this tremendous conceptual jump, it is appropriate to call psychoanalysis a paradigm in the Kuhnian sense.[8] However, it is not a paradigm
which replaces a weaker predecessor but one which made explicable many
features of people's behaviour which had been to all intents and purposes
inexplicable. In this it differs from the Copernican paradigm change,
which replaced one explanation of planetary phenomena with another.

Now Freud's theories were built upon clinical experience, namely
the analysis and study of a number of patients. They made internal sense,
but it was by no means clear that these were the only interpretations of
the effect of the unconscious on conscious behaviour, and various rival
schools grew up, usually as a breakaway from Freud (who found it difficult
to cope with serious criticism). Jung, originally the favoured son, split
away from Freud (or rather was banished) and became much more
mystical. Later, he did not even pretend to be scientific. Adler stressed
the search for power and the sense of inferiority (he invented the notion
of the 'inferiority complex'). These were perhaps the two most important
defectors, founding alternative theories of the unconscious and its relation
to the conscious mind.[9]

The multiplicity of theories, and the apparent freedom of choice
between them, is in part responsible for the alleged non-scientific nature
of psychoanalytic theory. Partly because of the complexity of a human
being's behaviour, one can get plausible interpretations of a person's
behaviour in either Freudian or Adlerian terms, just as one can get a
plausible account of the international system by assuming that its
behaviour is a consequence of either a capitalist or a communist conspiracy. Thus, a major issue is whether such a discrepancy of views is
inherent, or whether it is possible to discriminate scientifically between
different theories of the influence of the unconscious on behaviour. I shall
briefly argue in the next section that such discrimination is possible.

The status of psychoanalysis

It can be argued that Freudian psychoanalytic theory has a claim to be
regarded as a genuine theory in a commonly understood sense, such as that
of Braithwaite.[10] Influential voices are raised against this position—Popper
and Medawar have already been mentioned; Eysenck holds that such a
claim is both unscientific and scientifically wrong, thus verging on some
sort of contradiction.[11] I suggest, though in this chapter I do not have
time to argue this in detail, that these critics are wrong.

First, I must explain the unsatisfactorily-named idea of a *theoretical concept.*[12] In many of the natural sciences, for instance physics, a number of concepts are 'invented' in order to give coherence to certain theories. I say 'invented' (though with trepidation) as no conceivable set of sense data can, even in principle, establish their existence. An example with which we are all familiar is 'the centre of gravity'. We cannot see, touch, smell or in any other way directly observe the centre of gravity of an object. This is not because of any deficiency of our senses, or of our observational equipment, but because it does not 'exist' in any normal observational sense. It 'exists' only in the context of a theory, where it plays a very powerful part in the analysis of physical bodies whose existence and behaviour is beyond the doubt of all but the most extreme sceptic. The unconscious can be regarded as a theoretical concept in the same way. It functions as a concept within the theory, as something which is inherently unobservable but whose behaviour has observable consequences. It is not only the unconscious which is a theoretical concept, but also the terms which are used to describe it. The observable consequences are the behaviour of the individual, and that which is most widely observed is speech behaviour. However, if we accept that speech behaviour consists of facts, and that these are not purely the instruments of arbitrary interpretation, then we have manifest facts which can be explained by reference to the unobservable unconscious. It is along these lines that an argument can be made for the scientific respectability of *some* theory of the unconscious. It does not follow that Freudian theory or any of the current rival theories is a correct theory. It merely 'suggests' (for such a summary argument does not 'establish') the possibility of developing a theory of the unsconscious.[13] There are, then, grounds for supposing that Freudian theory is not as unscientific as some of its critics allege.

Despite the somewhat distrustful attitude of many psychoanalysts to the notion of testing in orthodox scientific senses, psychoanalytic theories have been subject to a great deal of testing. Freud himself was uneasy about exposing theories to test, and remained suspicious of statistical arguments. He argued that, because of the great heterogeneity of the subjects (individual psychological processes are very complex, interacting systems), very large samples would be needed in order to determine anything. This presumably left open the possibility of statistical testing of psychoanalytic propositions which would not then have been feasible for lack of sufficient numbers of cases. However, very large numbers of cases are not available, so this objection to statistical testing is weakened. In any case, Freud (as was a common weakness amongst doctors of his day) was a little vague about what the statistical testing of anything meant.

I rely in what follows on the extraordinarily diligent research of S. Fisher and R. P. Greenberg,[14] and on a slightly earlier work by Paul Kline.[15] In this research, they analyse all the work they could find (and they have looked in some obscure places) that has attempted to try to see which parts of Freudian theory are substantiated and which are not. Given the widespread view of the untestability of psychoanalysis, one of their concluding comments is worth quoting: 'We have actually not been able to find a single systematic psychological theory that has been as frequently evaluated scientifically as have Freud's concepts.'[16] Fisher and Greenberg's book is a review of a very large number of studies of varying degrees of rigour. These studies often contradict each other, but Fisher and Greenberg make serious efforts to sort out the sources of contradiction and, given the wealth of material, find that there is remarkably little in the way of outright contradiction in rigorously performed, and comparable, results.

I shall very briefly outline their findings. As I stressed earlier, it is important to distinguish between psychoanalysis as therapy and the Freudian theory of the mind. If his theory of the mind is correct (or at least constitutes a scientific research programme),[17] then one would suppose that some form of effective therapy could be based on it. However, as far as the therapy is concerned, the conclusions are fairly negative. They conclude that we can divide people suffering from some neurotic condition (say depression) into three groups: those who receive no treatment but who nevertheless come out of the depression spontaneously; those who receive Freudian treatment; and those who receive other forms of treatment. They found that people who receive treatment do better than those who receive no treatment, but that there is no clear superiority of Freudian treatment over any other or vice versa; what seems to matter is treatment of some sort.

If we return to the Freudian *theory* of the mind, then things become rather brighter. Most of the propositions directly stated or implied by Freudian theory come out reasonably well, such as, for example, theories of homosexuality. The only area of the theory which comes out badly is the theory of dreams. Perhaps oddly, given its intuitive appeal, the concept of dreams as wish-fulfilment is more or less ruled out by the existing evidence, as is the proposition that it serves a sleep-preserving function. While this might disappoint the supporter of psychoanalysis, it represents a perverse form of encouragement. A refutation establishes the theory's scientific nature, and the fact that the refutation is of something which is intuitively appealing (that is, conforms to our commonsense view of the world) supports its basic usefulness as something more than a systematization of commonsense using a complex vocabulary.

Thus, stealing directly from Kline, Fisher and Greenberg, I counter the view that Freudian theory cannot be regarded as scientific because of its untestability, with the response that, on the contrary, it has been widely tested and has survived many of these tests. It is then quite proper to regard this as a scientific research programme of good standing. The response to Popper's query, 'what evidence would cause anyone to abandon a belief in psychoanalytic theory?', is that no single piece of evidence would, any more than would be the same in almost any other theory. Rarely is a single proposition, even a generalization, critical to a theory. However, if the hypotheses which form Freudian analysis had been systematically shown to be incorrect, then one would abandon (or at least should abandon) the Freudian programme as a likely contender for a theory of the unconscious mind and pursue some of the other rivals, or, indeed, start afresh. In good Lakatosian terms, this is a research programme which is in some sort of progressive shift. It would be useful if more psychoanalysts were less defensive about testing and perhaps began to perceive the need for looking at psychoanalytic theory as being a scientific research programme. The various analytic schools of thought are contending programmes, and therefore attempts to discriminate between theories by testing become important.

Psychoanalysis and political attitudes

As far as the political scientist is concerned, psychoanalysis has potential relevance to two classes of problem. First, it is relevant to the discussion of decision-making, whether done by individuals or by groups such as cabinets. Second, it is applicable to general attitudes in a society. In the case of individuals, it would seem particularly relevant to the study of people like Stalin; in the case of societies, to such phenomena as Nazism. Indeed, it would seem difficult to analyse something like Nazism without some reference to whatever unconscious anxieties, hatreds or whatever lay behind it. However, the study of the unconscious is not relevant only to pathological conditions; we can use psychoanalytic concepts to analyse stable and liberal, as much as authoritarian, societies. There is nothing particularly 'normal', in a statistical sense, in stable liberal societies, either now or throughout history, though the author happens to prefer them. Except statistically, 'normality' is not a particularly easy concept to interpret psychologically, whether applied to individuals or groups.

Given that Freud worked with individual patients, it is not therefore surprising that, inasmuch as he had a coherent view of politics at all (and

I have suggested that his political perspicacity was low), it seemed to be a mixture of a 'Great Man' theory and some rather pessimistic views about human society *en masse*. The majority of 'psychohistories' implicitly (or explicitly) lie in the 'Great Man' tradition. In many ways, Freud would have fitted in better with those evangelical nineteenth-century nonconformists who believed in individual salvation, rather than with those who saw the Golden Age as coming through Chartism, trade unions, or in later years, the Labour Party. Because of the individualistic approach to human behaviour (natural enough given his primary occupation as a therapist), the implications for society as a whole are unclear. Thus, Fromm, a Freudian who has been interested in society as a whole, explicitly states that Marx is the much more significant figure of the two.[18] Writers in psychoanalytic veins have tended to work at the individual level, hoping perhaps that by a sufficiently comprehensive analysis at the individual level one can build up an analysis of society in due course.

However, the bigger political questions are whether psychoanalytical modes of thought can give us significant insights into such things as the rise of Nazism. It *may* be that the surmised absence of one of Hitler's testicles would explain his personal behaviour, while Napoleon's supposed penile inferiority does the same for him. However, the movements that they dominated can hardly be attributed to expressions of sympathy for these deficiencies. Lasswell's view, expressed in 1933, that Nazism was a yearning for the old political values, with Hitler as a Mother figure (*sic*), is scarcely compelling.[19] At least, as far as Hitler's role is concerned, this does not mean that a consideration of the unconscious in mass psychology is irrelevant and that Freudian theories have nothing to say. If nothing else, it points to features which more economistic views of human motivation miss out, whether these are the cruder versions of Marxism or 'Miracle of the Market Place' theories. Thus, for example, unemployment causes not only poverty but anxiety, and people may not always respond to anxiety as Milton Friedman would wish.

Yet, I am far from clear that psychoanalytic theory can add much to an awareness of society based on a reasonable degree of sensitivity to ordinary human experience. At the micro level, however, it is very different. We are conditioned to regard political decision-making as sets of rational responses to situations, given a reasonably coherent set of values. This is commonly not the case. While Leo Abse's rather manic psychoanalytic dash through the British Parliament of the sixties may not be terribly profound, it gives a much more coherent picture of political motivation and behaviour than most.[20] It may be a less flattering portrait of the human condition than some of us might have wished, but nevertheless it sees the human condition as something which lends itself to improvement, at least in principle. Quite how this is to be achieved is unfortunately not a question to which we can give a ready answer.

Still at the individual level, the best known application of psychoanalytic theory to political behaviour has been by Lasswell[21] and the work which has followed this tradition. Using a quasi-psychoanalytic technique, Lasswell interviewed in depth many patients in psychiatric hospitals who had been involved in political activity. He succeeded in relating political belief to a more general portrait of their personality expressed in psychoanalytic terms. A more recent approach of the same sort is by Davies, who interviewed, in a more informal manner, people who were not, at least officially, psychologically disturbed.[22]

While this is extremely interesting, it is somewhat limited in the insight it throws on mass political behaviour. We undoubtedly get a richer picture of the personality types who become communists, authoritarians and so on, while the typology alone enables a much fuller portrait of political attitudes. This, though useful, is all that is achieved. It would be more fruitful if we could say something more profound about human behaviour in general. At the slightly more complex level of social groups, the attempts to apply general notions of the recognition of the significance of unconscious factors in behaviour have had more sympathetic attention in business decision-making than in political circles. The use of T groups and other face-to-face groups as devices for examining the less obvious features of one's own behaviour, as well as that of others, is characteristic of business organizations rather than the civil service or political office holders. For example, it is not coincidental that De Board writes *The Psychoanalysis of Organisations* from Hendon Management College, and not from the Civil Service College.[23] However, the application of such approaches to groups is still, of course, just a stage up from the individual decision-maker. Its significance is for the tinkerer with social systems rather than the large-scale theorist. In this role, it may cast doubts on classical models of micro decision-making processes, such as the theory of games (though a gold mine may exist if some integration between formal rational choice theory and psychoanalytic theory could be made). Significant though this is, it leads perilously close to 'Great Man' theories of social behaviour.

Improvability and the unconscious

The psychoanalytic perspective has both an optimistic and a pessimistic aspect. It is optimistic in that it is essentially a doctrine of change and improvability; it is pessimistic in that it supposes that, collectively at least, we are only improving from a very poor initial position.

The portrait of mankind as it appears in the Freudian view is not a particularly flattering one. We try to dress up our unconscious drives in a variety of tolerable social clothes to make us fit for society, but in this attempt we often fail. The Freudian view is at least consistent with that of some of the ethological writers who argue that we are not very many generations away from much more primitive beings. In this view, drives, which might have been adaptive for small groups, are not adaptive but lethal in a complex society.[24]

While the Freudian theory might enable people to come to terms with the complex, sexually-based issues which affect them at an individual level, it leaves a great deal to be said about the problem of social order at the societal level. Despite the obvious problems which individual violence raises, this is really a relatively minor issue. Murder is an extremely rare phenomenon. However, while all, or almost all, societies deplore such personal violence, they applaud certain sorts of institutional violence. For example, the soldier is an honoured figure in most societies. Internally, societies seem to cope moderately well with the problem of violence, at least as far as lethal violence is concerned. Amongst the survival characteristics we may have inherited from our primitive fore-bears, there is also the habit of co-operation. Whether we fail to kill our neighbour when it is to our advantage due to a fear of the police, possible unpleasant experiences in the after-life, or because we have some basic co-operative urges, is debatable, but I think decidable, though not on current knowledge. Its decidability depends on future developments in the theory of the unconscious.

It is at least arguable that we have strong drives, left over from tribal society, to co-operate with relatively small groups of people. This makes for effective survival in either a hunting or a farming context. For groups to band together to fight other similar groups again provides a useful survival function in the search for food. However, these drives provided survival functions for humans or their immediate ancestors only when these beings were relatively few in number and possessed no weapons, or only simple ones. In a world which is heavily populated with highly-armed humans, such drives are of doubtful value. The aggressive attitudes to out-groups serve no purpose.

While it is true that violence internal to a society has harmed some groups, such as Jews and negroes, it is international violence which is the most characteristic form of lethal human aggressive behaviour. However rationally we purport to analyse 'defence', we are for the most part fascinated with the concept of violence. Most people, particularly males, enjoy vicarious violence and some appear to enjoy actual violence. That this involves deep unconscious drives seems to be the most coherent explanation. It is not, however, clear what to do about it. It certainly seems foolish to ignore it. If the aggressive drives are as strong as the sexual drives, then to ignore it is about as useful as to hope, as some puritans have done, that sexual intercourse would be practised purely for the purposes of reproduction—a view still held officially by the Roman Catholic Church. The urge to violence may be deplorable but it is there and, unlike sex, frequently lands societies in great trouble and discomfort. On present showing, it might very well end up by rendering the human race extinct.

The problem is how to organize society in the recognition that its members have deep violent drives. How one does this is by no means clear. For a start, it would seem that it would be better to recognize that the urge for violence exists. We go through rituals of deploring war, but in fact most people rather enjoy it, particularly if it causes them little personal inconvenience. The considerable popularity of the Falklands War in Britain stemmed from the combination of all the martial myths with a certain illusion of virtue, and only the minimum of direct inconvenience to the average citizen. However, if we face the reality that we like violence and do not regard it as a regrettable necessity, then we might be part of the way to reducing it. At the same time, we must recognize that these are very deep drives indeed. The problem is about as easy as trying to amalgamate a monastery and a nunnery while still retaining the principle of chastity. It would be a near impossible task, but its only hope of success would be for the members of the community to recognize their sexual feelings explicitly and not try to pretend that they do not exist. Similarly, an overt recognition that violence is positively liked, for poorly understood reasons, might at least provide some initial step towards coping with it at both the individual and societal level. As a panacea for world peace, this proposal might lack zest, or even much hope, but the other solutions, from Arms Control to Universal Love, do not seem to be achieving a great deal.

I earlier quoted Freud as being, like Marx, a theorist whose aim was to alter things as much as to explain them. This does have important implications, for it illustrates a basic feature of the psychoanalytic viewpoint— that people are changeable. In some ways it is a superbly optimistic view of human nature, in that while we might be born close to the animals, full of dread from a primal fear of loss of the breast, wracked with guilt from lusting (albeit unconsciously) after our mother or father from a remarkably early age, we can in due course acquire liberation and life-long happiness after some suitably long (and expensive) period of psychoanalysis. It is not, I think, a doctrine of perfectibility but a doctrine of improvability. Despite its strongly Jewish origins—Freud was very consciously Jewish, and the only non-Jewish member of the Vienna group who remained within his circle was Ernest Jones, a Welshman—it is a very puritanical doctrine. Liberation is usually achieved only after suffering.

Perhaps more to the point, it is a doctrine of individual liberation, not collective liberation. While Marx operates on the macro-scale, Freudian therapies are strictly micro-phenomena, and it then becomes a problem about how to relate the improvability aspect of psychoanalytic thought to society as a whole. What is individually an optimistic doctrine can collectively be a pessimistic doctrine in that, while we can learn to live with society, we cannot alter it (unless, of course, we believe in the possibility of a Psychoanalyst-King). We can, perhaps, look toward social improvement by improving methods of child-rearing, but inasmuch as Dr. Spock is our nearest approach to the psychoanalytic social engineer, the results have been of ambiguous benefit.

My conclusion is one of moderate optimism. Psychoanalysis is a theory of the mind, which, at the level of the individual and the small group, is a theory that can help us improve things, even if rather modestly. Its development at the societal level is less clear, though there seems no reason why there should not be significant developments in the theory. Indeed, it seems important that this should be done. It is a matter of both puzzlement and concern that people accept the significant possibility of mass extinction with equanimity. This may well be a perversion of some instinct which, for more primitive beings, served some positive function. However, for the current world, it is important both to explain it and to alter it.

Notes

1. Freud, S., *Civilization and its Discontents*, in *Collected Works*, J. Strachey (trs.), London, Hogarth Press, Vol. XXXI. (In citations to Freud's work, the date given is that of its original publication in German, not the Hogarth Press, English Edition.)
2. Freud, S., and Bullitt, W. C., *Wilson: A Psychological Study*, London, Weidenfeld & Nicolson, 1967.
3. Freud, S., *Thoughts for the Times on War and Death* (1915), op. cit., Vol. IV.
4. Freud, S., 'Analysis of a Phobia in a Five Year Old Boy' (1919), op. cit., Vol. X.
5. Popper, K., *Conjectures and Refutations*, London, Routledge & Kegan Paul, 1963.
6. Medawar, P., *The Hope of Progress*, London, Methuen, 1972.
7. Johnson, P., *Enemies of Society*, London, Weidenfeld, 1977.
8. Kuhn, T., *The Structure of Scientific Revolutions*, 2nd Edition, Chicago, Chicago University Press, 1970.

9. Roazen, P., *Freud and his Followers*, London, Allen Lane, 1976.
10. Braithwaite, R. B., *Scientific Explanation*, Cambridge, Cambridge University Press, 1955.
11. Eysenck, H. J., and Wilson, G. D., *Experimental Study of Freudian Theories*, London, Methuen, 1972.
12. See Braithwaite, op. cit., for a fuller explanation.
13. A similar argument is discussed in Farrell, B. A., *The Standing of Psychoanalysis*, Oxford, Oxford University Press, 1981. I also develop this analysis in my forthcoming book, *The Scientific Analysis of Social Science*, London, Frances Pinter, 1983.
14. Fisher, S., and Greenberg, R. P., *The Scientific Credibility of Freud's Theory and Therapy*, Hassocks, Harvester Press, 1977.
15. Kline, P., *Fact and Fantasy in Freudian Theory*, London, Methuen, 1972.
16. Fisher and Greenberg, op. cit.
17. The terminology and concepts are those of Lakatos, I., 'The Methodology of Scientific Research Programmes', in Lakatos, I., and Musgrave, A., *Criticism and the Growth of Knowledge*, Cambridge, Cambridge University Press, 1970. Lakatos was hostile to psychoanalysis and would have disliked this application of his concepts.
18. Fromm, E., *Beyond the Chains of Illusion*, New York, Abacus, 1980 (first published 1962).
19. Reported in Rogow, A., 'A Psychiatry of Politics', in Rogow, A. (ed.), *Politics, Personality and Social Science in the 20th Century*, Chicago, Chicago University Press, 1969.
20. Abse, L., *Private Member*, London, Macdonald, 1973.
21. Lasswell, H., *Psycho-Pathology and Politics*, 1930. Reprinted with a new 'afterword' in New York, Viking Press, 1960.
22. Davies, A. E., *Skills, Outlooks and Passions: a Psychoanalytic Contribution to the Study of Politics*, Cambridge, Cambridge University Press, 1980.
23. De Board, R., *The Psychoanalysis of Organisations*, London, Tavistock Publications, 1978.
24. Since Konrad Lorenz wrote *On Aggression*, London, Methuen, 1966, this has become a popular genre. Two more restrained and convincing accounts are Washburn, S. L., 'Conflict in Primate Society', and Chance, M. R. A., 'Resolution of Social Conflict in Animals and Man'. Both are in de Reuck, A., and Knight, J. (eds), *Conflict in Society*, London, J. and A. Churchill, 1966.

8   Feminism and human nature

RUTH LEVITAS

'Feminism' does not in itself entail any particular view of human nature; yet the issues of what that nature is, if it exists at all, whether it is a unitary phenomenon, or whether one should more properly talk of separate male and female human natures, are crucial both to debates *within* feminism, and to debates between feminists and anti-feminists. In this chapter some of the conceptions and misconceptions of human nature implied in these debates, and their wider significance, will be explored. In so doing, two points need to be borne in mind. First, feminism is not a homogeneous body of thought, and the positions outlined here are illustrative thereof, rather than providing a complete coverage. Second, such unity as does exist among feminists is based on a shared recognition of, and opposition to, the social subordination of women, but does not entail agreement about the causes and roots of this subordination, or, therefore, about how best it may be overcome. As a result, unity on the topic of human nature is a negative unity, that is, a unity about what human (particularly female) nature is not, rather than about what it is. This arises from recurrent confrontations with anti-feminists, who use arguments about 'human' nature to claim that women are different from men in many ways which explain, justify and render inevitable their inferior position in society. Because feminists deny this, and are committed to political change, they must necessarily dispute that biological or psychological differences between the sexes either justify or make inevitable the oppression of women; there is no reason why they should agree about exactly what such differences are or their implications. Moreover, as we shall see, there are differences between feminists on the topic of human nature that are as marked as those between feminists and anti-feminists, and indeed there are strong similarities between some feminist and anti-feminist positions.

Given this negative unity, the most useful place to start is with the view of human nature that feminists reject. This is also appropriate because it is the ground on which most popular debate takes place; for much of what feminists have had to say about human nature has been less from a desire to elaborate what that nature is than from a persistent need to refute the claims made about it by others.

The fallacy of 'naturalism'

There is a long tradition in English social thought of invalidating objections or proposed alternatives to the prevailing social order by arguing that the present mode of operation is 'natural', and stating, or often merely implying, that attempts at change would be impractical and fail because they were 'unnatural'. There are, in fact, a number of logical flaws in this sort of argument, but the use of 'naturalness' as a justification for the social order puts debates about human nature at the centre of *any* struggle for social change. This is nowhere more true that in relation to feminism, where the undoubtedly innate physical difference between the sexes is capable of almost infinite extrapolation into psychological and social spheres.[1] Janet Sayers has documented how every advance in the rights and opportunities of women has been resisted on the grounds of their peculiar nature, and how supposedly scientific evidence has been marshalled to the support of this resistance. Thus it was argued until relatively recently that girls should not be educated, since the energy used in the development of the mind would result in the enfeebled development of the reproductive system and render them less capable of bearing and rearing children. Further, since their brains were smaller and lighter than those of men, they were in any case less *able* to be educated.[2]

The main contemporary body of 'scientific' thought which is used to legitimate the unequal social positions of men and women on the grounds of naturalness is known as sociobiology. Sociobiologists seek to explain the social behaviour of all species, from insects to humans, in terms of a biological constitution evolved by natural and sexual selection.[3] In doing this, use is made of the concept of 'inclusive fitness'. It is argued that, in any species, the genes of those individuals who leave more viable offspring than others will come to be predominant in the population. Therefore, those with a genetic predisposition to behaviours which result in maximum reproduction are, by definition, most 'fit', and they will perpetuate those genes, and therefore those behaviours, at the expense of others. Even apparently 'altruistic' behaviour may be accounted for in these terms, since risking or sacrificing one's own survival for others may be beneficial in terms of gene-survival, provided the others concerned are genetically close relatives such as siblings or offspring. A crucial element in the argument is that the behaviour which maximizes the likely number of viable offspring is different for males and females; eggs, we are told, are expensive, sperm cheap. The best strategy for males is to impregnate as many females as possible, but to avoid having to put any effort into rearing resultant offspring—especially as it is difficult for males to be certain that the off-spring are, biologically, theirs. The most 'fit' males—in the sense of those whose genes would be most likely to come to be predominant in a popula-tion—would be those who are aggressive in competing with other males, and 'philanderers' in relation to females. Conversely, females maximize their chances of rearing viable offspring, and thus their genetic representa-tion in the population, by being 'coy': that is, avoiding sex until they are reasonably certain that the male *will* invest some effort in nurturing, a task which falls naturally to females as bearers and rearers of young. In humans, this leads to a situation where men are selected for being naturally larger, stronger, more aggressive, and relatively sexually promiscuous, while women are naturally smaller, weaker, nurturing and sexually discriminating—and here 'naturally' means 'genetically'. As Barash puts it:

> Sociobiology demonstrates that male–female behavioural differences are consistent with the basic biology of maleness and femaleness. Because they make such a small investment in their sex cells, males are generally selected to be less fussy and more promiscuous than females, and to compete with other males for access to females. This disparity explains why . . . men are generally more aggressive than women.[4]

Support for this notion that evolution has led to a genetically deter-mined difference between male and female natures which underlies the sexual division of labour is sought from three sources: from genetic 'logic', from ethology, and from social anthropology. All three kinds of evidence have been criticized on grounds of accuracy and relevance.[5]

What is said about the differences in male and female natures is only a particular application of a general theory about the relationship between genes and behaviour. Here a writer like Wilson, a major influence in the discipline, is much more careful than some. He says: 'in human beings the genes do not specify social behaviour.'[6] However, he also claims that 'genes . . . influence . . . the behavioural qualities that underlie variations between cultures',[7] and that the primary function of an organism (including a human being) is not to live for itself, or even to reproduce other organisms, but to act as a temporary carrier for genes.[8] The argu-ment that there is a genetic basis to behaviour is, none the less, quite ambiguous. Wilson portrays the counter-view as total environmentalism, in which the existence of any genetically transmitted human nature is denied in favour of a hypothesis of infinite malleability. Quite apart from the fact that this too would be a statement about human nature, it is not a view that anyone holds. As Harris puts it:

> Much confusion arises from the fact that sociobiologists present the concept of a genetically controlled 'biogram' or human nature, as if there is a significant body of informed opinion asserting that human beings are not genetically programmed to be predisposed toward certain behavioural specialities. In principle there can be no disagreement that *Homo sapiens* has a nature. . . . As every science-fiction fan knows, a culture-bearing species whose physiology was based on silicon rather than carbon and that had three sexes instead of two, weighed a thousand pounds per specimen, and preferred to eat sand rather than meat would acquire certain habits unlikely to be encountered in any *Homo sapiens* society. . . . Hence the disagreement about the human biogram is entirely a matter of substance rather than of principle—that is, precise identification of the content of the biogram.[9]

What is really at issue is not whether human beings have a nature in the sense of a biological, material existence involving genetic transmission, but whether observable behaviours can be properly said to be genetically caused. Wilson recognizes that environmental factors are necessary for the expression of genetic potential, and that learning plays a role in human behaviour, but he also argues that there is a genetic basis for differences in behaviour between individuals, races and genders—sometimes, it appears, simply because such differences can be observed to exist. Thus:

> In hunter-gatherer societies, men hunt and women stay at home. This strong bias persists in most agricultural societies and on that ground alone, appears to have a genetic origin . . . the genetic basis is intense enough to cause a substantial division of labour even in the most free and egalitarian of future societies.[10]

This is a quite different position from that of environmentalists who would argue that human beings are not so programmed, and that it is human nature to be reliant on learning and culture for the expression of whatever genetic potential exists—that *what* is learned is culturally determined (whereas Wilson argues that we are genetically programmed to learn certain things more easily than others).

An important similarity between the protagonists in this debate is that they commonly adopt deterministic arguments, whether it is the genes or the environment, or whatever mixture thereof, that constitutes the determining factor.[11] Three points arise here. First, attempts to calculate the degree of heritability of a trait, such as intelligence or aggression (that is, trying to decide 'how much' is due to heredity and how much to environment), are misguided; the conditions necessary for the statistical tests used are not, and cannot be, met.[12] More importantly, the nature/culture dichotomy implied here is misleading. What is inherited is not discrete genes, but systems of genes linked together which can interact with each other and with the environment in many different ways. It is not that characteristics are programmed in the genes and brought out by the environment, but that this interaction is a prerequisite of any development at all, in which the respective roles of 'genes' and 'environment' defy quantitative assessment. These gene systems allow developmental flexibility, whereby the same genotype can give rise to different phenotypes (or observable characteristics), while also permitting canalization, where different genotypes will tend to result in similar phenotypes. This makes it logically impossible to separate genetic and environmental effects, and absurd to argue for genetic or environmental causation *per se.* [13]

An example of this first problem also serves to illustrate the second point, which is that this kind of deterministic argument itself misses an important feature of human nature—the reflexive ability which allows us to intervene in the developmental process. The condition known as PKU (phenylketonuria) is used to 'prove' the case for both sides. It undoubtedly involves a genetically-linked disorder, namely, the inability to break down phenylalanine, a compound present in protein. The indirect result of this is severe mental retardation—which can be entirely avoided by environmental adjustment to a diet low in phenylalanine. It would make no sense to say that the effect on an untreated child was caused by either genetic abnormality or diet, or 50 per cent by one, 50 per cent by the other. It is 100 per cent caused by the *interaction* of these two factors. However, the crucial factor about the incidence of PKU is rather different:

> . . . the most significant points are, not that it is genetically transmitted nor that its effects are environmentally remediable, but that we are the sort of species (1) that investigates conditions of this sort and (2) that can choose to intervene socially on the results discovered. Even more important is the fact of what we can achieve by such intervention.[14]

Third, these points bear on the issue raised earlier about the legitimating force of the term 'natural' in relation to social behaviours and organizations, and the implication that anything else, especially if produced by conscious intervention, would be 'unnatural'. Here, the popular understanding of 'natural' is that which is least affected by the environment and most produced by genes; and what is 'natural' is good. The effects of intervention, required, for example, in the treatment of PKU, cannot properly be called 'unnatural' since it is the nature of the species to be able to act in this way, and the lack of intervention cannot possibly be deemed preferable. Since all behaviour is produced by the interaction of organism and environment, the distinction between 'natural' and 'unnatural' behaviour remains contentious at the level of description. Its main use is ideological, in placing positive values on some outcomes and negative values on others. The way in which sociobiologists use the term 'natural' ignores this constant process of interaction, and elides 'natural' with 'biological' and with 'genetic'.

It is claimed, however, that this account of the genetic basis of the sexual division of labour is purely descriptive, and merely tells us what must be taken into account when choosing social arrangements which do not correspond to our natural inclinations. This claim is at best disingenuous, at worst dishonest. Statements are made, such as: 'we are . . . primed to be much less sexually egalitarian than we appear to be';[15] 'polygyny is the biologically "natural" state of *Homo sapiens*';[16] 'after the child is born, a woman is biologically primed to nurse it';[17] 'male parenting in human . . . beings is not nearly as innate as modern sexual egalitarians might wish it to be.'[18] These cannot be expected to be read as having no bearing on the evaluation of the social order. Still less can Wilson's claim that the genetic origin of the sexual division of labour is immutable be regarded as non-evaluative. Explicitly or implicitly, sociobiologists, especially in their more popular writings, do make judgements about existing and potential social arrangements. Indeed, it is on this that their popularity depends.[19] They cannot, therefore, abdicate all responsibility for these judgements.

Differences within feminist thought

Sociobiological accounts of the sexual division of labour portray human nature as dichotomous. The reproductive roles of the sexes cause selection for sex-linked personality traits, producing different male and female natures, and having a strong causal effect on social organization. One would expect that feminist views of human nature would oppose such biological determinism, but in fact this is not universally the case. Radical feminism also regards the reproductive process as the cause of the social subordination of women in a very direct way, and similarly posits the naturalness of the mother–child bond as well as sex-linked psychological and personality differences. Explanations of how this results in the oppression of women, as well as prescriptions for its termination, vary. Thus, Shulamith Firestone's analysis is strikingly close to that of Wilson, although she regards pregnancy as an imposition foisted upon women for the sake of the survival of the species, rather than as a means by which particular combinations of genes reproduce themselves.[20] Because women bear children, and because of the long period of dependence of children upon adults, particularly their mothers, pregnancy and childcare make women naturally dependent upon men. In Firestone's view, the inequality resulting from this can be overcome only by artificial reproduction, which will remove the fundamental biological inequality. This is tantamount to agreeing with Wilson's argument that a substantial sexual division of labour will of necessity persist in the future.

Where radical feminists differ from sociobiologists is less in the description of events than in their evaluation. In spite of sociobiologists' protestations to the contrary, there is a strong implication that explanation is legitimation. With radical feminists this is not so, although biological determinism always creates severe problems for overcoming women's oppression. Another version of radical feminism illustrates this different evaluation, while at the same time providing an alternative explanation.

In *Of Woman Born*, Adrienne Rich writes:

. . . female biology . . . has far more radical implications than we have yet come to appreciate. . . . The ancient, continuing envy, awe and dread of the male for the female capacity to create life has repeatedly taken the form of hatred for every other female aspect of creativity;[21]

and

. . . the male mind has always been haunted by the force of the idea of dependence on a woman for life itself, the son's constant effort to assimilate, compensate for, or deny the fact that he is 'of woman born'.[22]

This account shares the view that women are biologically destined to bear and rear children, but argues not that this makes women dependent on men, but men dependent on women: resentment of this, and fear, and envy, lead men to dominate women. This is possible because men are in general physically stronger and, the argument implies, more aggressive than women. In this formulation, male dominance is purposive (whereas sociobiology does not concern itself with human motives and purposes, only with behavioural tendencies). In itself, this is an advantage, but the explanation is unsatisfactory on several counts. It is historically speculative, failing to explain why women were unable collectively to resist such oppression. Also, it begs the question why men should be so envious of the ability to give birth (an ability Firestone holds in low esteem), rather than thanking God daily they were not born women.

In this view, then, the antagonism between men and women is biologically given. The solution that most radical feminists look to is, therefore, one of separatism and a re-evaluation of femaleness. In some accounts this involves a celebration of biology which is almost as mystical as that supposedly generating male jealousy:

> The feminist vision . . . will . . . come to view our physicality as a resource, rather than a destiny. In order to live a fully human life we require only *control* of our bodies; we must touch the unity and resonance of our physicality, our bond with the natural order, the corporeal ground of our intelligence.[23]

Yet in others there is a more rational assertion that the traits found in women because of their maternal role are more desirable than those found in men (co-operation, care for others, rather than competitiveness and aggression, and the need to dominate in society). How this could ever happen, though, if biology is the cause of the present state of affairs, is unclear.

The alternative to biologism is not, as Wilson claims, a denial of human nature, or a claim that this is entirely socially constructed. Nor is it a claim that the male/female difference is socially constructed, but rather, as Barrett argues, that 'biological differences . . . are the basis upon which specific gender identities of masculinity and feminity are constructed',[24] and that '. . . the social construction of gender division massively outweighs any basis in biological differences.'[25] What biologism does is to confuse the biological categories of sex with the social categories of gender. Liberal feminism, which perhaps comes closest to Wilson's dystopia of total constructivism, has been very largely concerned with elucidating the ways in which gender is socially constructed through processes of socialization. Nevertheless, it is not possible to do this without at least implicitly conceptualizing human nature; this is clear from one account which urges that the issue should be side-stepped.

In *The Sceptical Feminist*, Janet Radcliffe Richards argues that feminists have been too ready to be drawn into debates about human nature, and too ready to reject the suggestion that there may be differences of psychology, personality and ability between men and women which are biologically based; they fear that conceding this would also concede that the social subordination of women was natural and legitimate.[26] She argues that the case for feminism can be made while reserving judgement about the nature and extent of differences which may exist.

The crux of the argument is as follows. When statements are made, even by the most virulent biological determinist, such as that 'men are stronger than women', they very rarely mean that 'all men are stronger than all women', but rather that, on average, 'men are stronger than women.' It will follow, therefore, that anyone making such a statement will concede that some women are stronger than some men. One cannot therefore justify a rule that 'women are not allowed to drives buses' on the grounds that they are less strong than men. Even if all women were too weak to drive buses (in which case the exclusionary rule would be redundant), so too would be all but a very few men; a test of strength would thus be needed, and there could be no grounds for a special and separate exclusion on the basis of sex.

One difficulty with the argument is that it works best where it can be demonstrated that such a rule is being applied. Many rules excluding women are both informal and unrelated to ability—for example, those which prevent women drinking alone in pubs. These may be directly discriminatory (she may not be served), or indirectly so (she may be harrassed or ostracized), but they have more to do with propriety than ability. There is always some notion here of a difference in nature which needs to be made explicit.

Second, the argument only works at all within a liberal–individualist framework. Liberal feminism generally rests on the assumption that social status should be achieved by individual effort and ability, and that what feminism is about is removing obstacles to the free competition of women alongside men in the labour market. As Sayers has observed, there are similarities between liberal feminism and sociobiology, in their views of society, if not in their views of human nature:

> Liberal feminism and sociobiology both have their roots, historically speaking, in the development of the free market society . . . the sociobiological account of sexual relations relies on the bourgeois ideology of the free market. . . . Whereas sociobiology elaborates this ideology to develop a biological determinist account of sex roles, liberal feminism has elaborated it to develop a concerted critique of sex discrimination and of biological arguments designed to justify that discrimination.[27]

Third, it is only possible to 'ignore' the issue of the natural difference in strength in so far as both parties to the argument are willing to accept, as a plausible hypothesis, a distribution of strength whereby on average men are stronger, but some women are stronger than some men. On the issue of infant care, even excluding breast-feeding, one would be quite likely to meet the contention that all women (apart from a few 'unnatural' ones) are more able to provide this than men. While the *logic* of the argument holds, however small the overlap between the sexes, its persuasiveness diminishes with that overlap.

Further, the degree of overlap, which is essentially a question of human nature, is at issue in actually demonstrating that women are discriminated against. Statements that women are over-represented in some areas and under-represented in others imply a conception of what a proper representation would be. That there are few women engineers, MPs and company directors only becomes culpable (rather than an interesting observation) when it is argued that these differences cannot be accounted for by 'natural' inability or disinclination on the part of women; the assumption that any inability or disinclination involved is socially produced is necessary for the identification of the problem.

Thus, in concentrating on the processes of socialization whereby gender is socially constructed, one does not make the issue of human nature go away. Explicitly or implicitly, a discontinuity between biological sex and social gender is posited, and human nature, as far as gender is concerned, is portrayed as far more malleable than biologistic accounts would concede. Yet although the separation of sex and gender is an important issue (just how important is shown by the sociobiologists' imperviousness to it!), showing how men and women are socialized into masculinity and feminity, it does not explain *why* this process should take place. And if biological determinism is rejected, then some other, social, explanation must take its place.

Social explanations

Marxist and socialist feminists have been concerned with providing explanations of this kind. In general, they locate the source of oppression in social structures—the economy and the family—and in the ideologies which exist alongside them. The role attributed to biology in these accounts varies. In Engels' version, the facts, that women bear children and are more certain of their relationship to them than men can be, are given a centrality in explaining women's oppression that is almost as great as in sociobiology.[28] The problem, he argues, arose when subsistence ceased to depend mainly on the appropriation of products in their natural state, and the economy became based on the domestication of animals. Herds constituted a form of surplus, and once there was a surplus to inherit, men found the preceding matrilineal descent system intolerable because they wished to pass on their property to their own children. In order to be able to do this, to be certain of paternity, men enforced sexual fidelity on women, and systems of descent became patrilineal.

An important element in this argument is that the wealth involved in the herds was socially defined as men's property, a fact which Engels attributes to a natural division of labour between the sexes. Both Marx and Engels (like Wilson) believed that the division of labour, whereby men were involved in hunting, fishing and war, and women in more domestic pursuits, is 'based on a purely physiological foundation.'[29] Thus, it is this biologically-based factor, plus the greater physical strength of men, which accounts for the origin of patriarchy.[30]

Among the many grounds on which Engels can be criticized are that, besides being historically speculative and accepting the quite spurious argument about physical strength causing the division of labour, there is no explanation of *why* men should be concerned to pass their acquired wealth to their biological descendants.[31] Indeed, one of the main criticisms levelled at sociobiologists' preoccupation with biological kinship is that anthropological evidence shows social definitions of kinship to be of much greater significance.[32]

In spite of the fact that Engels locates the origin of patriarchy in the emergence of a specific mode of production, his explanation is still substantially biologistic. It has, as Barrett observes, proved remarkably difficult to construct a general explanation of patriarchy independent of capitalist organization which does not involve biologism.[33] Paradoxically, though, in stressing the dependence of women's oppression on the mode of production, Engels opens up the whole issue of the relationship between production and reproduction to which socialist feminists have addressed themselves. Thus he writes:

> According to the materialistic conception, the determining factor in history is . . . the production and reproduction of immediate life. . . . On the one hand, the production of the means of subsistence . . .; on the other, the production of human beings themselves, the propagation of the species. The social institutions under which men of a definite historical epoch . . . live are conditioned by both kinds of production. . . .[34]

And it is clear that it is not so much the biological process of reproduction but the social mediation of this in a particular historical context that causes the social subordination of women, and which therefore leaves open the possibility of their future emancipation. He asserted that 'It will . . . become evident that the first premise for the emancipation of women is the reintroduction of the entire female sex into public industry. . . .'[35] Further:

The emancipation of women becomes possible only when women are enabled to take part in production on a large, social scale, and when domestic duties require their attention only to a minor degree. And this has become possible only as a result of modern large-scale industry, which not only permits of the participation of women in production in large numbers, but actually calls for it, and moreover, strives to convert private domestic work into a public industry.[36]

The final, unelaborated clause here is crucial, since it does not distinguish between domestic labour as social reproduction and as biological reproduction,[37] and it is difficult to see how the latter could become a public industry. Thus, although Engels argues that both social production and biological reproduction are conditioning factors on social institutions, he subsequently treats the emancipation of women as primarily dependent upon their entry into social production, and fails to detail how this relates to the reproductive roles of men and women.

Later attempts to relate modes of production and reproduction have taken two directions. The first has elaborated the relationship between women's role in the family and the overall mode of production;[38] the second strand has tried to supplement Marxism with psychoanalysis, so as to show how the social construction of sex differences, but not those sex differences themselves, contributes to the reproduction of patriarchy. The most influential example of this second strand has been Juliet Mitchell's *Psychoanalysis and Feminism*.[39] While her interpretation of Freud remains contentious,[40] what is important here is the denial that biology, rather than its social interpretation, can be regarded as having any causal effect upon society:

> Although there is an obvious *use* of the biological base in any social formation, it would seem dubious to stress this. For there seems little evidence of any biological priority. Quite the contrary; we are confronted with a situation that is determinately social. This situation is the initial *transformation* of biology by the exchange system. . . . This is not, of course, to deny that, as in all mammalian species, there is a difference between the reproductive roles of each sex, but it is to suggest that in *no* human society do these take place in an untransformed way. . . .[41]

Because of this insistence on the dominance of social mediation over biological differences in sex and reproductive role, Mitchell denies the importance of the technological transcendence of biology prescribed by Firestone. Biology does not need to be made redundant; it already is. Far from the Oedipus complex being a description of a natural law of human development, it becomes 'the universal law by which men and women learn their place in the world.'[42] But like patriarchy, whose universal aspects are 'the exchange of women and the cultural taboo on incest', these are differently expressed under each specific mode of production.[43] As far as capitalism is concerned, the demands of exogamy and incest avoidance for the propertyless classes are actually irrelevant, and there is a contradiction between the ideology which presents the nuclear family as natural, and the way in which the Oedipus complex is expressed within it.

The main problems with Mitchell's account, aside from the interpreta-tion of Freud, concern the extent of autonomy of the ideological sphere. Thus, she says, 'we are . . . dealing with two autonomous areas: the economic mode of capitalism and the ideological mode of patriarchy.'[44] This raises a specific problem, noted earlier, of an independent 'cause' of patriarchy outside biology/psychology—i.e. outside human 'nature'.

Conclusion

Mitchell's account probably comes closer than most to what Wilson rejects as total environmentalism. The objection is unwarranted: it does not con-stitute a denial of human nature, but an assertion that this nature is always encountered in socially mediated forms (and, therefore, that much of what Wilson claims is natural is in fact social). It is clear that all versions of feminism *must* adopt some stance on the topic of human nature, although one cannot, even in the most general way, contrast 'feminist' and 'anti-feminist' accounts. Radical feminism has strong descriptive similarities with sociobiology, seeing reproduction as a direct cause of the social order. Liberal feminists focus on the way in which gender is socially produced, and imply a discontinuity between gender and sex, as well as a mallea-bility of gender to social process which itself constitutes a statement about human nature. Socialist and Marxist feminists try to identify the structural causes which underlie this social production of gender within the processes of production and reproduction. The insistence on the mediated forms in which human nature is always encountered is perhaps the most important contribution of feminism to our understanding of the matter. Neverthe-less, it is an insight recurrently denied by radical feminists as well as by sociobiologists, just as it is always open to the danger of sliding into either biologism or environmentalism.

This is not a problem specific to feminist theories. It stems from the problem Timpanaro raises, and unwittingly illustrates, when he argues that the biological givens of illness, ageing and death should be treated as fundamental to a materialist analysis of society. He says both that these are universally and necessarily unpleasant experiences, and that they are of course only ever experienced in socially mediated forms.[45] This has recently been taken up by others seeking to take account of biology without lapsing into biologism.[46] The difficulties are that social scientists have generally avoided engaging with biology, and are relatively ignorant of biological ideas; also, that our nature is such as to make intrinsically problematic the distinction of nature and culture, and thus the identification of processes of social mediation. In general, over the last decade, it has been feminists who have pioneered study in this field, albeit with particular reference to female 'nature'. It is clear from the expansion and claims of sociobiology that such work needs to continue if there is to be any hope of challenging the 'naturalness' of the existing social order, whether the impetus for change is socialist, feminist, liberal or anything else; for the claim that the present order cannot be made more egalitarian demonstrates the centrality of the debate about human nature for the future.

Notes

1. The precise nature and extent of 'undoubtedly innate physical difference' is, of course, itself a matter of debate.
2. Sayers, J., *Biological Politics*, London, Tavistock, 1982, esp. chapters 2 and 6.
3. There are, of course, differences between sociobiologists; but in terms of the basis of the discipline, and its claims about human nature, legitimate generalizations can be made.
4. Barash, D., *Sociobiology: The Whisperings Within*, London, Fontana, 1981, p. 63.
5. See in particular Janson-Smith, D., 'Sociobiology: So What?', in Brighton Women and Science Group, *Alice Through the Microscope*, London, Virago, 1980; Montagu, A., (ed.), *Sociobiology Examined*, Oxford, Oxford University Press, 1980; Sahlins, M., *The Use and Abuse of Biology*, London, Tavistock, 1977.
6. Lumsden, C. J., and Wilson, E. O., *Genes, Mind and Culture*, Cambridge, Mass., Harvard University Press, 1981, p. 349.
7. Wilson, E. O., *Sociobiology*, Cambridge, Mass., Harvard University Press, 1975, p. 550.
8. Ibid., p. 3.
9. Harris, M., 'Sociobiology and Biological Reductionism', in Montagu, op. cit. pp. 319–20.
10. Wilson, E. O., 'Human Decency is Animal', *New York Times Magazine*, 12 October 1975, cited in Sayers, op. cit., p. 29.
11. On this point, see Midgley, M., 'Rival Fatalisms', in Montagu, op. cit. pp. 15–38.
12. Open University, *Intelligence and Creativity*, E 201, Block 6, pp. 44–9.
13. Ibid.
14. Barker, M., 'Human Biology and the Possibility of Socialism', in Mepham, J., and Ruben, D. H. (eds), *Issues in Marxist Philosophy*, Vol. IV, Brighton, Harvester Press, 1981, p. 60.
15. Barash, op. cit., p. 47.

16. Ibid., p. 64.
17. Ibid., p. 56.
18. Ibid., p. 88.
19. Both Wilson and Barash have written books on sociobiology which are mainly about other animals (Wilson, *Sociobiology*, op. cit., and Barash, D., *Sociobiology and Behaviour*, London, Heinemann, 1978); both books follow the pattern of ending with a short and avowedly speculative chapter on the possible implications for human beings. Both have then gone on to write more popular books entirely about human nature (Wilson, E. O., *On Human Nature*, Cambridge, Mass., Harvard University Press, 1978; Barash, *Sociobiology: The Whisperings Within*, op. cit.). This suggests a certain ambivalence on their part about the scientific nature of their claims.
20. Firestone, S., *The Dialectic of Sex*, London, Paladin, 1972.
21. Rich, A., *Of Woman Born*, London, Virago, 1977, pp. 39–40.
22. Ibid., p. 11.
23. Ibid., p. 39.
24. Barrett, M., *Women's Oppression Today*, London, Verso, 1980, p. 213.
25. Ibid., p. 224.
26. Richards, J. R., *The Sceptical Feminist*, Harmondsworth, Penguin, 1982.
27. Sayers, op. cit., p. 175.
28. Engels, F., *The Origin of the Family, Private Property and the State*, in Marx, K., and Engels, F., *Selected Works*, London, Lawrence & Wishart, 1968.
29. Marx, K., *Capital*, Vol. I, London, Lawrence & Wishart, 1974, p. 332.
30. There are a number of ambiguities involved in the use of this term. For an account of the theoretical problems involved, see Barrett, op. cit., pp. 10–19.
31. The argument is spurious because there is overwhelming anthropological evidence that women have not been predominantly engaged in lighter work than men.
32. See especially Sahlins, op. cit.
33. Barrett, op. cit., p. 15.
34. Engels, op. cit., p. 449.
35. Ibid., p. 501.
36. Ibid., pp. 569–70.
37. On this distinction, see Barrett, op. cit., pp. 19–29.
38. e.g. Zaretsky, E., *Capitalism, the Family and Personal Life*, London, Pluto, 1976.
39. Mitchell, J., *Psychoanalysis and Feminism*, Harmondsworth, Penguin, 1975.
40. See Barrett, op. cit., pp. 53–62.
41. Mitchell, op. cit., p. 407.
42. Ibid., p. 409.
43. Loc. cit.
44. Ibid., p. 412.
45. Timpanaro, S., *On Materialism*, London, New Left Books, 1975.
46. See especially Rose, S. (ed.), *Against Biological Determinism* and *Towards a Liberatory Biology*, London, Allison & Busby, 1982. The papers in these two volumes constitute the proceedings of a conference at Bressanone, Italy, in March 1980, organized by the Dialectics of Biology Group.

9 Work and human nature

JOHN STREET

> Men are never satisfied with their wages. I suppose it's human
> nature.   A Shop Steward[1]

People need to work. This is a statement about human nature, and one
which might find common agreement. But, as with all such consensus, a
wealth of disagreement lurks beneath the surface. For some people, the
need to work may be tied to the need to survive; for others, it may be
tied to the realization of human freedom. Indeed, there will be as many
accounts of the need to work as there are descriptions of human needs.
Since no single book, let alone one chapter, could do justice to them all, I
shall concentrate here on a particular interpretation of the need to work,
one which focuses on the link between freedom and work.

The emphasis on freedom is appropriate for two reasons. First, those
political writers who have devoted most attention to work have done so
with an eye for the emancipatory potential of work reform.[2] Second, the
theories of human nature examined earlier in this book have placed considerable emphasis on freedom in their accounts. Thus, it would seem that,
if we wish to give work a prominent place in a theory of human nature, we
would be well advised to examine the coherence of its connections with
freedom. The logic of this argument is best understood by asking what we
mean by the general category of 'human nature'.

Human nature refers to the ensemble of fundamental characteristics
which help to define what it is to be human and which any good society
must recognize. Such characteristics are not confined to those identified
by biologists and zoologists (human nature is not just 'natural' in the sense
of natural science).[3] On the contrary, it is evident that human nature is the
legitimate territory of the student of politics.

When political thinkers consider human nature, their discussions turn
toward the idea of free choice. In the exercise of choice, human beings
express their nature. Different theories of human nature emerge from
disagreements over the balance between freedom and practical necessity,
and from dispute about the range of possibilities open to human beings.

Broadly, conservative theorists emphasize the limits of choice, attaching their theory of human nature to the solid foundations of physical and social permanence; while liberal theorists stress the range of available choices, drawing a picture of human nature in which nothing is fixed and anything is possible; and socialist theorists combine a limited notion of choice with a distrust of permanence, producing a portrait of a developing human nature bonded to the passage of history.[4] To talk in such sweeping terms is, of course, to identify only the vaguest of outlines; the details are revealed only when we narrow our gaze. We study human nature, not in its entirety, but through the eyes of a single writer or by concentration on a single idea or activity. Work is an example of the latter.

By asking what political significance can be attached to the idea of work, we can gain some insight into its pertinence to a theory of human nature. In doing so, however, we have to be aware that work does not automatically announce itself as a feature of human nature. Its significance is determined by the degree to which freedom is appropriate to the understanding of work. The resolution of this issue comes in a variety of forms, but tends to fall within the boundaries established by freedom and necessity. At one end, there is the view that work and freedom are antonyms; at the other end, the view that they are synonyms. If work is seen purely as an animal activity, by which we satisfy basic physical needs, then the political side to human nature will be revealed in those activities which human beings engage in once they are freed from the need to work. If, however, work is held to constitute a major part of freedom itself, then it will be inextricably tied to our perception of human nature.

The view of work as 'an articulation of need, a definition of co-operative means, in what is felt and known to be a common condition', is a rejection of the idea of work as primitive animal activity.[5] At the core of this argument is the belief that work is crucially important to the way in which individuals see themselves. It is this link between self-perception and work that establishes the bond between work and human nature. In this interpretation, work takes on an importance and a meaning which cannot be captured by a mere description of the physical activity of the worker. Work is valued in itself as well as for the ends it realizes. People need to work, because working is a central feature of human nature. The plausibility and coherence of this view is the concern of this chapter. Our examination is best begun by asking how (and then why) work might be thought to be imbued with qualities inherent in an apparently mundane ritual.

The importance of work

In contemporary society the importance of work is suggested by the way
in which people describe themselves. When we ask someone what they do
or who they are, they tell us about their work (or its absence). As Mike
Cooley has noted:

> If you ask anybody what they are, they never say, 'I'm a Beethoven
> lover', or 'a Bob Dylan fan', or 'a James Joyce reader', they say 'I'm
> a teacher', 'an engineer'. People relate to society through their work.[6]

This process by which work and self-esteem are linked can find expression in a variety of ways. For example, a dull job can lead the worker to
see himself as worthless, as is the case with this Ford worker: 'You don't
achieve anything here. A robot could do it. The line here is made for
morons. It doesn't need any thought. . . . It's bad when you *know* you're
just a little cog.'[7] Alternatively, apparently uninspiring tasks, such as
making washing machines or sinks, can induce a sense of pride. One worker
at Fisher-Bendix protested at the closure of his factory: 'We had the Rolls-
Royce of washing machines . . . the Rolls-Royce of sinks—the only one-
piece sink in the country—a masterpiece of engineering it was. The lads
were proud of it.'[8] Although these two workers provide very different
accounts of their work, they are linked by one common assumption: that
how you feel, how you regard yourself, can be significantly affected by
work experience. This fairly straightforward claim is, of course, confirmed
by the research of industrial psychologists, who advocate changes in work
patterns as a means of creating a contented workforce.[9] A sense of happiness
seems dependent upon the sense of purpose (or purposelessness) that can
be attributed to a particular job. A job that can be described as 'worthwhile'
or 'useful' can induce a sense of pride in the worker; where a job appears
worthless or useless, the worker feels a failure. This suggests an ingrained
sense of the importance of work to how we see others and how we regard
ourselves.[10]

The connection between self-understanding and work seems to feature
prominently in our society, and clearly helps to explain the reaction to unemployment. But to recognize the common assumption, that work can have
a direct effect upon the self-perception of an individual, is quite different
from arguing that work holds the key to human happiness, or that work is
central to our view of human nature. To be able to develop an argument
along these lines, we have to look more closely at the mechanisms by which
work and self-perception are linked. So far we have only established that
if people work they are likely to make a connection between their job

and the way they see themselves. We have not established any reason why they should want or need to work at all.

To do this we have to look at the source and character of the importance attributed to work. We need to examine the meaning of work, to see what connection—if any—can be ascribed to the idea of freedom.

The meaning of work

It may well be contended that the connection between self-perception and work derives solely from the dominant social code of the society. Such links that exist between self-esteem and work are seen, therefore, as the consequence of a particular social definition of work, that the link between work and self-esteem is part of the protestant work ethic, itself a necessary corollary of work in industrial society.[11] In other words, although we may evaluate people in terms of their work, this does not indicate any universal or fundamental connection which would be appropriate to a theory of human nature. This conclusion might be drawn from E. P. Thompson's writings. He argues that work was redefined with the emergence of industrial capitalism, and that new justifications were needed for new kinds of labour. For him, 'The factory system demands a transformation of human nature, the "working paroxysms" of the artisan or outworker must be methodised until the man is adapted to the discipline of the machine.'[12] Emergent industrial capitalism, therefore, required new forms of behaviour and new reasons for acting. Those in authority needed to devise a method whereby suitable workers were produced. As Thompson writes elsewhere, 'new disciplines, new incentives, and a new human nature upon which these incentives could bite effectively' were the goals which confronted a nascent industrial society.[13]

In this sense, attitudes to work appear to reflect social needs. But such an analysis would be too crude. We have to ask why it was necessary to justify the new work ethic, and why this justification was expressed as part of a moral code. We cannot explain such things in terms of the development of social needs in the light of technical change. It is not the same sort of social change as is engendered by, say, the shift from the horse-drawn transport to motorized transport. Thompson himself argues that the change from agrarian to industrial life, and the change in work thereby entailed, involved more than a matter of social adjustment. Instead, individuals were subjected to a 'psychic ordeal in which the character-structure of the rebellious pre-industrial labourer or artisan was violently recast into that of the submissive industrial worker.'[14] Whether or not we agree with the detail of Thompson's description of the change in human behaviour following industrialization, we certainly cannot see those changes simply as the consequences of new sets of orders issued by a new ruling class to a subservient class.

While we may concede that the particular meaning given to work served the interests of those who managed and owned industry, this does not explain the means by which work was redefined to advance those interests. To change the way people work, it was necessary to change people. It involved an appeal to morality, to the way individuals saw and understood themselves. Implicitly, the attachment of individuals to their work exists independently of the particular needs of any given society. We are confronted with the suggestion that the need to work is part of our nature, that it cannot be separated from the idea of our humanity.[15] But to establish this moral importance, and thereby to suggest a strong connection with a political portrait of human nature, is not to define in any detail the character of either the morality or the human nature involved.

While historical and sociological evidence does point to a close link between work and human nature, we are still uncertain as to how the connection actually functions. We need to look more closely at the way in which work is evaluated and regarded. The meaning of work may exist independently of a given society, but this does not establish any particular connection with freedom or any other political value.

The value of work

Some jobs are seen as more interesting, rewarding or important than others. The standards applied vary. Such criteria as wealth and influence are but two candidates on a long list. This is made most clear by the failure of industrial psychologists (and others) to reach any agreement as to how satisfaction might be measured. No manageable set of criteria seems to present itself.[16] But we cannot leave things with the simple assertion that money is not enough. Consider this description by a clerk:

> The basic fact remains though, that, in common with other jobs I've had it [the clerk's job] has no value as work. It is drudgery done in congenial surroundings. . . . You are there for the money, no other reason.[17]

The implication is that work *ought* to provide more than money, that work should have a value beyond that established by the cash nexus. The tone of this complaint presupposes that work should furnish other qualities. But what might such qualities be? When Huw Beynon, in his book, *Working for Ford*, asked some of the workers what they would like to be doing, he received these replies:

I'd like to work on a newspaper, I'd like to meet people . . . find out the facts about people's problems.

I'd just like to be able to go into work of a morning without being scared of what you're going to face. A clerical job I suppose.

I'd like to have been able to be a doctor. I wouldn't want a bossy job or a factory job.

I'm very interested in helping the working class. You know I'd really like to *do something*.[18]

Even in their dreams, these workers spoke of other jobs, not of lying about on sun-drenched beaches. They spoke of doing something, of using their faculties, of changing the world, of helping others. They did not talk of money. This does not seem to be a matter of merely romantic or senti-mental hope; it seems to refer to a genuine desire for a certain kind of work. It was always work that seemed to hold the key to fulfilment.

The ideal form of work, according to the Ford workers, embodies those values which are generally held to represent the 'good life'. Work is required to allow for freedom of expression, self-development and equality. Which-ever value is selected, no evaluation is based solely on financial reward. There is a persisting tension between freedom in work and freedom *from* work. Thus, like the industrial psychologist, we are driven to the conclu-sion that there is no single scale of values by which work may be judged. This conclusion is more important than it might at first appear. We are not just saying that it is impossible to identify all the criteria by which a job is evaluated. Rather, we are saying that there are at least two discrete *forms* of evaluation. On the one hand, work is valued for the opportunities it provides; work functions as a machine for producing benefits to be enjoyed away from work. In this dimension, job satisfaction is understood in terms of the efficiency with which work is organized or the comfort in which it is done. Jobs are evaluated in the weighing-up of discomforts against benefits. Work is judged *instrumentally*, in terms of what is gained and what it costs. The benefits of work are extrinsic to it. On the other hand, this form of evaluation has to be contrasted with the one which con-centrates solely on the work itself. Here, satisfaction derives from feelings experienced in the actual conduct of work. Work is expected to conform to those values associated with the 'good life'. Thus, the value attributed to a job is not determined by the access it allows to other goods, consumed or enjoyed away from work, but by the satisfaction to be derived in the work seen as a part of an entire social existence. Work is valued *expressively*. Here, the benefits of work are intrinsic to it.[19]

Hence, it might be argued that the ideal job would maximize both intrinsic and extrinsic values. It is an ideal appealed to by advocates of industrial democracy, who contend that participation will increase both the efficiency of an enterprise (hence improving the size of the profit to be re-distributed) and the responsibility of the workers (hence ensuring a high level of job satisfaction). Such plans are, however, not so easily realized.[20] At issue is the definition, which must refer to the effort being expended in the production of goods or provisions of services. The precise character of this effort will itself depend on the costs thought to fall upon workers in particular forms of employment. Therefore, the absence of participatory opportunities will be regarded as a cost by one side, but irrelevant by the other side. Not only can there be little agreement as to what constitutes efficiency, but also there are too many independent variables which may affect the success of an organization. The argument has to be taken at the level of why participation might be valued. In seeking an answer to this, we are driven to consider the two dimensions along which work is valued. If its extrinsic or instrumental qualities are emphasized, then participation will be considered expendable, provided that a sufficiently large wage packet is available. If, on the other hand, work is viewed as intrinsically rewarding, then the organization of work will stand on a par with the economic rewards.

Ultimately, the argument about industrial democracy is an argument about the value of work, and the latter turns on the competing tensions established by the different scales upon which work can be evaluated. What is significant is that these two scales suggest quite opposite ways of relating work and human nature. The instrumental scale suggests that human nature is peripheral to work but central to consumption, while the expressive scale reverses the order. The link between work and human nature must reside somewhere between these two extremes. It cannot be exclusively expressive or exclusively instrumental, at least not if we are going to take seriously the idea that factories are not simply institutions for self-development, or the idea that human beings are different from machines. We need, therefore, to examine the competing claims, and, more particularly, see what assumptions have to be built into a theory that asserts the centrality of work to a conception of human nature.

The instrumental view of work

According to the instrumental view, human beings were not destined for work or, at least, work should not take on the guise of some fundamental human purpose. From this perspective, work is seen simply as a means to an end. The classic representation of this view is found in the *Affluent Worker* studies.

> . . . the primary meaning of work is as a means to an end, or ends external to the work situation; that is, work is regarded as a means of acquiring the income necessary to support a valued way of life in which work itself is not an integral part.[21]

Work is just a way of meeting material needs. The bond that binds workers to work is determined by the calculations of the worker. If the economic benefits outweigh the costs then the worker regards work as worthwhile. He or she holds no hope of intrinsic rewards.

If it is possible for work to be regarded as purely instrumental, then we effectively destroy the possibility of a bond between work and human nature. If work functions purely as a means of servicing a life outside of work, then whatever external or environmental factors are held to affect or shape human nature, they do not include work. Theories of human nature would be obliged to concentrate on consumption or leisure or political activity. They would be no more concerned with the role of work than nutritionists would be concerned with the design of knives and forks. This is not to suggest that work, even in its instrumental form, plays no part in the life of the individual. At the simplest level, it determines the shape of his or her day; it imposes restrictions of both time and location. It may even help form the aspirations of the worker. But if work is instrumental, these changes of behaviour relate only to habit and not to character. There are good reasons for rejecting this version of the work–human nature relationship. The attribution of instrumentality implies that work provides the means for satisfying desires that exist independently of it; work is endured, not enjoyed. But is this a coherent picture? Will any job be acceptable provided the pay is sufficient? Or if not, what criteria are employed to distinguish the acceptable from the unacceptable? The answers to these questions will turn on what is at stake in the endurance of the means. The means have to be described; the problem is how. Even if we accept that people are prepared to work 'just for the money', we still have to explain why such an explanation is valid. An adequate account will require reference to personal circumstances, and these will be tied to expectations; and both of these will, in turn, have to be set in the context of what the job involves for the worker in terms of physical and psychological costs.[22]

An instrumental orientation to work is based upon a calculation, and balancing, of costs. The instrumental worker cannot afford to be indifferent to his work; he recognizes its unpleasantness, but in so doing he justifies it by reference to a valued private existence. But while an instrumental evaluation may involve a weighing of costs and benefits, it cannot provide for the way in which costs or benefits are themselves identified, or indeed for the process of calculation itself.[23] The instrumental worker has to identify what is boring, uncomfortable, unpleasant about his job. To be able to do so, it is necessary to refer to how life could otherwise be constituted, to know how the job could be more or less boring, etc. These assessments must be derived from some prior understanding of individual worth and its connection with work. Work is judged inadequate for its failure to provide a proper source of choice and responsibility. It is against these standards, and the idea that work could be organized to respect the qualities of the worker, that an instrumental attitude is adopted. Without such assumptions, it is difficult to present instrumentalism as a coherent idea.

Thus, an instrumental approach to work may constitute a strategy in a battle in which workers recognize that work effectively denies them their dignity; it may exist in conjunction with a desire to maintain self-respect and to seek work arrangements which would acknowledge this worth. This form of strategic withdrawal, whilst acknowledging that work does not offer much intrinsic reward at present, presumes that it could in the future.[24]

Two important points emerge from the instrumental interpretation of work. First, it is clear that the decision to view work instrumentally may not reflect any particular desire to do so. Although some empirical evidence may suggest that workers do view work instrumentally, we should not conclude that this indicates any fundamental truth about the nature of work and individual responses to it. The instrumental approach may simply be a recognition that nothing better is available. Secondly, even if the instrumental attitude reflects a freely chosen approach to work, it cannot encompass all the feelings generated by work. The instrumental view must itself allow for the expressive view, or at least some view which recognizes that work is expected to provide intrinsic rewards.

Marx: from the instrumental to the expressive view of work

For Marx, instrumental work is a lesser form of human endeavour. His criticism of instrumental labour rests on the distinction between animal and human activity. Instrumental labour is comparable to the former because it serves only to satisfy animal needs: eating, drinking and procreating. When work is directed to such goals, it has no positive, creative aspect: 'Labour is *external* to the worker, it does not belong to his essential being; he therefore does not confirm himself in his work, but denies himself.'[25] Of course, it is not simply the arduousness of this kind of work that Marx denounces. It is its lack of freedom and its inability to satisfy genuine human needs, that is, its failure to provide an outlet for man's expressive and creative ability. Under communism, work is transformed; it loses its instrumental character. Lucien Sève explains that, for Marx, 'communism puts an end to the historical era of alienated, fragmented, exploited labour, reduced to being merely a *means* of "earning one's living".'[26]

When Marx talks of work under communism as 'self-expression', as 'self-realisation' and as 'really free', two assumptions are made about work and human nature. First, he assumes that work can provide the opportunity for the expression of man's creative capacities. Second, he assumes that these creative capacities are directly related to the core of human existence, to human nature itself.[27] Human beings are distinguished from other creatures by these very abilities. It is, therefore, one of the major crimes of capitalism that it reduces human labour to instrumental (animal) labour. In his rejection of instrumental labour, Marx appears to commit himself to an unqualified acceptance of labour as expressive. In using terms like self-expression, he suggests to the reader the idea of the creative artist. Further, he evokes a particular image of the artist as someone who expressed themselves through their art. But, for Marx, worthwhile work is not to be confused with spontaneous creativity; rather it involves the deliberate development of self-control. It is this move toward self-control, and away from the external control represented by instrumental labour, that Marx sees as the realization of freedom. And in the discovery of freedom is the revelation of man's true nature. Freedom, for Marx, comes through control. In overcoming obstacles, the individual is liberated, particularly when those obstacles are replaced by 'aims which the individual himself posits.'[28] Under these conditions, an individual engages in 'self-realization, objectification of the subject, hence real freedom, whose action is, precisely, labour.'[29] Freedom is work, but it is not idleness or playfulness.[30] Work is the scientific transformation of nature. It is this process which allows man to come to identify his nature. Freedom comes through greater understanding, and greater understanding leads to greater control.

This conception of work, and the notion of freedom to which it appeals, suggests a strongly developmental notion of human nature. The direction of change is toward socialism and communism, toward a world in which labour is neither forced upon, nor external to, the worker. The revelation of this final state comes through the activity of work, itself guided by science. The link between freedom and work is directly related to the source of social change, which is inspired by the idea of scientific progress. The process of transforming the world, and thereby revealing man's true nature, involves the manipulation of nature through the objectivity of science. Socialism is the logical outcome of this progress. Such a line of development is, paradoxically, highly instrumental in character.[31]

Work is the manipulation of nature, albeit as a way of realizing socialism. Marx's objection to the use of machinery under capitalism did not derive from a mistrust of machinery *per se*, but from the way in which workers were used as the extension of machines. It was class, not mechanization, that was the barrier to socialism.[32] There is no threat to Marx's account of human nature in work being done with a machine, provided the technology operates to help realize the full extent of man's capacities. But there are problems in this analysis. Not least, there is the doubt suggested by the idea that an individual's capacities are realized in this particular form of work.

Within Marx's critique of work in capitalism and in his evocation of work under communism, there are a set of images and ideas which do not fit neatly into the assumptions which guide his criticism of instrumental work. Without the emphasis on creativity and individuality, Marx cannot establish the grounds for distinguishing forced or instrumental labour from free labour. If socialism and social change are treated as determined and mechanical, then there is no need to be concerned about the absence of the creative, expressive dimension. However, if people expect their work to realize freedom of the artistic type, and if Marx wishes to establish an ethical critique of capitalism, then his conception of work cannot function only as an agent of social transformation. Marx's account of work and human nature seeks to accommodate both ideals, but they lie uncomfortably together. The spontaneity of expressive freedom does not fit easily with the discipline of scientific freedom. Furthermore, they suggest very different accounts of human nature. On the one hand, there is the developmental model suggested by the process of material change; on the other, there is the image of creative individuality.[33]

Those who do seek a connection between work and human nature find themselves caught. They have to reject the purely instrumental account, which, were it to be coherent, would sever the connection between work and human nature. As a result, they have sought to emphasize the expressive view of work, and thereby to establish a connection between work and human nature. But in making this shift along the lines suggested by Marx, they find themselves confronting two competing and incompatible visions of freedom and of human nature. This state of affairs suggests one final possible resting-place: a view of work as exclusively expressive.

The expressive view of work

Once again, the relationship between work and human nature is established through the medium of freedom. This time, though, the freedom is that appealed to in Marx's critique of instrumentalism, rather than in his vision of freedom as scientific progress. In its extreme form, this idea of work takes on the appearance of radical individualism, an image vividly evoked by Oscar Wilde: 'The pleasure that one has in creating a work of art is purely personal pleasure. . . . The artist . . . is indifferent to others.'[34] Under this guise, work, and the freedom it entails, suggest a version of anarchism. Work becomes precisely what we choose to define it as, just as some artists choose to define piles of bricks or four minutes' silence at the piano as art. To give art or work this eclecticism is to deprive it of meaning and of a specific connection with universalistic human nature. To treat work simply as any form of personal expression is to lose the sense of what work is, to lose the distinction between it and leisure. Furthermore, it makes it impossible to know what is being expressed. To meet both these concerns, work has to be viewed as a public act. In the words of Raymond Williams, work has to involve the common recognition of a common condition.[35] The kind of freedom appealed to, then, is not that of the private individual, but rather of the collective aspirations of those who work. It is this kind of freedom, neither that of scientific progress nor that of private choice, that expressive work must be said to realize.

Work comes to constitute the way that individuals describe and identify their common identity. The analogy with art is still there, not in the comparison with spontaneous creativity, but in the comparison with the meaning of art for its audience. Work and art are to be connected in the sense that they both, according to William Morris, 'tell of men's aspirations for more than material life can give them.'[36] Work, then, represents the means by which individuals come to register their existence. Hence we can understand the responses to work reported at the beginning of this chapter, where we found the desire to see work as meaningful and useful. It had to serve a social and a personal purpose. This is not, though it may seem so, the same version of work which Marx attributes to communism, where work's purpose is identified solely in the realization of socialism and material change. In the expressive account, work has to provide *in itself* —not just as a means of social change—the opportunity for collective identification and self-realization. While Marx is right to see freedom as emerging through the exercise of disciplined self-control (in contrast to the 'freedom' of anarchic liberalism), his concern with a particular mechanism of social change causes the creative side of work to be subsumed by material necessity. Moreover, expressive work need not be anarchic or individualist. It can conform to regular patterns and co-ordinated organization, but such disciplines cannot be dragooned for the mechanical advance of socialism.[37] It must be supposed that if workers' control or industrial democracy are to be considered desirable goals, it is because work can be 'meaningful'. That is, it must be supposed that work can constitute a substantial part of what we understand by the idea of human freedom.

Though the argument of this chapter has led to this point, to the linking of human nature and work, it must be clear that this does not amount to a claim that all work is an expression of human nature, even in the most ideal of all worlds—work is inevitably instrumental, in the sense that it is the means by which nature is manipulated. The expressive element is located in the organization of that work, and in the accompanying opportunities for choice. Though such an idea owes much to Marx, it is not confined to his writings. Indeed, it is perhaps best described in the works of William Morris, where the creative, expressive side of work allowed for the development of individual capacities, not in isolation, but in the shared understanding of a community. He wrote:

> A man at work, making something which he feels will exist because he is working at it and wills it, is exercising the energies of his mind and soul as well as of his body. Memory and imagination help him as he works. Not only his own thoughts, but the thoughts of the men of past ages guide his hands; and, as a part of the human race, he creates. If we work thus we shall be men, and our days will be happy and eventful.[38]

Morris did not regard work as the sum total of human existence. There were other freedoms to be enjoyed and explored away from the workshop, but these freedoms were not superior to those derived from work. A job or a craft was not a means to an end, but was an end in itself. In this sense, work is part of human nature by means of the opportunities it provides for freedom, a freedom that is not just individual expression, but collective expression too. Thus, for Morris, people need to work as a way of physically surviving, as a way of realizing individual capacities, and as a way of establishing the traditions and character of the community to which they belong. Work, in its present form, may well fail to achieve these ends; this does not prove that it never did, or never can. The expectation that it might underlies much of the criticism made of contemporary work.[39]

These criticisms are linked to a view of human nature, in which work plays a prominent part. In both the social codes surrounding work and in the statements of workers, we find a view which places work at the centre of a conception of what it is to be human. In the link between freedom and work lies our understanding of human nature. Whereas instrumental work, if such exists, appears to bear no close relationship with human nature, expressive labour presupposes a direct link. Were work to be treated instrumentally, then we would be forced to conclude that it constituted an interesting footnote to human nature, but no part of the main text. The revelation of human nature would come in the ends for which work was the means. However, as we have noted, the instrumental account is inadequate in that it fails to encompass the full range of responses to work. Work, it seems, means more than a convenient device to reach a given end. This suggested the possibility of exploring Marx's conception of work, and his attempt to give work a meaning. The problem was that the meaning is never entirely clear. Marx's trust in science and the scientific method provided a rather uni-dimensional account of freedom, in which human nature was relegated to the result of determined scientific progress. It, too, failed to capture the full complement of responses to work. And hence we found ourselves emphasizing the 'forgotten' side of Marx's thesis: the idea of work as expression. In this we found the strongest link to human nature, since, in this interpretation, work became the language with which individuals announced their common humanity.

Notes

I would like to thank Ian Forbes, Graeme Duncan, Angela Jameson and George Sulzner for their criticisms and their help.

1. Quoted in Zweig, F., *The Affluent Worker*, London, Heinemann, 1961.
2. See, for example, the works of William Morris, Karl Marx and G. D. H. Cole.
3. See Hampshire, S., 'The Illusions of Sociobiology', *New York Review of Books*, Vol. XXV, No. 15, pp. 64–9.
4. See Chapters 2, 3 and 4 in this volume.
5. Williams, R., 'The Meanings of Work' in Fraser, R. (ed.), *Work*, Harmondsworth, Penguin, 1968, p. 280.
6. Cooley, M., quoted in Goldwyn, E., 'Now the Chips are down', in Forester, T. (ed.), *The Microelectronics Revolution*, Oxford, Basil Blackwell, 1980, p. 301.

7. Quoted in Beynon, H., *Working for Ford*, Harmondsworth, Penguin, 1973, p. 114.
8. Quoted in Clarke, T., *Sit-In at Fisher Bendix*, Nottingham, Institute of Workers' Control, p. 9.
9. See, for example, Locke, E. A., 'What is Job Satisfaction?' *Organisational Behaviour and Human Performance*, Vol. 4, 1969, pp. 309–36.
10. Goldthorpe, J., and Lockwood, D., *The Affluent Worker: Industrial Attitudes and Behaviour*, Cambridge, Cambridge University Press, 1968, p. 11.
11. Tawney, R. H., *Religion and the Rise of Capitalism*, London, Pelican, 1938.
12. Thompson, E. P., *The Making of the English Working Class*, Harmondsworth, Penguin, 1972, pp. 396–7.
13. Thompson, E. P., 'Time, Work-Discipline and Industrial Capitalism', *Past and Present*, No. 38, 1968, p. 57.
14. Thompson, *The Making of the English Working Class*, op. cit., p. 404.
15. See Williams, op. cit., p. 291.
16. See Locke, op. cit., pp. 333–4.
17. Quoted in Williams, op. cit., p. 287.
18. Benyon, op. cit., pp. 113–15.
19. See also Mason, R., *Participatory and Workplace Democracy*, Illinois, Southern Illinois University Press, 1982, chapter 5.
20. See Weinstein, W. L., 'Bullock and the Business Enterprise', *Director*, January 1978.
21. Goldthorpe and Lockwood, op. cit., pp. 38–9.
22. See Connolly, W. G., *Appearance and Reality in Politics*, Cambridge, Cambridge University Press, 1981, chapter 3.
23. See Plamenatz, J., *Democracy and Illusion*, London, Longman, 1973, p. 104.
24. This kind of strategy is described in Nichols, T., and Beynon, H., *Living With Capitalism*, London, Routledge & Kegan Paul, 1977, p. 193.
25. Marx, K., 'Economic and Philosophical Manuscripts' in *Early Writings*, Harmondsworth, Penguin, 1975, p. 326.
26. Sève, L., *Man in Marxist Theory*, Sussex, Harvester Press, 1978, p. 327.
27. See, for example, Marx, K., 'Excerpts from James Mill's Elements of Political Economy' in *Early Writings*, op. cit., pp. 277–8; also Clayre, A., *Work and Play*, London, Weidenfeld & Nicolson, 1974, chapter 5.
28. Marx, K., *Grundrisse*, Harmondsworth, Penguin, 1973, p. 611.
29. Ibid., pp. 611–12.
30. Ibid., p. 612.
31. See the argument made by Habermas, J., *Knowledge and Human Interests*, London, Hutchinson, 1973.
32. Marx, K., *Capital*, Vol. 1, London, Dent, 1957, chapter 13.
33. See Marx, *Early Writings*, op. cit., pp. 277–8.
34. Wilde, O., *Selected Letters*, Oxford, Oxford University Press, 1979, p. 81; also Stoppard, T., *Travesties*, London, Faber & Faber, 1975, pp. 37–8.
35. Williams, op. cit., p. 280.
36. Quoted in Thompson, E. P., *William Morris*, London, Merlin, 1977, p. 656.
37. See, for example, Lenin's frustration with workers' control schemes immediately following the 1917 Revolution.
38. Morris, W., 'Useful Work and Useless Toil', quoted in Thompson, *William Morris*, op. cit., p. 642.
39. For example, Schwartz, A., 'Meaningful Work', *Ethics*, July 1982; Jones, B., *Sleepers, Wake*, Sussex, Wheatsheaf, 1982, chapter 9; and Skillen, A., *Ruling Illusions*, Sussex, Harvester, 1977, chapter 2.

10 Bureaucracy and human nature

JEFFREY SEDGWICK and GEORGE SULZNER

The typical way of addressing the issue of the 'fit' between bureaucratic organization and human nature is to focus on either the efficiency of bureaucracies (that is, the extent to which bureaucratic organizations have sufficient flexibility and adaptability to facilitate an appropriate choice of means to ends), or on the prospects for meaningful democracy in an increasingly bureaucratized environment. The former issue is at the foundation of the writings of Robert Merton, Peter Blau and Herbert Simon.[1] The latter issue figures prominently in the writings of Gaetano Mosca, Robert Michels and John Stuart Mill.[2] This chapter, however, pursues a different line of argument. It will attempt to show that a consistent and coherent view of the problematic relationship between bureaucracy and human creativity animates the writings on administration of two major writers, one European and one American.

Undoubtedly, the best-known theorist of bureaucracy in Europe is Max Weber. In the United States, however, it is the writings of Woodrow Wilson that are assigned to virtually every student of public administration. What is striking about these two is the extent to which themes articulated by Weber are echoed in the thinking and political actions of Wilson. In particular, the views of both regarding the nature of appropriate political leadership are essentially the same; both advocated what might be called a plebiscitarian democratic leader. Such a leader was thought to be necessary to sustain individual creative activity, an essential element of human nature, in the midst of the routinizing forces of rationalization and bureaucratization in the modern world.

This argument is important if one is to understand practical political issues such as the perennial drive in the United States for civil service reform. The advocates of such reform in this century typically defend their proposals as necessary for the establishment of democratic responsibility. Put briefly, most civil service reform proposals are designed to enhance the accountability of professional public servants to elected public officials, particularly the president. Such accountability is deemed necessary if the president is to be held responsible by the voting public. In so far as the public endorses a particular candidate for the presidency, ought not the operation of the executive branch reflect the policies and priorities of the winning candidate? Seen from this perspective, the administrative apparatus of the executive branch is made accountable to the public through its subordination to the elected chief executive who in turn is directly responsible through election to the public.

The argument just recounted, that administrators ought to be clearly subordinate to an elected chief executive, is precisely the justification for the latest reform of civil service in the United States. Indeed, such reforms conform to what is known as the executive responsibility model of personnel administration. It is important to realize that such reform is grounded in a modification, if not outright rejection, of the Madisonian and Hamiltonian theories of American government articulated at the Founding. More precisely, the Wilsonian attempt to establish a plebiscitary presidency, along the lines of Weber's recommendation, involved a re-formulation of the basis of executive power in the United States.

Max Weber: bureaucracy, rationality and human nature

Much of the debate over the works of Max Weber has centred on the efficiency of his ideal-type of bureaucracy, and whether it is truly descriptive and, therefore, of use in empirical research. Such debate, however, fails to illuminate the essence of Weber's understanding of human nature and his notion of the prospects for humanity in an increasingly bureaucratized and rationalized world. In highlighting these aspects of Weber's work, it is clear that he was deeply influenced by both modern liberalism and Nietzschean pessimism. As Wolfgang Mommsen comments:

> The central issues of his sociological works as well as of his political thought are without exception related to his growing anxiety about the future of the liberal societies of the west, in an age of rapidly expanding bureaucracies. He was convinced that the universal advance of bureaucratic forms of social and political organization was bound to place the principles of individual liberty and personal creativity in jeopardy. He perceived that the slow but steady ossification of the social systems in the west could only [be] prevented by social and political institutions which would guarantee maximum dynamism and leadership.[3]

To begin to understand such fears, it is necessary briefly to review Weber's thoughts on authority and rationality.

Weber's study of history led him to the conclusion that there were essentially three different foundations for authority. These different foundations were not in practice distinct, for they could be intermingled in a particular historical example. None the less, the three were conceptually distinct, and this is reflected in Weber's ideal-type description of them.

First, there is charismatic authority. Charisma obviously resides in a particular person; hence, charismatic authority refers to a situation where 'the governed submit because of their belief in the extraordinary quality of the specific *person*.'[4] Weber lists magical sorcerers, prophets, leaders of hunting or booty expeditions, warrior chiefs, Caesarist rulers and, on occasion, political party heads as examples of such rule. Each has in common the ability to display some outstanding characteristic which charms or entices others to follow. Clearly, Weber's inclusion of sorcerers and prophets indicates that the attachment or bond between leader and led need not be the product of reasoned reflection. Indeed, mystical and supernatural appeals are to be expected. In contemporary usage, to call a leader charismatic is to imply an extra-rational appeal or a bond between leader and led which appeals to the followers' passions.

The legitimacy of charismatic rule for Weber depended on a display of the leader's ability to provide for the welfare of his followers. A constant demonstration of such ability is necessary to sustain charismatic authority; once the mass fails to believe in the ability of the charismatic individual, both his authority and his legitimacy dissolves.[5] Thus a charismatic leader is of necessity a dynamic leader, constantly active, needing to prove both the existence and legitimacy of his authority. Such activity, in addition, is irrational. In Weber's words,

> . . . charismatic rule is not managed according to general norms, either traditional or rational, but, in principle, according to concrete revelations and inspirations, . . . It is 'revolutionary' in the sense of not being bound to the existing order: 'It is written—but I say unto you . . .!'[6]

Charismatic leadership historically has led to the second ideal-type of authority, 'traditionalism'. In Weber's work, traditionalism refers 'to the psychic attitude-set for the habitual workaday and to the belief in the everyday routine as an inviolable norm of conduct.'[7] The most common historical form of traditionalism is patriarchalism. Weber argues that the rule of father over household, freeman over slave and prince over subjects are all patriarchial forms of authority. Traditional and charismatic authority are in practice closely related. Traditional authority depends on outbursts of charismatic authority to inject new laws into the traditional practices of a community. And charismatic authority routinely degenerates into traditional authority, especially over the problem of succession.

Whichever method of succession is chosen, be it election, consecration, or inheritance, rules of succession come to govern. And such rules, over time, become traditional.

But traditional authorities rarely remain simply traditional. The rationalization and routinization of succession leads to rationalization in other aspects of patriarchal rule as well. As charismatic rulers attempt to institutionalize their rule and make it less conditional, their staffs become transformed from disciples or followers into officials. Historically, such officials are necessary supports in the attempt of traditional leaders to overcome rival status groups. The clearest example is the rivalry in medieval society between king and aristocracy. The success and power of the king was enhanced by his acquisition and firm possession of administrative resources.

Perhaps the three central elements of such administrative means are the courts, the military, and the treasury. Within these organizations, the transformation from traditional or charismatic authority to bureaucratic authority begins. Again quoting Weber:

> . . . in legal authority, submission does not rest upon the belief and devotion to charismatically gifted persons, like prophets and heroes, or upon sacred tradition, or upon piety toward a personal lord and master who is defined by an ordered tradition, or upon piety toward the possibile incumbents of office fiefs and office prebends who are legitimized in their own right through privilege and conferment. Rather, submission under legal authority is based upon an *impersonal* bond to the generally defined and functional 'duty of office.' The official duty —like the corresponding right to exercise authority: the 'jurisdictional competency'—is fixed by rationally established norms, by enactments, decrees and regulations, in such a manner that the legitimacy of the authority becomes the legality of the general rule, which is purposely thought out, enacted, and announced with formal correctness.[8]

In this passage, one can see the essential characteristics of bureaucratic authority—rationality and impersonality. Further, one can see that rationality refers not necessarily to efficiency, but rather to deliberation and formality.

From Weber's perspective, the danger of such rationality is that it is necessarily impersonal. It is his argument that charisma, which is strongly attached to the person, erodes when confined within the permanent institutions of a community. The decline of charisma, in turn, reduces or diminishes the importance of individual actions. Consider Weber's characterization of bureaucrats as opposed to politicians. In his essay,

'Politics as a Vocation', Weber juxtaposes the genuine official and the political leader. The official is said to be apolitical, impartial, dispassionate and 'without scorn or bias.'[9] The political leader, on the other hand, is passionately committed to a cause for which he is always prepared to fight. The official is considered honourable only in so far as he is prepared to execute conscientiously the order of superior authorities, even when such orders run contrary to the official's personal conviction. Political leaders, however, are honourable only in so far as they claim personal responsibility for their actions. The essential quality of the official is self-denial; the essential quality of the political leader is passionate commitment to a cause or a calling of an intensely personal nature.

To define the essential qualities of the official and politician in this way is to highlight the threat bureaucratization (with its rationalization and routinization) poses to politics and political leadership of an intensely personal kind. But what, one might wonder, is the peculiar attraction of an intensely passionate, personal political rule? Why, in short, is charisma so much to be preferred as a type of authority? The answer to this question is that Weber's conception of human nature stressed the importance of individual free initiative. To be fully human was to be able to search out and choose a set of values for oneself, and to put those values to the test by living one's life in accordance with them. Mommsen comments that Weber followed Nietzsche in believing that there was no foundation for values other than the spontaneous decision of the personality.[10] Human nature resides in the act of choosing one's values, not in having made the correct choice.

Such a view of human nature suggests the inhumanity of rationality (understood as deliberation and formality). There is no foundation by which forms governing choice can be legitimately grounded, nor is deliberation necessary for spontaneous choice. What is needed for a fully human life is *personal* responsibility and room for *personal* initiative. Charismatic political leadership provides the opportunity for the exercise of such personal initiative, and checks the spread of bureaucracy by 'breaking the deadly rule of routine'. By altering the political horizons of an increasingly ossified, rationalized society, charismatic rule preserves the possibility of a fully human life. Indeed, in so far as charismatic leadership displays a commitment to values which contrast with the status quo, the resulting tension between the professed value and the empirical reality generates social change in an otherwise stagnant world.

Weber's belief in the necessity of both charismatic leadership and free individual initiative led him to advocate a plebiscitary-democratic form of leadership as most appropriate for the modern world. By subordinating officials or bureaucrats to such a leader, the bureaucratic threat to human nature could be restrained. To see Weber's theories put into practice, one need only turn to the United States, where Woodrow Wilson made an intellectual and political career by giving life to Weber's ideas.

Woodrow Wilson and the nature of executive power

Both the writings and the political actions of Woodrow Wilson reveal a deep-seated rejection of American politics as conceived by James Madison and Alexander Hamilton and embodied in the Constitution of the United States. The root of Wilson's unease with the traditional understanding of American politics was that it was too concerned with moderation and checks and balances. The overemphasis on restraining immoderate ambition was revealed most clearly in the lack of effective and dynamic leadership. Such leadership was necessary to provide vitality and a sense of direction in American politics.[11] On the surface, the problem of poor executive leadership would appear to be attributable to the state of political parties in the United States during the last half of the nineteenth century. But Wilson correctly perceived the problem to be more deep-rooted. The moderate nature of American political parties, and their desire to build electoral coalitions even by deliberate obfuscation of political choices, was due to the Constitutional framework of American political life. Whereas Wilson preferred to judge political arrangements by their capacity for change through dynamic leadership and the closeness of the relationship between the leader and public opinion, the Constitution reflected a concern for maintaining institutional checks and balances, which facilitated deliberation, thus slowing the pace of political change.

In *Federalist 10*, James Madison argued that the fatal flaw of democracy is the rise of majority factions, for such factions decide public issues 'not according to the rules of justice and the rights of the minor party, but by the superior force of an interested and overbearing majority.'[12] Madison's cure for the problem of majority faction (or majority tyranny) was not to eliminate the causes of faction, but rather to control its effects. This was accomplished by multiplying the number of factions until each was a small minority of the whole community. In order to achieve any political influence in such a fragmented setting, each faction would be required to compromise as the basis for coalition with other minority factions. The result would be slim electoral majorities built up by a process of moderation and compromise.

However, Madison noted a small problem with this scenario. There are different sources of faction, and not all sources of faction produce groups equally amenable to compromise. Madison argued that there were, in fact, three distinct sources of faction: interests, opinions and passions. Of the latter two, Madison noted

> A zeal for different opinions concerning religion, concerning govern-ment, and many other points, as well of speculation as of practice; an attachment to different leaders ambitiously contending for pre-eminence and power; or to persons of other descriptions whose fortunes have been interesting to the human passions, have, in turn, divided mankind into parties, inflamed them with mutual animosity, and rendered them much more disposed to vex and oppress each other than to co-operate for their common good.[13]

What is striking here is the open reference to the dangers of charismatic leadership in the second half of the quotation. For Madison, opinion and passion were unsafe bases for politics since neither produced factions amenable to compromise. History is virtually littered with examples of martyrs either to the 'true cause' or to the 'true prophet'. There are, on the other hand, very few martyrs among the 'interested'. For the sake of moderation and compromise, Madison opted for a politics of interest-based factions. Further, he established stability as a prime political virtue; stability facilitated an orderly deliberation of political proposals. Change would be preceded by the opportunity for mature and sober reflection on the issues of the day. And change would, itself, be moderate.

What seemed to Madison to be a stable, moderate, and therefore potentially just or non-oppressive form of politics, appeared in Wilson's eyes to be a stagnant, moribund evasion of responsibility. What Wilson wanted was growth and change. As one commentator puts it:

> Ultimately Wilson was, in a literal sense, a Progressive; he had a strong preference for change or 'growth', alternating between an enlighten-ment vision that history inevitably brought progress and a more limited Darwinian concept that continuous adaptation was necessary to sustain and nourish society.[14]

Such growth and change came, for Wilson as for Weber, from the dynamic political leader sustained by a close personal mandate from his followers. In a vigorous rejection of Madison, Wilson noted that no living thing in nature can survive if its organs are constantly checking one another.[15] What is needed is energy or an energetic political leader, not stability and moderation. In this way, Wilson tried to dismiss the constitutional foundations of American politics in favour of a more plebiscitary rule. However, it is worth noting that the Founders agreed that an energetic executive was a necessary element in good government. The lack of such energy (centred in the executive) was their major criticism of the discarded Articles of Confederation.

To understand the disagreement between Wilson and the Founders, one must focus not on the amount of presidential power, but on its source. It would appear that the Founders wished their president to think of his power as legal or institutional; at the very least, they did not want that power to be understood as popular. The reason executive power could not be popular in origin was that the Founders expected the executive to check the power of the legislature when legislative initiatives were unwise or unjust. But what was the source of legislative power? It was popular support or mandate. Hence, if the executive was expected to check the legislature (the Founders referred to the Congress as 'the legislative vortex'), then his source of power would have to be different from that of the legislature. Thus, when Alexander Hamilton specified the ingredients which constitute energy in the executive, he referred only to constitutional or structural aspects of the office, such as a unitary as opposed to multiple executive, duration in office, adequate provision for support, and competent powers.[16] Hamilton did not speak of any personal attributes leading to energy, nor did he mention public support or popular opinion.

Even the method of presidential selection set forth in the Constitution militated against executive reliance on public opinion. The president was selected by electors who were chosen by their states for that purpose only. Electors met only once, and never as a whole body; rather, they met on the same day in their respective state capitals thereby preventing any possibility of eager candidates lobbying them or otherwise attempting to gain favour (and votes). In addition, the majority of states prior to the nineteenth century did not permit direct election of presidential electors. Rather, the typical pattern was for the people to elect members of the upper house of the state legislature, who in turn elected the electors, who in turn selected the president. Surely such an indirect method of election prevented a credible claim to executive power based on public mandate!

For Wilson, then, the whole notion of institutional or legal sources of energy was absurd. Executive energy came from the person, not the office. His argument was aimed at undermining the Founders' notion of representative government based on a formal, constitutionally-articulated division of legal powers. In its place, Wilson proposed not forms and laws but public support and following. Political leadership was to be informal and extra-institutional. The solution to the nation's problems lay in a leader whose energy derives from the admiration and confidence of the people who have entered into a direct, one-to-one relationship with the president through the mechanism of direct (or nearly direct) election of the chief executive.

This formulation of executive power or leadership has a number of important implications. First, it tended to de-legitimize Congress as a political voice, just as it increased presidential responsibility and authority. If, as Wilson claimed, the president had a direct relationship to the people through which he received his power, then what was the status of the Congress? He offered that Congress was no more than

> . . . a collection of men representing each his neighborhood, each his local interest; an alarmingly large proportion of its legislation is 'special'; all of it is at best only a limping compromise between the conflicting interests of the innumerable localities represented.[17]

The president, by contrast, was the only national voice in politics; he speaks for the nation, not for one or a collection of special interests.

Second, Wilson's theory of executive leadership puts the political party in a new light. No longer is the president a faithful party worker, put forth by a stable electoral organization with long-term interests and orientations. Rather, the party becomes a mere instrument for presidential use if needed for electoral purposes. Of course, in a system with open primaries to select candidates, a party, as opposed to an *ad hoc* temporary coalition of personal adherents, is unnecessary.

Third, the notion that the nation speaks through the president logically leads to the proposition that the entire executive and administrative apparatus of the government should be subordinated to the public through the person of the chief executive or president. Whereas under the Founders' conception of government the nation was said to speak through the interplay of the various branches of government and through the Constitution itself, under Wilson the nation would speak only through the president. Only the president faces the nation as a whole for its endorsement or rejection of his leadership; consequently, in so far as officials are to serve the nation, they do so by serving the president.

One of the best measures of Wilson's success as a leader is his ability to change the way Americans have thought about their government. A notable example is civil service reform. Since the Wilson presidency, the dominant justification for civil service reform has been to subordinate the executive branch to executive leadership and authority. In the discussion that follows, it is striking the extent to which the themes articulated by Max Weber and Woodrow Wilson are repeated in advocating practical reforms in the American civil service.

Perspectives on civil service reform in the United States

The directing motive underlying civil service reform changed significantly during the twentieth century in the United States. Reform in 1883, Nigro writes, 'meant starting the process of eliminating the spoils system and of implementing a merit system based on the use of competitive examinations in filling federal jobs.'[18] This led to the development of a perspective on reform labelled as the 'protectionist' school, whose adherents were committed to the idea of keeping the personnel function insulated from the influence of chief executives and other instruments of political pressure.[19]

Wilson, as early as 1885, and two years after the passage of the Pendleton Act, noted the salutary effects of accountability which he hoped would not be lost in the newly-reformed, politically neutral civil service. He wrote, in *Congressional Government*:

> If there be one principle clearer than another, it is this: that in any business, whether of government or of mere merchandising, *somebody must be trusted*. . . . In order to drive trade at the speed and with the success you desire, you must confide without suspicion in your chief clerk, giving him the power to ruin you, because you thereby furnish him with a motive for serving you. . . . And human nature is much the same in government as in the dry-goods trade. *Power and strict accountability for its use* are the essential constituents of good government . . . these are the influences, the only influences which foster practical, energetic, and trustworthy statesmanship.[20]

Gradually, without any direct acknowledgement of their linkages to Wilson, students of personnel administration began to criticize the 'protectionist' orientation on several grounds. First, it was regarded as lacking the dynamism needed for efficient administration of human resources. Operationally, policies were produced which undermined merit by creating personnel systems wrapped in red tape and procedural requirements which, it was alleged, obstructed the hiring or promoting of the best and the removal of the inadequate. Second, the 'protectionist' focus on neutral competence unacceptably blunted the competing need for democratic accountability in public administration. An alternative perspective, known as the executive responsibility model, was developed. This attempted to rectify the above defects by borrowing heavily from the private sector experience, with its emphasis on providing political executives (elected and appointed) with the structures and techniques required for the efficient and energetic running of government. A principal element in this approach,

Felix and Lloyd Nigro observe, 'is control by the chief executive of the "tools of management", of which personnel is one. . . .'[21] Adherents of the executive responsibility model were not satisfied with personnel systems that measured success in terms of staving off politics. To them, this was a much overemphasized value because the new, complicated industrial society required efficient and effective public services. Thus personnel administration should concentrate on the recruitment and retention of professionally-trained public servants who could implement the priorities of political executives. Both a competent *and* a responsive government was necessary.

These rival conceptions of civil service reform battled for ascendancy for over forty years following the publication in 1937 of the report of Franklin Roosevelt's Committee on Administration Management. With the passage of the 1978 Civil Service Reform Act, however, the executive responsibility model emerged triumphant. Alan K. Campbell, the principal architect of the reform, clearly affirms this point when he writes, 'The history of the evolution of the Federal Civil Service has been primarily one of increasing the protections of career members. . . . The new emphasis is to modify these protections sufficiently to encourage initiative, flexibility, and productivity.'[22] This emphasis has resulted in the establishment of a set of 'presidentially-inclined' administrative roles for federal civil servants. Accountability to presidentially-appointed executives is enhanced by grouping 'positive personnel' functions in a presidential agency, the Office of Personnel Management, and relating this structural reform to operational changes in assigning, evaluating, rewarding and disciplining career administrators.[23]

Not surprisingly, the 1978 Civil Service Reform Act served as a catalyst for state reform efforts. By 1980, thirty-two States, largely spurred by the federal example, were pursuing civil service reform programmes based in most instances on the national pattern. Since the federal legislation centred on the executive responsibility model, it is to be expected that this model also oriented the reform constructs in the states as well. This was certainly the case, for example, with the 1981 Massachusetts Civil Service Reform Act. A more detailed look at it will illustrate its mirroring of the 1978 federal legislation, its responsiveness to the executive responsibility model, and its concern with bureaucratic stagnation.

The Massachusetts Civil Service Reform Act

The civil service remedies contained in Chapter 767 of the laws of Massachusetts are intended to 'restucco the outside walls and renovate the inside rooms' so that, in its streamlined form, the Massachusetts Civil Service would be able to meet its contemporary obligations. These obligations were set forth by the Special Commission on Civil Service as (1) selection on the basis of qualification and merit; (2) equity in job compensation; (3) elimination of political influences and the prevention of discrimination; and (4) establishment of the most effective use of human resources.[24] The legislation hinges, however, on three types of reforms whose main purpose is the achievement of the fourth objective, establishment of the effective use of human resources. This focus is consistent with the dominant executive responsibility model approach to civil service reform. The carrot and stick incentives used in assigning, evaluating, rewarding and disciplining career administrators (reflecting private personnel management practices) are not present to the same degree in the Massachusetts legislation as they are in the 1978 Federal Act. Nevertheless, much of the retooling of the personnel machinery in Massachusetts was along the lines of private business organization. Private business practices of personnel management were thought superior with regard to enhancing flexibility and accountability, since private businesses typically treat staffing as a management prerogative.

The Act provides for the reorganization of the old Division of Personnel Administration in the Executive Office of Administration and Finance and for a significant reallocation of personnel responsibilities between the former Division and the Civil Service Commission.[25] The Division now becomes a Department headed by a Commissioner of Personnel Administration—hereafter referred to in this chapter, as in the Act itself, as the personnel administrator—rather than by a Deputy Commissioner. The old Bureaux in the former Division are replaced by new Divisions of Management Services, Information Services and Technical Services, led by Deputy Commissioners within the new Department of Personnel Administration. The commissioner and deputy commissioners of the Department of Personnel Administration are appointed by the Secretary of Administration and Finance (himself a gubernatorial appointee) for terms concurrent with the governor's. Contrast this with the pre-reform practice of vesting personnel powers in a civil service commission headed by commissioners serving staggered terms which overlapped governors' terms in office. The impact of this aspect of the reform is to increase executive influence over staffing. The reform structure conforms generally to the current alignment of personnel units in many business organizations, and reflects as well the growing institutional status of human resource management activities in various enterprises in the United States.

Furthermore, the traditional rule-making authority of the Massachusetts

Civil Service Commission is given to the personnel administrator in addition to assigning new responsibilities for administering various features of the legislation. The Civil Service Commission is transformed primarily into a reviewing and appellate body. Its principal mission under the Act is to police the merit system by reviewing the rule-making activities of the personnel administrator, by hearing appeals alleging violations on the civil service law, rules and procedures, and by launching investigations on its own or others' initiative.[26]

The correspondence to the division of personnel management responsibility at the federal level between the Office of Personnel Management and the Merit System Protection Board is striking. Similar to the federal reform, personnel administration in the state service is more 'executively inclined' than previously. Likewise, there is a harmony in the rationale, as in both cases it was claimed that Civil Service Commissions, making rules and then adjudicating interpretations of those rules, were confronted with an inherent conflict of interest which could only be resolved by a functional and institutional separation. Moreover, with the decision to keep the Massachusetts Civil Service Commissioners on part-time duty, it was thought that redirecting responsibilities to a 'beefed-up', more responsive and broadly organized Department of Personnel Administration would promote the quality and accountability of personnel administration in the state. Implicitly, this is a rejection of Michel's Iron Law of Oligarchy, and suggests an orientation toward democratizing the workplace. It is not a propensity of human nature that undermines bureaucratic organization, but the form of the structure acting on humans which can prove deleterious.

Undoubtedly, the most dramatic reform of administrative practice in Massachusetts is mandating of performance evaluations in the legislation.[27] Strange as it may seem, performance evaluations were not required for state or municipal employees prior to the enactment of this statute. No feature, perhaps, of the previous system was subject to greater criticism in the press and among the attentive public who were interested in the administration of the civil service. Under the present Act, the personnel administrator, in conjunction with representatives of collective bargaining units to be evaluated and (at the municipal level) representatives of the Massachusetts Municipal Association, shall determine the form, method and general criteria of a performance evaluation system for all civil service employees.

Interestingly, while the evaluations do not have to be used in future personnel actions, there surely is the expectation that they will be so utilized. For example, one of the six 'basic merit principles' of the system, listed in Section 10 of the Act, is 'retaining of employees on the basis of adequacy of their performance, correcting inadequate performance, and separating employees whose inadequate performance cannot be corrected; . . .'[28] Instituting regular performance evaluations, it was envisaged, would go a long way towards boosting merit within the state civil service. This reflects the attempt to take account of the performance of people in the lower echelons of an organization. It is assumed that *all* the members of a bureaucracy are equally to be credited with creative and dynamic potentialities, the expression of which should not be restricted but encouraged. At the level of theorizing about human nature, this represents a combination of the liberal view of the free and creative individual, and the Skinnerian belief that such qualities can be evinced and enhanced by a judicious mixture of reward and punishment.

Again we have a close parallel with federal civil service reform. Naomi B. Lynn, writing about the 1978 Civil Service Reform Act, points out that

> . . . performance appraisals receive more emphasis . . . than does any other aspect of personnel management. CSRA requires each agency to set up new performance systems that . . . are to service as the basis for merit pay, removal or demotion of unacceptable performers, and other personnel decisions.[29]

Additionally, other sections of the Massachusetts law are constructed to encourage state administrators to act confidently and aggressively in their employee relations.[30] The personnel administrator is, in Section 14(p), directed to provide training programmes and technical expertise to the various state agencies on the substantive and procedural issues involved in disciplinary personnel actions. Furthermore, the appointing authority's position in disciplinary actions is strengthened in Section 20. Previously, the burden of proof rested entirely with the appointing authority. Now the appellant will have full rights restored only if by a preponderance of evidence the employee establishes that the action was based on a harmful error in the application of rules and procedures, based on factors not related to the fitness of the employee to perform in the position, or an error of law. It is possible to find sections of the 1978 CSRA which served as the genesis for the Massachusetts rendering. Both versions seek to address the conventional wisdom today that the United States public service suffers from a 'country club' atmosphere, in which overly-relaxed approaches to work are never reprimanded and may even be rewarded. The proposed remedies draw heavily from private sector methods and are influenced by the 'bottom-line' mentality allegedly practised there.

The final area of change examined is directed toward improving the quality of state public administration. All states have in the past decade faced the problem of attracting talented personnel to the service and providing incentives for improvement once individuals are employed. This approach to bureaucracy, then, concerns itself with all employees, and hence the nature of men and women, rather than the more restricted issues of leadership, rationality and efficiency. Following the lead of the federal government in instituting a Senior Executive Service for its top-rated civil servants, Massachusetts, in *Chapter 767*, created a Career Management Service.[31] The target group, as in the CSRA, is the top echelon among the career professionals. No more than 6 per cent of the total positions in any secretariat can be designated as career management slots, and only 30 per cent of the Career Management Service can be incumbent positions. The Career Management Service legislation, like its federal counterpart, provides a trial period for employees entering the service, and a safety net within the regular grades for those who voluntarily or involuntarily leave its ranks. While the Massachusetts version does not include bonuses for superior performance, it does set salaries for the following year on the basis of an evaluation of the current year's work. Since bonuses have been one of the most controversial and ineffectual components of the CSRA package, it is probably salutary that they were kept out of *Chapter 767*.[32]

The SES and the CMS were designed to provide a cadre of high-level managers who would hold a 'rank-in-person', thus giving political executives more flexibility in fitting talents to problem situations. They also aimed to make career executives more accountable for the productivity of subordinates. Further, these concepts recognize that, in the past, initiative and ambition were often stifled by the civil service system. Monetary rewards were limited, career ladders hardly visible, and discretion circumscribed. Advancement was often channelled into line-management positions, and many administrators, with mainly subject-matter competence, were forced to function as reluctant and sometimes relatively unskilled managers to receive higher pay. In brief, both the SES and the CMS hold out the expectation for public administrators that the challenges and rewards of public management will begin to approximate those of private business, and the consequence will be the energizing of the government service. Although the liberal-capitalist view of human nature employed here looks to be the same as Forbes's description of Marx's first notion of human nature, it has a significant difference. The problem of work and human nature itself is addressed, and the radical expressivist position, outlined by Street, wins substantial endorsement. However, this has only a partial application, and must be augmented by the liberal view which taps the inherent dynamism of free creativity under the motivating conditions of competition and reward.

Conclusion

The examination of state and federal civil service reforms has revealed an underlying concern for flexibility, dynamism and accountability to elected political executives. While growth is in many respects an expected component of the American way of life, its organizational dimensions have always been suspect. The 'dead hand of the bureaucracy', with connotations of undue formalism, multiple clearance points, excessive rules and regulations, and inefficient redundancies, has always been a pejorative phrase dear to the heart of most Americans. The intent of recent reform legislations has been to preserve individual creativity, without and within public organizations, by trying to make them accountable to the dynamic leadership of external political executives, and, more recently, responsive to internal structures and leader relationships patterned after the practice of American business. Woodrow Wilson, as we have already noted, provided an early rationale for this approach and, surprisingly, even Max Weber might have been sympathetic to it. At a conference in 1909 at Vienna, he startled his fellow sociologists with the observation that while many were impressed with the technical superiority and high morality displayed by the German bureaucracy, it had not accomplished as much as the governmental organizations of France and America which were 'linked to a purely business officialdom, which is easily open to corruption', and oriented toward 'private capitalistic expansion. . . .'[33]

Still, the American response has its dangers. Bureaucratic accountability to political executives and legislators, as Weber noted, has often meant excessive favours, which undermine public purposes and result in the corrupt dealings which are too frequently a part of American state and local government practices. And, as the experience of Watergate showed, strict subordination of bureaucracy to plebiscitary democratic leaders may subvert justice and the public interest when such leaders turn demagogic. Madison's fears of a passionate politics and charismatic leadership are well taken.

At the most fundamental level, bureaucratic reforms revolve around competing visions of human nature. On the one hand, human nature is understood to be fulfilled through reasoned deliberation on public issues. Such deliberation depends on moderation and formalisms. On the other hand, human nature is understood to be fulfilled through spontaneous affirmation of personal values. Such affirmation depends on creativity, flexibility and dynamism. Modern bureaucracy creates problems for both visions of human nature; but it much more directly threatens the latter.

Notes

1. See, for example, 'Bureaucratic Structure and Rationality', in Merton, R. K., *Reader in Bureaucracy*, New York, Free Press, 1952; Blau, P., *The Dynamics of Bureaucracy*, Chicago, University of Chicago Press, 1955; and Simon, H., *Administrative Behavior*, New York, Free Press, 1965.
2. See, for example, Mosca, G., *The Ruling Class*, New York, McGraw Hill, 1939; Michels, R., *Political Parties*, New York, Free Press, 1949; and Mill, J. S., *Principles of Political Economy*, Toronto, University of Toronto Press, 1965.
3. Mommsen, W. J., *The Age of Bureaucracy*, New York, Harper & Row, 1974, p. xiii.
4. Weber, M., in Gerth, H. H., and Mills, C. W. (eds), *From Max Weber*, New York, Oxford University Press, 1958, p. 295.
5. Ibid., p. 296.
6. Ibid.
7. Ibid.
8. Ibid., p. 299.
9. Ibid., p. 95.
10. Mommsen, op. cit., p. 7.
11. Wilson, W., 'Leaderless Government', in Baker, R. S., and Dodd, W. E. (eds), *College and State*, 2 vols., New York, Harper Brothers, 1925, Vol. 1, p. 339.
12. Hamilton, H., Madison, J., and Jay, J., *The Federalist*, New York, Modern Library, 1937, p. 54.
13. Ibid., p. 55.
14. Ceaser, J., *Presidential Selection*, Princeton, Princeton University Press, 1978, p. 174.
15. Wilson, W., *Constitutional Government in the United States*, New York, Columbia University Press, 1908, p. 57.
16. Hamilton *et al.*, op. cit., p. 455.
17. Wilson, W., *Congressional Government*, as quoted in Ceaser, op. cit., p. 181.
18. Nigro, F. A., 'The Politics of Civil Service Reform', *Southern Review of Public Administration*, 3 (September, 1979), 198.
19. Nigro, F. A., and Nigro, L. G., *The New Public Personnel Administration*, Itasca, Illinois, F. E. Peacock, 1981, p. 98.
20. Wilson, W., *Congressional Government*, New York, Meridan Books, 1956, pp. 186-7.
21. Nigro and Nigro, op. cit., p. 93.
22. Campbell, A. K., 'Civil Service Reform as a Remedy for Bureaucratic Ills' in Lane, F. S. (ed.), *Current Issues in Public Administration*, New York, St. Martin's Press, 1982, p. 299.
23. Huddleston, M. W., 'The Carter Civil Service Reforms: Some Implications for Political Theory and Public Administration', *Political Science Quarterly*, 96:4 (Winter 1981-2), 617-18.
24. The Commonwealth of Massachusetts, *Report of the Chairman of the Joint Committee on Public Service on H6500*, Boston: Joint Committee on Public Service, 1981, p. 6.
25. The Commonwealth of Massachusetts, *Chapter 767: An Act Providing for Certain Improvements of the Personnel Administration in the Commonwealth*

and its Political Subdivisions, Boston: Office of the Secretary of State, Advance Copy, 1981, Sections, 1, 4, 12, 14, 16 and 24.
26. Ibid., Section 11.
27. Ibid., Section 15.
28. Ibid., Section 10(d).
29. Lynn, N. B., 'The Civil Service Reform Act of 1978' in Hays, S. W. and Kearney, R. C. (eds), *Public Personnel Administration: Problems and Prospects*, Englewood Cliffs, New Jersey, Prentice-Hall, 1982, p. 351.
30. The Commonwealth of Massachusetts, *Chapter 767*, Sections 18, 20 and 14(p).
31. Ibid., Sections 22 and 23.
32. Lynn, op. cit., p. 352.
33. Albrow, M., *Bureaucracy*, London, Macmillan & Co. Ltd., 1970, p. 64.

11 War and human nature

STEVE SMITH

For very obvious reasons, the phenomenon of war has been the major concern of writers on international relations. Not only has war been such a destructive and prevalent feature of international society, it has also been at the centre of attempts to conceptualize and explain the relationship between domestic and international societies. The object of this chapter is to examine the major perspectives from which the occurrence of war has been explained in terms of one aspect of their explanations: their conception of human nature.*

The basic argument of this chapter derives from the rather obvious assumption that attempts to explain why war occurs have, either explicitly or implicitly, a conception of human nature. Having established that some conception of human nature underpins these various perspectives, this chapter will attempt to illustrate the precise nature of these conceptions. The main argument of this chapter is that the major explanations of war have fundamental epistemological problems that derive in essence from their conceptions of human nature.

For the purpose of structuring the discussion, this chapter will analyse the major perspectives from which war can be explained according to the well-known division adopted by Kenneth Waltz in his book, *Man, the State and War.*[1] He argues that in any search for the causes of war, as distinct from the cause of a particular war, one of three levels is used. These three levels are: the nature of individuals, the internal structure of the state, and the structure of the international system. This threefold distinction of the levels from which war can be examined will be extended by introducing specific writers and, more saliently, by linking these levels to the paradigms that have dominated the subject-area of international relations since its development as a separate subject. Hence, the level of the nature of individuals will be linked to realist explanations of international relations, the level of the internal structure of states to Marxist explanations, and the international systems level to idealist explanations.

Realism, individuals and war

The most common explanation of war derives explicitly from a very clear conception of human nature: this is, of course, the view that war results from the essentially selfish nature of human beings. To quote Waltz: 'the focus of the important causes of war is to be found in the nature and behaviour of man. Wars result from selfishness, from misdirected aggressive impulses, from stupidity.'[2] In the literature of international relations this viewpoint has been at the heart of the 'realist' school. Realism arose as a response to the failure of the previous dominant school of thought—idealism—to explain the central features of the international system in the 1930s. Idealism based its interpretations of international relations on the essentially liberal view of the manageability of international problems; individuals were basically good and had been corrupted by the selfish interests of leaderships. The associated prescriptions for ensuring stability and peace, international law and the role of mediation (as enshrined in the League of Nations) were so evidently discredited by events in Manchuria, Abyssinia and, above all, by the nature of German foreign policy in the late 1930s, that realism emerged, claiming to be able to explain these events.

This explanation was based on a very straightforward view of human nature. This is most succinctly outlined in what became the classic text of realism, Hans Morgenthau's *Politics Among Nations*,[3] first published in 1948. Morgenthau starts from the premiss that realism is to be distinguished from idealism since, whereas the latter concentrated on 'the essential goodness and infinite malleability of human nature. . . . The other school believes that the world . . . is the result of forces inherent in human nature.'[4] Specifically, he argues that realism is based on the belief that politics 'is governed by objective laws that have their roots in human nature.'[5] This human nature 'has not changed since the classical philosophies of China, India and Greece endeavoured to discover these laws.'[6] The central feature of this fixed human nature is interest defined in terms of power. As he writes:

> We assume that statesmen think and act in terms of interest defined as power, and the evidence of history bears that assumption out. That assumption allows us to retrace and anticipate, as it were, the steps a statesman—past, present, or future—has taken or will take on the political scene. We look over his shoulder when he writes his dispatches; we listen in on his conversation with other statesmen; we read and anticipate his very thoughts.[7]

This view of human nature enables Morgenthau to distinguish rigidly between the analysis and explanation of international relations, and statements to do with ethics and morality; this is also the central concern of the other major founding father of realism—E. H. Carr, in his work, *The Twenty Years' Crisis*.[8] As such, this view provides the basis for their attacks on idealism; for Morgenthau, 'Realism maintains that universal moral principles cannot be applied to the actions of states in their abstract universal formulation';[9] for Carr, 'The course of events after 1931 clearly revealed the inadequacy of pure aspiration as the basis for a science of international politics.'[10]

Of course, this conception of human nature has been very widely used as a basis for explaining war. Indeed, Waltz, in his book, discusses this view in the context of the work of St. Augustine, Spinoza and Niebuhr.[11] However, it is precisely because Morgenthau's work so clearly altered the direction of the discipline that his views have been outlined here. Furthermore, Morgenthau is so explicit on his conception of human nature:

> It is this ubiquity of the desire for power which, besides and beyond any particular selfishness or other evilness of purpose, constitutes the ubiquity of evil in human action. Here is the element of corruption and of sin which injects even into the best of intentions at least a drop of evil and thus spoils it.[12]

Three points should be made about Morgenthau's view of human nature. The first is that it does allow him to develop a most coherent and elegant theory of international relations, which gives him a very clear answer to the question of why wars occur. It also allows him to propose means for preventing war, through a reliance on the balance of power. Secondly, it must be pointed out that his theory has been very widely accepted in the subject-area; as a recent paper by John Vasquez notes, even the quantitative school of international relations is based on the realist paradigm—he calls this the 'colour it Morgenthau' thesis.[13] Finally, this conception is virtually identical to the dominant view of human nature held by politicians; as Robert Rothstein has argued, realism was

> . . . particularly attractive to an emerging generation of statesmen whose views had been formed as a response to the failure to stop Hitler before it was too late and who were thus predisposed towards a doctrine which would guarantee that the same errors would not be committed against Stalin.[14]

However, despite the coherence and attractiveness of such a view of the causes of war, the fact is that any theory which is based on a view of human nature as evil and selfish has to answer the criticism that this conception is unsubstantiated. If this one claim is removed from realism, then its coherence as a theory of war and international relations vanishes. Morgenthau does not support his claim that human nature is evil and selfish in depth; he merely asserts it as correct.

Basically, there are two major explanations of human aggression located in a fixed conception of human nature: the frustration-aggression approach and the biological-instinctive approach. Each of these explanations locates aggression within a conception of human nature. The frustration-aggression approach argues that aggression occurs because of the existence of frustration. As argued in the classic work of this approach, frustration is 'an interference with the occurrence of an instigated goal-response at its proper time in the behavioural sequence.'[15] Similarly, aggression is defined as a 'sequence of behaviour, the goal-response to which is the injury of the person toward whom it is directed.'[16] The basic argument of this approach is that aggression is a secondary drive induced by frustration; hence aggression presupposes the existence of frustration and therefore frustration leads to aggression. The problem with this approach is simply that it requires one to accept that all aggression is the result of frustration; this poses the question of whether frustration is the necessary and *sufficient* condition for aggression.

The effect of this problem has been largely to discredit the original formulation of the argument. However, writers such as Leonard Berkowitz[17] have attempted to reformulate the approach in the light of this objection. Specifically, Berkowitz introduces the notions of aggression-evoking cues and learning experience, which together significantly water down the determinist relationship between frustration and aggression posited in the original formulation of the approach. Nevertheless, significant problems remain. As Falk and Kim argue:

> The tendency to simplify and reduce the determinants of human aggression into a single cause has resulted in defining 'frustration' in such broad terms as to make the concept almost circular, in which the cause (frustration) and the outcome (aggression) can each be cited as evidence of the other.[18]

Furthermore, they argue that non-frustrating causal variables provide additional explanations of aggression. Finally, they point out that aggression is by no means the only response to frustration.

The dominant explanation of human aggression located in a conception of human nature has been the biological-instinctive approach, as pioneered by Lorenz, Storr and Ardrey,[19] and more recently developed by the sociobiologists, notably Edward Wilson.[20] Its roots, of course, go back to Freud,[21] for whom the inclination towards aggression was an instinctual disposition in human beings; group violence could therefore be seen as a simple extension of the individual death instinct.

Nevertheless, it is Lorenz and Ardrey who provide the most sustained arguments at this level. For Lorenz, aggression is phylogenetically programmed: it is, therefore, instinctive behaviour inherited from our ancestors and essential for adaptation and survival.[22] Being instinctive behaviour it is independent of experience and environment. Lorenz characterizes aggression as a release of the build-up of specific energy in the organism—the hydraulic mechanism—which requires regular discharge. This discharge may require a stimulus, but if none is forthcoming the organism may actively search for a stimulus. This, of course, is one of Lorenz's major claims: 'Following a more or less extensive period of "damming", the entire motor sequence can be performed *without* demonstrable operation of an external stimulus.'[23] Lorenz clearly holds this belief with considerable conviction: 'There cannot be any doubt, in the opinion of any biologically minded scientist, that intraspecific aggression is, in Man, just as much of a spontaneous instinct drive as in most other vertebrates.'[24]

For Lorenz, contemporary human beings suffer from having insufficient outlets for their aggressive desires. Given the problems of overcrowding and overpopulation, this results in large-scale conflict. In animals, Lorenz argues that those species that are harmful to each other (i.e. those with claws and fangs) ritualize conflict and, through the mechanism of the appeasement gesture (as in the well-known case of the wolf exposing its throat), inhibit intra-species conflict. Human beings, though, being harmless to each other in terms of a lack of claws and fangs, have not developed this inhibiting mechanism; therefore, given overcrowding, intra-species conflict will occur. The only solution for Lorenz is the diversion of aggressive impulses through catharsis; hence his, and his followers', concentration on finding outlets for aggressive impulses.

Lorenz's work has become extremely popular, especially in its popularized form (as in Ardrey's work); it has also been subjected to a massive amount of criticism. In a compendious survey of this criticism, Samuel Kim outlines the major problems in Lorenz's argument.[25] At a conceptual level, Kim argues that Lorenz does not adequately define aggression— it is merged with the concept of instinct—so that cause and effect are merged, omitting intent or perception. In terms of the methodology employed, Kim argues that:

Instead of the formulation of operational hypotheses that can be empirically verified, or the development of theses based on evidence, one finds an unrestrained mixture of metaphorical reasoning and dogmatic conviction, a persuasive confusion of analogy and homology, and an unabashed exercise in cross-species extrapolation and long inductive leaps.[26]

This is compounded by Lorenz's reliance on anthropomorphism; hence he consistently talks of animals in human terms and vice versa. This combination results in a set of inductive leaps, both between and within species.

However, the major criticism of Lorenz's work concerns his use of evidence. Kim cites at some length the major criticisms of Lorenz's work on animal aggression and demonstrates that, on the one hand, Lorenz's views on animal aggression are simplistic, and, on the other, that there are numerous problems in moving from statements about contemporary animals to statements about either contemporary human beings or their ancestors. In terms of the evidence on human aggression the fundamental doubt over Lorenz's account comes from the fact that many neurophysiologists reject the instinctive-hydraulic model. Similarly, the concept of territoriality is not supported by examining the behaviour of the nearest primates to humans.

Of most salience to this chapter, though, is the criticism that Lorenz does not distinguish between individual territoriality and group territoriality. Whilst even individual territoriality varies widely according to a host of intervening variables, empirical evidence on the link between overpopulation and war-proneness fails to establish any correlation.[27] Fundamentally, Lorenz's work does not demonstrate that group violence is an innately determined drive. Even at the level of the individual, Kim concludes:

The Lorenzian theory cannot account adequately for human aggression because it is insensitive to the relative importance of different causal variables, such as sex, age, social class and organization, culture, ecological habitat, frustration (deprivation) level, experiential factor, and inherited and/or learned predispositions of individuals.[28]

Attempting to explain the occurrence of war in terms of human nature therefore suffers from massive problems. Given the flaws in Lorenz's work, we can argue that the evidence simply does not support the claim that aggressive behaviour, either in individuals or in groups, is innate. Those who argue that it is have the further problem of explaining why some

individuals and some societies are peaceful. Accepting that genetic endow-
ment sets parameters for human behaviour, it is nevertheless very difficult
to accept that something called human nature, which is specifically
aggressive and self-interested, causes war. As Falk and Kim argue:

> The concept of human nature, which assumes so much uniformity of
> human behaviour in time and place, is hopelessly inadequate in explain-
> ing why some people are so peaceful and others so war prone or why
> the same people are peaceful and violent at different times under
> different situations.[29]

As Corning has noted, there are many causal variables involved in collective violence, and aggression is certainly not a unitary phenomenon.[30] In
the words of Margaret Mead's famous essay, 'Warfare is only an invention
—not a biological necessity.'[31] Indeed, most current research on aggression
is now based on a third theory, that of social-learning, in which aggression
is seen as a learned response to specific environmental stimuli.

For Morgenthau and Lorenz, then, their assumptions concerning human
nature allow them to develop comprehensive theories that explain war.
The fundamental problem, though, is that their claims concerning the
aggressive and selfish character of human nature are simply not supported
by the evidence. This does not detract from the attractiveness of their
a priori theories, but it does significantly detract from those theories'
explanatory power.

The state and war

As Waltz notes,[32] it is this dissatisfaction with theories based on human
nature that has led many writers to argue that war occurs because of the
internal structures of certain states. They argue that human nature is too
simplistic a term to explain why some states are warlike and others are
not. Hence they see specific types of states as causing war. Now this
position has been argued by a very wide variety of thinkers who, in turn,
see certain kinds of states as peaceful and others as warlike. The most
obvious schools of thought are the liberal and the Marxist, although the
recent revival of Islam suggests a further position. Nevertheless, each of
these schools argues that war arises because some states are inherently
aggressive; to be more precise, each argues that if only a certain type of
internal structure for states were universalized, peace would obtain.

Although this approach will be discussed mainly in terms of the Marxist
approach, it is salient to mention the strength of the liberal perspective.
For liberals such as J. S. Mill, Bentham and, more recently, Woodrow

Wilson, universalization of liberal principles of government would produce world peace. This does not mean that human nature would be changed, nor does it imply that international processes and structures would require amendment; rather, it is a direct claim concerning the peace-enducing qualities of specific liberal arrangements. To give the best example, Woodrow Wilson's approach to preventing future wars was based on the peace-enhancing characteristics of democracy (as specified in his fourteen points). At the end of the First World War the dominant conception among liberal thinkers was that having made the world safe *for* democracy, it was now necessary to make the world safe *by* democracy. The establishment of democratic regimes would reduce the dangers of war breaking out since it would prevent states being used for the 'sinister interests' of a dominant minority.

The Marxist viewpoint, to the extent that it is possible to talk of *the* viewpoint, is the clearest example of reasoning at this level of analysis. The essential point for Marx is that international relations can only be understood by reference to the states partaking in these relationships. In other words there can, for a Marxist, exist no separate theory of inter-state relations; the theory is to be developed via an understanding of the constituent actors. The essential underlying factor in Marxism is that human beings are shaped by the environment in which they live, with, in the final case, the determining factor being that of the economic structure of that environment. '(Thus) the first premise of human history', writes Marx, 'is the existence of living human individuals. Thus the first fact to be established is the physical organisation of these individuals.'[33] He develops this by stating that the all-important premiss of human existence is:

> That men must be in a position to live in order to make history . . . The first historical act is thus the production of the means to satisfy the needs, the production of material life itself.[34]

Thus Marx is starting from the statement that the production of the means to support human life—and next to production the exchange of things produced—is the basis of all social structure; that in every society that has appeared in history the manner in which wealth is distributed and society is divided into classes and orders is dependent upon what is produced, how it is produced and how the products are exchanged.

The *ultimately* determining factor in history is therefore the economic structure of society. As Engels wrote:

> More than this neither Marx nor I has ever asserted. Hence if somebody twists this into saying that the economic element is the *only* determining

one he transforms that proposition into a meaningless, abstract, sense-less phrase. The economic situation is the basis, but the various elements of the superstructure . . . also exercise their influence upon the course of the historical struggles.[35]

Given this ultimate determining force, the character of the state reflects the economic forces within it. Hence, Marx and Engels write that,

. . . the ideas of the ruling class are in every epoch the ruling ideas i.e. the class which is the ruling material force of society, is at the same time its ruling intellectual force. . . . Each new class which puts itself in the place of the one ruling before it, is compelled, merely in order to carry through its aim, to represent its interest as the common interest of all the members of society.[36]

The state, for Marx and Engels, is therefore '. . . the state of the most powerful, economically dominant class, which through the medium of the state, becomes also the politically dominant class.'[37]

On the basis of this conception of the state, international relations are determined by the economic forces within states. Thus Marx and Engels write: '. . . The relations of different nations among themselves depend upon the extent to which each has developed its productive forces, the division of labour and internal intercourse.'[38]

Hence, one of the effects of the overthrow of capitalism would be to transform the nature of international relations, not by transforming either human nature or the international system, but by altering the internal structure of the state. Therefore, a world of communist states would be one in which the 'international rule will be peace, because its national ruler will be everywhere the same—Labour.'[39] Since war was the mani-festation of the class struggle on the international level, and as communism would abolish the class struggle, then it follows logically that war would likewise disappear.

Now, common to both the liberal and the Marxist view of the causes of war is a very important conception of human nature: that human beings are essentially formed by their environments. It assumes that if all states were organized along certain specified lines, then war would disappear. This implies two things: first, that human nature would be moulded by 'good' states so as to reduce any incentive for war; second, that the inter-national political system would require no structural modification to ensure peace.

The dominant criticism of this viewpoint has been levelled at the Marxist account of war. Specifically, the major criticism is summed up by Waltz as: 'Is it capitalism or states that must be destroyed in order to get peace, or must both be abolished?'[40] To pose the question the other way: would a world of socialist states be a peaceful world? The usual answer to this question is that in a socialist world both states and capitalism would be abolished, thereby ensuring peace. However, this is a dissatisfying answer in that states were seen by Marx as units of societies during, at least, the transitional phase to communism. Hence, even if they were to disappear in a communist world, why should we accept that the transitional phase, in which states continued to exist, would be peaceful? Furthermore, there is considerable ambiguity in Marx and Engels' work over the nature of the state in communist society (see Engels *On Authority*).[41]

Indeed, Berki claims that 'the very existence of international relations poses a serious, and perhaps intractable, *problem* for Marxism . . . since international relations presuppose the horizontal division of mankind into nations or states.'[42] Since Marxism claims that international relations is a secondary phenomenon, removed from the 'real' causes of conflict, it follows that removing capitalism will remove conflict; yet, Berki argues, separate national identities do exist. Hence, any socialist world would take one of two forms: either it would be one of hegemony, that is the domination of strong nations over weak ones, or it would be one of a community of independent nations, in which case it would be essentially similar to the existing world system.

These criticisms emerge fundamentally from the conception of human nature offered in Marx's account. For Marx, human nature is ultimately determined by productive forces. Now, if human nature is ultimately determined by economic forces, why will a world of socialist states be peaceful, given the economic antagonism inherent in a world of finite resources? Unless we replace the sovereign state system with a world government, and this removes the discussion from this level of analysis to the next, why should we expect fundamental economic conflict to be managed peacefully? Does the achievement of socialism within a state remove the effect of the asymmetrical distribution of resources between states? Clearly it does not. Thus, as a direct consequence of Marx's own view of human nature, we would expect conflict to persist as long as separate states, with separate interests, existed. Of course, this problem is exacerbated by the realization that since human nature is ultimately determined by economic forces, the type of socialism achieved in each state will differ, in that it will be in response to different mixes of productive forces. This is even more problematic since states will become socialist not only at different times but also at different stages of development.

The major difficulty for the Marxist account of war is that human nature is not simply ultimately determined by productive forces. Certainly, if we examine war we find that wars start for a variety of reasons: some, to be sure, are fought for economic reasons, but many are not. Indeed, much of the contemporary work on international conflict reveals the role of systemic processes on war. Hence, war may be the outcome of arms races, status disequilibrium, fears of insecurity, nationalism, religious disagreements, border disputes, etc. It is certainly very difficult to see, for example, Sino-Soviet conflict as essentially economically determined; thus, it may well be more profitable to see war as a systemic phenomenon, determined by great power security rivalry or polar configuration. Added to this, a world of socialist states, with differing definitions of socialism could well exhibit the same features of mistrust and insecurity as characterize contemporary international relations.

Therefore, the Marxist account of war is problematic exactly because of its view of human nature: if it is ultimately determined by economic forces why should these cease to be important in a world of socialist states? If other factors determine human nature, then why will changing two variables, the economic and political systems, remove the other reasons for war? More generally, it is important to note that such evidence as exists does not support the contention that any one type of state is more warlike than others. For these reasons, explaining war at this level of analysis is unsatisfactory because of the conception of human nature supporting it.

The international system and war

Historically, the third level of explaining war, the nature of the international system, has been of significant importance in the discipline. As has already been noted, it is war which so characterizes the distinction between domestic and international society: thus much of the literature in international relations relates to the ways in which order is maintained in international society. Most texts start from the premiss that international and domestic societies are fundamentally different, and that war is the most notable example of this distinction. Put simply, the lack of a government above states and the consequent absence of enforceable law are seen as the reasons why war, as a phenomenon, occurs.

Indeed, that is the conclusion of Waltz's analysis. In his memorable words, 'wars occur because there is nothing to prevent them.'[43] Paradoxically, although this view dominates the discipline it may be the conclusion of rather different analyses. These reflect two very different conceptions of human nature.

The first is the view of human nature held by the idealist school of thought. This school, which dominated the discipline from around the end of the First World War to the outbreak of the Second, believed that, above all, war was the result of misperception and misunderstanding. In the classical liberal vein, the view was that if only international society could be so changed as to build in some mechanisms for ensuring mediation and conciliation, then war would be prevented; hence, the idealists' faith in the League of Nations. By building in to the system a set of structures and processes that would allow 'rational' discussion to occur, it would be possible to allow the essentially 'good' nature of human beings to flourish. This perspective, based on the then dominant conceptions of why the First World War had occurred, clearly has a very specific view of human nature: it is essentially 'good', requiring only the establishment of appropriate mechanisms to enable it to be manifested. War occurred not because of, but despite, human nature; remove the requirement for hasty action, allow misperceptions to be transcended, and human nature would ensure peace. That this viewpoint was so cataclysmically discredited by the way in which the Second World War occurred is ample indication of its fundamental weakness. Just as assuming human nature to be selfish presents serious problems, so does assuming it to be inherently good. To believe that war occurs only because of misperception is simply incorrect. There are numerous examples of aggression being undertaken by states with a very clear conception of what is at stake. This does not mean that wars do not occur because of misperception; it does mean that not all wars do. The evidence, therefore, clearly indicates that as mediation and conciliation have failed to prevent war, this view of human nature is simply untenable. Of course, the viewpoint can be salvaged by a theory of real interests but this involves well-known epistemological pitfalls.

The second conception of human nature at this level is that reflected in the calls for world government. Indeed, this has been the dominant prescription for avoiding war. The argument is simply that war can be prevented only by world government; this world government would impose the same structure on international society as exists in domestic society, namely, enforceable law and rule-making. In the words of Rousseau, the way to prevent war 'is to be found only in such a form of federal government as shall unite nations by bonds similar to those which already unite their individual members, and place the one no less than the other under the authority of the law.'[44] As war results from international anarchy, it can be abolished only by abolishing this anarchy. The analogy with domestic society suggests the conception of human nature involved in this argument: it is that human nature is selfish and therefore requires control by a body above the individual and, in turn, the state.

The fundamental problem with this viewpoint is that its prescription is only true by definition; whereas the idealist's prescription is aimed at abolishing war, this perspective would only abolish war in name. Since war is defined as conflict between sovereign states, then transcending state sovereignty by establishing world government would abolish war in name only. Since this perspective is based on a view of human nature as selfish, why should we believe that a world government would remove the reasons for conflict? This conflict would take the form of civil war within the world state rather than war between sovereign states. It is, therefore, only true by definition that establishing a world government would remove war. The tautological nature of this argument is entailed in its conception of human nature.

Although Waltz is very explicit in discussing the connections between the three levels of explaining war,[45] he nevertheless concludes that the third level is essential in any explanation of the causes of war. The important point, though, is that the third level cannot deal with the causes of war; it can really only describe the framework within which war occurs.

Conclusion

This chapter has examined three levels at which explanations are offered for the causes of war. Each level has been shown to involve certain conceptions of human nature. It has been argued that, in each case, it is this conception of human nature that ultimately undermines the prescriptions offered for avoiding war. On the one hand, those explanations of the causes of war that involve an explicit conception of human nature turn out to be inconsistent with the evidence. On the other hand, most explanations involve a conception of human nature at a secondary, implicit level; this conception has to be inferred from the statements about war. However, this conception, without exception, then turns out to reduce the coherence of the prescriptions for eliminating war by containing elements that suggest that the motives for conflict will still remain.

What is central to the argument of this chapter is that these theories of the causes of war, which have been very popular in the literature, are ultimately eroded in their explanatory power because of their conceptions of human nature. Thus, whilst it is common to see the work of Morgenthau and Lorenz attacked because of their explicit theories of human nature, it is less common to see the second, and especially the third, levels attacked for this reason; obviously this is because neither level has to rely upon an explicit conception of human nature. Hence we see that at each of these levels, very different conceptions of human nature may be involved—liberal/Marxist at the second level, idealist/Hobbesian at the third. Yet it is essential to realize that these levels also fail to establish a coherent theory of the causes of war because their implicit conceptions of human nature are inconsistent with their prescriptions. As has been noted previously, this is especially so with regard to the third level, where the explanatory power of the Waltzian perspective is a commonplace in the literature.

All this, of course, raises one fundamental question: can we construct a coherent theory of the causes of war with an explicit conception of human nature? To answer this, it is necessary to distinguish between three uses of the term 'human nature': the first means simply behaviour as revealing something about human nature; the second uses human nature to talk of a human essence, that is, something intrinsic to being human; the third concerns a viewpoint on how human nature is determined. Now, the explanations that have been examined in this chapter tend to fall in the first two categories. For this reason, it is argued that attention should be concentrated on specifying the parameter of the third level, that is stating explicitly the conception of human nature that is adopted for the purposes of constructing an explanation.

An alternative to this method is that of Singer's Correlates of War project.[46] In this project, Singer and his associates have spent some twenty years examining the correlations obtaining between the occurrence of war and a vast array of structural characteristics. The problem, of course, is that no theory is utilized for examining these relationships; it is hoped that theory will emerge from the results of the correlations. Singer has been very strongly attacked for this methodology,[47] but claims that no viable theory exists. Whilst the perils of induction seriously reduce the likelihood of any theory emerging from this project, the results it has produced can provide the basis for the development of explanatory analysis. That this has not yet happened clearly reflects the difficulties involved in this mode of theorizing.

To return to the question of whether it is possible to create a theory of the causes of war with an explicit conception of human nature, it is necessary to respond with a two-part answer. Of course, it is possible in principle to do so, but this is much more likely to be successful if the third use of the term is employed. This would require consideration of the long-standing debate in social science about Free Will and Determinism; it is by the examination of this relationship that a coherent view of how human nature is to be conceptualized can emerge. Such a view, by seeing behaviour as determined by structural forces mediated through images and belief systems, could then serve as the basis for an examination of why war occurs. By combining empirical work on the sources of individual aggression —as in social-learning theory—with the work on the structural factors influencing the level of war (the concept of polarity is an example), it might be possible to explain why war occurs. What is clear is that the theories examined in this paper ultimately fail to provide a coherent explanation directly because of their explicit or implicit reliance on a specific conception of human nature. Abandoning a fixed conception of human nature, as involved in either of the first two uses discussed above, may well be the best starting-point for probing the age-old question of why war occurs.

*   I would like to thank Bob Berki and Mort Schoolman for their comments and help on an earlier draft of this Chapter.

Notes

1. Waltz, K., *Man, the State and War*, New York, Columbia University Press, 1959.
2. Ibid., p. 16.
3. Morgenthau, H., *Politics Among Nations*, Fifth Edition (revised), New York, Knopf, 1978, pp. 3–15.
4. Ibid., p. 3.
5. Ibid., p. 4.
6. Ibid.
7. Ibid., p. 5.
8. Carr, E. H., *The Twenty Years' Crisis*, London, Macmillan, 1939.
9. Morgenthau, op. cit., p. 10.
10. Carr, op. cit., p. 9.
11. Waltz, op. cit., pp. 16–41.
12. Morgenthau, H., *Scientific Man Versus Power Politics*, Chicago, University of Chicago Press, 1946, pp. 194–5.
13. Vasquez, J., 'Colouring it Morgenthau: new evidence for an old thesis on quantitative international politics', *British Journal of International Studies*, Vol. 5 (3), 1979, 210–28.
14. Rothstein, R., 'On the costs of realism', *Political Science Quarterly*, Vol. 87 (3), 1972, 351.
15. Dollard, J., et al., *Frustration and Aggression*, New Haven, Yale, 1939, p. 7.
16. Ibid., p. 9.
17. Berkowitz, L., *Aggression: A Social Psychological Analysis*, New York, McGraw-Hill, 1962.
18. Falk, R., and Kim, S., *The War System: An Interdisciplinary Approach*, Boulder Co., Westview, 1980, p. 79.
19. See Lorenz, K., *On Aggression*, New York, Harcourt, Brace & World Inc., 1966; Storr, A., *Human Aggression*, New York, Bantam, 1970; Ardrey, R., *The Territorial Imperative*, New York, Atheneum, 1966.
20. Wilson, E., *Sociobiology: The New Synthesis*, Cambridge, Mass., Harvard, 1975; and *On Human Nature*, Cambridge, Mass., Harvard, 1978.

21. Freud, S., 'Why War?' in Bramson, S., and Geothals, G., *War*, New York, Basic Books, 1968, pp. 71-80.
22. This summary of the work of Lorenz is based upon the excellent one in Kim, S., 'The Lorenzian theory of aggression and peace research', reprinted in Falk and Kim, op. cit., pp. 82-115.
23. Quoted ibid., p. 85.
24. Quoted ibid.
25. Kim, op. cit.
26. Ibid., p. 90.
27. Ibid., p. 102.
28. Ibid., p. 103.
29. Falk and Kim, op. cit., p. 78.
30. Corning, P., 'Human Violence: Some causes and implications' in Beitz, C., and Herman, T. (eds), *Peace and War*, San Francisco, Freeman, 1973, pp. 119-43.
31. Mead, M., 'Warfare is only an invention—not a biological necessity', *Asia*, Vol. 40, 1940, 402-5.
32. Waltz, op. cit., pp. 80-1.
33. Marx, K., and Engels, F., *The German Ideology*, London, Lawrence & Wishart, 1970, p. 42.
34. Ibid., p. 48.
35. Engels, F., 'Letter to Joseph Bloch', in Feuer, L., *Marx and Engels: Basic Writings*, London, Fontana, 1969, pp. 436-7.
36. Marx and Engels, *The German Ideology*, op. cit., pp. 64-6.
37. Engels, F., 'Origins of the family, private property and the state', in Feuer, op. cit., p. 431.
38. Marx and Engels, *The German Ideology*, op. cit., p. 43.
39. Marx, speaking at General Council of the First International 1870-1871, cited in *Minutes*, Moscow, 1967, p. 328.
40. Waltz, op. cit., p. 127.
41. Engels, F., 'On Authority', *Selected Works Vol. 2*, Moscow, 1973, pp. 376-9.
42. Berki, R., 'On marxian thought and the problem of international relations', *World Politics*, Vol. 24, 1971, 80.
43. Waltz, op. cit., p. 232.
44. Quoted ibid., p. 185.
45. Ibid., chapter 8.
46. For an overview, see Singer, J. D., *The Correlates of War Volumes I and II*, New York, Free Press, 1979 and 1980.
47. See Hoole, F. W., and Zinnes, D., *Quantitative International Politics*, New York, Praeger, 1976, chapters 2-6.

12 Conclusion

IAN FORBES

Ultimately, this volume does not provide any definitive answers to the question 'What is human nature?'. But to phrase the question in this manner is, in an important sense, misleading. Certainly, a common problem is the absence of a framework necessary both for productive enquiry into human nature and the ordering and comprehension of the results of that enquiry. This has led some, in a confused way, to suppose that *human nature* is nebulous, the study of it artificial, and any conclusions irrelevant. What the preceding chapters have shown, in a variety of ways, is that such a view is mistaken, and why. On the one hand, contributions are made to an image of human nature, but such an image emerges only fitfully and partially (and always in the context of the requirements and possibilities inherent in the particular study). However, these chapters tell us more about what we are *not*, than they ascribe positive or negative features to our nature. On the other hand, they amply demonstrate the extent to which beliefs and assumptions about human nature already permeate and affect thought and action of all types, and on all levels. It is in this sense that human nature must exercise the minds of political analysts. Even without being able to ask the empirical question of what human nature is, and without knowing the 'real' nature of men and women, the central focus of this volume is on a second question, namely, the role of existing views of human nature.

Indeed, this is the hard core to the analysis of politics and human nature. As Nietzsche argued, the truth of a belief is much less important than the impact of its use in human society. This is clear in many places throughout the volume, where very similar beliefs about human nature serve quite different purposes for different thinkers and political programmes and movements. Nor is it always possible simply to infer, conversely, that similar sets of political ideals and goals must rest upon comparable assumptions about men and women. As such, our principal concern must be with the concept, not the content, of human nature, and its relation to political thought and practice. In his Introduction, Steve Smith sets out six key aspects of an examination of the concept of human nature, such that the status of the various models detailed in this volume only partly rests upon their descriptive merit, and greatly depends upon logical coherence in the use of evidence and argument. This reflects two complementary beliefs on the part of the editors: first, that human nature is not so much an empirical question as a problem which deserves articulation and analysis in political thought and practice; second, that the current uses of the concepts of human nature lack rigour. It is used implicitly, or as a convenience, when it ought to be a carefully utilized theoretical tool.

Such issues are addressed by Graeme Duncan, whose chapter establishes that the study of human nature is something that involves research into politics specifically and social science generally. That is, we constantly seek explanations for, and an understanding of, human activity and motivation, and attempt to delineate the parameters within which they are manifested. But this generalized commitment and involvement, while not random in its resultant insights, produces no straightforward or cumulative addition to our knowledge of human nature. Even more problematic is the transformation of that knowledge, or interpretation, into policy that actually employs a better understanding of ourselves and society. Clearly, these are difficulties that are elemental to political theory and practice.

In the first place, it is essential to recognize that the use of assumptions about men and women does not necessarily imply a weakness in the construction of theoretical method. Only when such assumptions are gratuitous, or unconnected with an analytical and explanatory framework, is the appeal to human nature simply a matter of preference, prejudice or convenience. The demand, then, must be for an account of human nature which is consistent with the other aspects of the political theory in question. Such an account must be able to contribute to the critical work of the theory, but must also be able to become the subject of that same critical process. What we require from a theory of society—a complex, interactive critique, model of the future, and theory of change—has also to be provided with respect to human nature. In other words, a *theory* of human nature must be constructed in order to move beyond *a priori* argument, and into the uncertain realms of evidence, proofs and logical choice between competing models and explanations.

Duncan makes his choice, but not always the basis for it, quite clear. For him, the candidates are roughly divided into those that are either radical or conservative or, more accurately, those that support an expansion of the expressive capacity of human beings in society, and those that tend to constrain and channel human propensities, and he prefers the radical models because they incorporate, on a practical level, appropriate values. Above all, he values freedom, even though he remains aware of the accompanying dangers and uncertainties that will arise, not as a result of our make-up, but from the possibilities of the social environment we construct and seek to control. In a clear way, then, Duncan's theory of human nature sustains and augments his view of society. As he sees it, political theory and human nature will always be thus intertwined and, equally, will be speculative, in the sense that 'testing' the validity of claims about human nature cannot be done in isolation from that other, and perhaps more important, aim, which is social change.

In the first of the chapters on specific thinkers and traditions, Forbes takes a fresh look at the conception of human nature implicit in Marx's thought. Forbes maintains that the assumptions about men and women employed by Marx did have a formative role in his theory as a whole, and that he created the means to generate a theory of human nature consistent with historical materialism. The connections between politics and human nature lie in the discussion of two human natures, a distinction made in several of the chapters. The first, and fundamental, nature is in terms of a universalistic abstraction (but not an abstract universalization), and the second is the historically mediated form of that nature. Of interest is the way that particular modes of production lead to particular expressions of our fundamental nature, and at issue is the concept of malleability, which is central to any political theory promising or offering widespread social change. Through an analysis of capitalist human nature, Forbes reaches two main conclusions, which reflect the need to include the individual as a category in radical social theory and his dissatisfaction with class-based politics and theories of change. Principally, he argues that the link between our fundamental nature and the dominant mode of production can produce forces for progressive social change. Second, and on a practical level, he sees such a possibility reflected in the emergence of non-class activism and the development of new forms and definitions of politics, all of which, nevertheless, are antagonistic to advanced capitalism and may anticipate the potentialities of a future, socialist society.

Paul Smart shows J. S. Mill to be one of the pioneers of a serious and self-confessed concern with the content and structure of human nature. Mill understood that any political and social theory emphasizing utilitarian social engineering must be equally clear about the human raw material it seeks to manipulate and improve. Mill's attempt to construct a *science* of human nature reflects his commitment not only to this idea, but also to the need for an analysis which conforms to the standards and practices of a scientific analysis of society. The product of his study was a working model of human nature of interesting but distinctly Enlightenment proportions, as one would expect. At the same time, however, Mill raised and tackled issues that remain contentious and problematic, and made some critical observations that bear further review. Much hinges on his perception that many thinkers had erroneously equated present experience with universal validity. Quite rightly, he also rejected the *a priori* approach of the English Romantics, but in the grey area between environmentalism and metaphysics Mill found it very difficult to erect a theoretical landscape of sufficiently materialist dimension. In the end, he had to settle for an uneasy combination of liberal values, casual laws of the mind, and the ultimately determining influence of the social environment. And, as Smart points out, even this formulation proved inadequate. In a sense, then, Mill's scientific study, conducted over many years, is a dismal failure, but, on the other hand, is ameliorated by his conception of, and commitment to, science, regardless of the difficulties it presented.

In clear contradiction of this view, the science of human nature may be thought a specious notion since, as Christopher Berry argues, conservatism purports to incorporate all the relevant knowledge that is needed. Much less a political view of society and humanity, conservatism gains its form and strength from an account of *naturalness*. Crucially, society is natural, but not in the Marxist sense that we are, by nature, social beings. Rather, what naturally happens to all individual humans is acculturation within a continuing social milieu. In his discussion of the themes of universality, acculturation and continuity, Berry shows how the conservative approach makes the connection between the fixed datum of social experience and the necessary features of the nature of humankind. Two things stand out in this account. First, the emphasis on language and the family makes the distinctions between politics and human nature on the one hand, and between politics and society on the other, seem artificial and unhelpful. Second, Berry demonstrates why continuity is so vital to conservatism. Here there are interesting parallels to be drawn with the Marxist account. Unlike liberals, both conservatives and Marxists have a clear understanding of the importance of history. As Forbes pointed out with Marx, so does Berry make plain that conservatives are aware of the difference between a universal abstraction and human nature *as it is expressed* under given conditions. They diverge markedly, however, with respect to the use they make of this insight. Conservatism wishes to preserve the formative elements of our second nature: social change is certainly necessary, but must always be achieved in the context of the dependence on social givens, not by their swift and crass rejection, which would be against nature and, therefore, impolitic.

Utopianism is the boldest of all doctrines concerning human nature. The linchpin, as William Stafford argues, is the dedication to the idea of the malleability of humankind, making conceivable the generation of a harmonious and happy social life. Owen's assertions are based on two premisses. He focuses entirely on the life that individual men and women experience and, as a result, is not able to establish universality sufficiently. Second, and more positively, he makes an important distinction between human nature and character. Malleability refers to character, such that a society constructed on the basis of an underlying and unchanging humanity is a possibility. However, as Stafford demonstrates, Owen's psychology may just be plausible, but cannot sustain his commitment to social equality. On the other hand, Godwin's acceptance of malleability is tempered by his refusal to relinquish character formation entirely to determination by the environment. His view reflects a greater awareness of philosophical arguments: he accepts that traits in human nature affect our ultimate character. Yet this ensures that there is, if anything, even less autonomy than Owen envisaged, and perhaps more moral imperatives— unusual for a thinker interested in the science of the mind, as Mill was soon to be. With B. F. Skinner we see a Utopianism of a totally different order. Here, malleability of human nature, not simply character, is at issue, and behavioural engineering is the appropriate manipulation of the environment, co-ordinating and employing the force of some traits to overcome others. Moreover, Skinner does have a science with which he feels confident, even though his moral views are not always at one with that science. There is good and bad in nature, but this is not to be discussed, only controlled. Utopianism is, *par excellence*, human nature *without* politics, and thus very different from conservatism, which sees politics as a tedious but minor necessity, or liberal and radical views, for which politics is a direct and vital result of the nature of humankind.

Vincent Geoghegan also deals with three major thinkers, representing this time the Frankfurt School. In a sense, their enterprise is as bold as that of the Utopians and, significantly, this chapter comes at the end of the first half of the book, to which point we have concentrated on the major traditions in political theory. Critical Theory marks the end of such neat divisions, in several ways. First, the Frankfurt School tried to come to terms with the new and sometimes alarming developments in the first part of this century, and in so doing widened significantly the scope of political theorizing. Second, Critical Theory signals the first modern attempt to synthesize theoretical accounts of human nature in society and the consideration of specific social issues from the perspective of the detail of human nature. Their contribution made it not only possible but imperative for political thought to interest itself with both levels, and the format of this volume seeks to reflect that development.

Horkheimer gave Marx's materialist method its most controversial task —the construction and examination of human nature under given historical conditions, a project that finds its echo in Forbes's chapter. However, as Geoghegan demonstrates, Horkheimer's attempt to establish human nature as a force for social change is only partially successful. Although he avoided the errors of Fourier and Owen, and recast our understanding of the family, his predictions have proved to be inaccurate, thereby underlining the complexity of the relationships between human nature, politics and society. Adorno, too, was concerned with the individual, and this emphasis, along with the dramatic integration of Freudian thought, should be set against the psychologism Stafford identified in Utopian thought. With Critical Theory, psychology became part of the *social* explanation of human nature. As such, Adorno saw the need to revise completely the framework of sociological analysis, such that it could properly deal with the individual as a psychological as well as a sociological entity, thus stressing the need for explanations that considered both planes of experience. Marcuse, along with Fromm, also drew inspiration from the work of Freud. Liberation is the key concept here, and it underpins a much more positive conception of the role of human nature, as well as its substance and content. This led Marcuse to apprehend the revolutionary nature of the women's movement, thus avoiding some of the interpretative mistakes that are detailed in Levitas's chapter. Above all, Marcuse recognized that the transition to socialism had to be psychologically, as much as it was structurally, plausible, and that this required a better understanding of human nature. Taken together, the Frankfurt School is most remarkable not for its achievements, but in that the Critical Theorists remained undaunted by the difficulty of theorizing about human nature, and that they made serious attempts to glean some practical sense out of the transitory elements within it.

It is fitting that a chapter on psychoanalysis heads the second group of contributions, since the information about human nature it entails and its implications for political theory and practice have an outstanding importance. Psychoanalytic theory stands at the forefront of modern attempts to establish the nature of men and women, principally because it deals exclusively with human beings. As Michael Nicholson points out, this theory not only offers an image of the form and content of human nature, but also incorporates the means to establish the validity or otherwise of those claims. However, if any credence is to be attached to the view of human nature provided by that theory, then we must first be concerned with the status of that theory. Nicholson concludes that psychoanalytic theory is indeed a scientific research programme in good standing. It meets methodological objections and produces useful results, thereby establishing not only that the pursuit of that theory is a valid exercise, but that human nature is tangible enough to be explored. One of the most telling findings is of great political importance. Aggressiveness, the drive to commit violence, presents itself as a basic propensity in human social action, one of the ramifications of which Smith explores in his chapter on war. However, the identification of such a drive is not necessarily connected to any solutions of psychoanalytic dimension. Thus, in reflection of one of the central themes of the volume, Nicholson concludes that, while psychoanalytic theory may lead to a better understanding of an improvable human nature, the application of that knowledge must always be the domain of politics.

Ruth Levitas's discussion of feminism and human nature deals with one of the clearest possible cases of the political uses of concepts of human nature. She shows the connections between any view of female nature and political and social policies to be direct and manifest. However, the repudiation of the models of human nature employed to subjugate women is the high point of feminist agreement on this issue. It is instructive to note that, within feminism, Levitas finds the same mix of arguments and assumptions canvassed in other chapters. Nevertheless, one underlying point becomes clear. The women's movement has shown, theoretically as well as practically, that the distinction between first and second natures is a crucial one. In other words, our fundamental nature, which can never be rigorously defined, can be conceptualized to incorporate uncertainty, along with specific characteristics such as biological differences between the sexes. Our second nature, however, is a *social* product, and reflects the impact of structures, choices and beliefs. Differences that exist between the status, position and ability of women and men, therefore, have to be understood as *gender* differences, where gender is a socially constructed category that has no relation to fundamental human nature. It is worth interpolating here that the same argument would hold for another issue not covered by this volume, namely, racism. Political differentiation and discrimination, then, cannot be in terms of human nature. However, as Levitas points out, while feminism establishes the centrality of the social mediation of human nature, it has yet, collectively or in individual expression, to accomplish a more detailed and integrated account of the interplay of nature and culture.

Even when dealing with competing and contradictory notions of work, the chapter by John Street shows that each of them is inextricably bound up with assumptions that relate to human motivations, needs or potentialities. A careful analysis of the details of that connection within the dominant models of work, however, highlights important inadequacies in those accounts. Freedom, also, is a central element in these models, but is only implicitly regarded as a basic human need. Street uses sociological and historical evidence to establish the importance, the meaning and the value of work. Work is at once a means of social definition and self-understanding, a universal yet complex human need (i.e. not related merely to survival), and a realm of human activity which encompasses choice and positive and negative freedom. These three perspectives demonstrate the centrality of our concern with human nature, and provide also the framework within which opposing views of work can be assessed. Instrumentalism opts for the conclusion that humans always seek freedom from work. Marx, on the other hand, acknowledges the possibility and existence of instrumental work, but insists that the full creative potential of human labour can only emerge under communal ownership of the means of production. However, the value of work, and the entailed discussion of freedom, presents difficulties for Marx's view, because it is at times implied that human nature is best described in terms of creative individuality, thereby undermining the communist ideal of scientific freedom, of work as self-control. This leads Street to prefer the expressive view of work, where work is consistent with our fundamental nature, just as it is a crucial component of the free *expression* of that nature. Finally, since the actual organization of work is always at issue, the expressive view makes the connection between work and human nature a directly political issue.

In their chapter on bureaucracy, Jeffrey Sedgwick and George Sulzner probe an aspect of the American response to the issue of politics and human nature. Here, bureaucratic organization is treated as an exemplar of the connection between a theoretical conception of human nature and its ultimate representation in the practical politics of the modern industrial state. We see, first, how Weber's view of human nature underpins his approach to bureaucratic theory and practice, and second, how Woodrow Wilson was influenced by him to such an extent that he changed the direction of policy on civil service reforms quite dramatically. Bureaucracy, the authors argue, must be seen as subordinate to a politics *of* human nature. Against the *realpolitick* of power and authority is set the commitment to creativity and autonomy, a clear echo of the expressivist view of work and human nature endorsed by Street. Accountability, then, is a solution which must be crafted in law both to achieve organizational rationality and efficiency and to enhance individual initiative and choice.

Organizational theory, therefore, always has an underlying context: as Sedgwick and Sulzner point out, it is alternative models of human nature that are fundamentally at issue, and the choice between them is of enduring political importance.

War is the subject of the last of the chapters concerned with specific issues, and Steve Smith shows that explanations for its occurrence depend fundamentally on a wide variety of conceptions of human nature. This is of more than a little political, and not merely academic, importance, since Smith establishes that there is a direct connection between assumptions about men and women and proposals for the prevention of war. The chapter focuses on the three perspectives which dominate the discipline, drawing out the relevant assumptions and subjecting them to critical scrutiny. The first, realist, perspective has a clear but simplistic view of a human nature dominated by selfish and aggressive drives, behaviourally mediated in the pursuit and exercise of power. However, this explanation of war rests upon *a priori* assumptions which cannot be validated, and has led to the second kind of approach, which concentrates on the internal structures of states, in the belief that some types are inherently aggressive. The liberal solutions call for the extension of democratic government, but the dominant environmental perspective remains the marxist approach. The view of human nature adduced here is that of economic determinism, such that a change in the structure of states would mean an end to exploitative class domination internally, and a cessation of international class struggle.

For Smith, as for Forbes, this is a glib environmentalism, such that this version of Marx's view of human nature proves not to be the solution to war, and actually undermines the entire approach to international relations. The third major perspective seeks to make the international system correspond to domestic society: war is in some ways an aberration which can be prevented. The solutions are as different as the conceptions of human nature from which they spring. Smith demonstrates, however, that neither the liberal nor the conservative account is capable of sustaining an adequate explanation of the causes of war, just as their solutions prove incorrect and vacuous, reflecting, in the end, on the views of human nature they employ. What this particular chapter establishes is that a *fixed* conception of human nature is usually mistaken, and always problematic, and that future research much consciously conjoin the study of human nature and the study of international relations.

This volume, then, clearly illustrates the indeterminancy of human nature, and the difficulty of assessing and theorizing about it. Indeed, the search for a human essence is problematic in two respects. First, it is not directly accessible, at least with the tools available to the political analyst. This makes it even more imperative for political analysts to be aware of the existence, and role, of assumptions about our fundamental, or first, nature. Second, universalistic assumptions about men and women are discrete entities, quite separate from discussion of the dynamic character of politics and society. The best example of this is provided in Nicholson's chapter. Although psychoanalytic theory produces an important finding concerning our fundamental nature, that theory is quite incapable of dictating the manner in which that knowledge ought to be used. Thus the realm of politics is not primarily to do with the *discovery* of human nature, but the adequacy of the various theories, and the effects and means of their implementation.

Having established the difficulties encountered when dealing with our first and unalloyed nature, this volume also demonstrates that there is another level of analysis. Here, attention is concentrated on a *second*, or mediated, concept of human nature, which views qualities of human nature always in the context of historical and social circumstances. Conceived in this way, human nature is of major political concern, because that nature is no longer abstracted from the political and social realities within which it is expressed. Whatever our basic nature, it can consist only of capacities and powers which emerge and have influence within our social selves. No theory of society, then, can hope to cling to one, fixed view of human nature. In the short term, such an approach can facilitate attempts to change society, to achieve humanly social goals like freedom, justice and perhaps a notion of equality, because assumptive base and ultimate aims are made clear. However, such change, were it to occur, would only highlight the transitory nature of these very elements. Other goals, or the same goals differently understood, would then be at issue, just as the view of human nature would be changed, in some ways more open, but in others more circumscribed. In this sense, political analysis needs to focus on the ways in which various theories of human nature are linked to prescriptions concerning society: above all, the crucial issues become the links between theory and evidence, and theory and prescription.

In politics, then, the search for an adequate account of human nature is not principally a question of ultimate truth or knowledge. Instead, it concerns an understanding that can be used in connection with specific social circumstances. Since the construction of this second nature involves the interplay of social forces and structures with our fundamental nature, we are entitled to be at once demanding of, and sympathetic to, the enormous variety of models of human nature. Several things must be demanded of an appeal to human nature. It should enable us to assess the grounds of that appeal, as well as the substance of the crucial assumptions themselves, such that the associated prescriptions and political implications can also be judged. Further, no assumption should only be a disguise for a prejudice, an ideal, a prescription or a justification. Nevertheless, we should be sympathetic to approaches that make a serious attempt to come to terms with human nature, whether they utilize new scientific insight or just fresh thinking. While positive results are not always forthcoming, and the beneficial effects of such study are by no means inevitable, the impetus to advance and enrich our understanding is worth maintaining.

The contributions of this volume also establish that it is vital to treat human nature as a political issue. Since human nature cannot be abstracted from the social and political environment, any account which does not incorporate the mediating links with social meaning and consequences is at best simplistic, and may prove politically persuasive but socially destructive. Sociobiology, for example, fails on two counts from this perspective. First, it assumes that human society is the same as animal society, making connections and drawing conclusions not just across species boundaries, but between behavioural bases that defy comparison. Second, it is also assumed that scientific discovery can be applied mechanically in human society, without taking into account the possibility that other human predispositions might dictate that certain aspects of our fundamental nature will be of secondary rather than primary significance. Taken together, this means that sociobiology cannot claim to be dealing with human nature *in society*, and thus cannot be applied in any straightforward fashion. On a general level, it is important to note that science, therefore, offers an approach to human nature that is no more intrinsically productive for political analysis than the speculative and metaphysical alternatives. They must be placed and constructed both in the context of political category and examination, and in a framework of evidence and testing. It might be difficult to relinquish the convenience of human nature as an independent variable in social scientific research, but this must be done in order to achieve results that are relevant.

Human nature is also political in a much more direct sense. Throughout the volume, certain views of human nature find constant reiteration and application. These competing, and ostensibly commonsensical, views are chiefly sustained and purveyed by the dominant political ideologies of our day. Yet such views—of selfish and apolitical humans, or of the free individual, or of the communal being—are all inaccurate by virtue of their partiality: indeed, their reproduction by modern societies is one of the chief obstacles to a better understanding of human nature. Thus, the pre-eminent problem for the political analyst is not simply that human nature is notoriously difficult to discern and define. Rather, it is that the commonsensical view of human nature constitutes a misleading shorthand which militates against our putting into effect even those few things we do already know about human nature. As long as this is the case, human nature is political, and politics has a task and responsibility to change this, both theoretically and practically. In a theoretical sense, this means that models of human nature, and their role within a theory, must be made explicit, and attention given to their adequacy, in terms of viability and evidential status. For practical politics, the connections between structures and human nature must always be recognized and explored, such that social change can be assessed, or even suggested.

Contributors

Christopher J. Berry is lecturer in the Department of Politics at the University of Glasgow. He has also taught at the University of Pittsburgh and at the College of William and Mary, Williamsburg. His publications include *Hume, Hegel and Human Nature* (Martinus Nijhoff, 1983) and numerous articles in intellectual history and political theory. His current research interests include an examination of differing concepts of Man in the Western experience.

Graeme Duncan is Professor of Politics at the University of East Anglia. He has previously taught at the Universities of Monash and Adelaide. His publications include *Marx and Mill* (Cambridge University Press, 1973), *Critical Essays in Australian Politics* (Edward Arnold, 1979), and numerous articles in political theory. His research interests include democratic theory, Australian socialism, and the politics of human nature. He is currently working on a book on democratic theory, and a study of the Australian Labour Party.

Ian Forbes is a postgraduate in the Politics Sector at the University of East Anglia. He has previously taught at Adelaide University and the University of East Anglia. His research interests include democratic theory, Marxism, theories of human nature and the thought of Friedrich Nietzsche.

Vincent Geoghegan is lecturer in Political Science at The Queen's University of Belfast. He has previously taught at the University of East Anglia. His publications include *Reason and Eros: The Social Theory of Herbert Marcuse* (Pluto, 1981), His research interests are The Frankfurt School, Socialism, and Irish Political Thought.

Ruth Levitas is lecturer in Sociology at the University of Bristol. She has previously taught at Huddersfield Polytechnic. Her publications include various articles on Utopianism and social movements. Her main research interests are in ideology and Utopian thought.

Michael Nicholson is Visiting Professor of Social Sciences at Carleton University, Ottowa. He has previously taught at various universities in Britain and the United States, and was Director of the Richardson Institute for Conflict and Peace Research from 1970-82. His publications include *Oligopoly and Conflict: a Dynamic Approach* (Liverpool University Press, 1972), *Conflict Analysis* (English Universities Press, 1971), and *The Scientific Analysis of Social Behaviour* (Frances Pinter, 1983), along with numerous articles in theoretical economics and international relations. His primary research interest is in the social scientific analysis of the causes of war.

Jeffrey Leigh Sedgwick is Assistant Professor of Political Science at the University of Massachusetts at Amherst. He has previously taught at the University of Virginia. His publications include *Deterring Criminals: Policymaking and the American Political Traditons*, and contributions to books on policy implementation and American federalism. His current research interests are in American federalism and criminal justice policy.

Paul Smart is a postgraduate in the Department of Politics, University of Keele. He is currently working on a comparative study of the political and ethical thought of J. S. Mill and Karl Marx.

Steve Smith is lecturer in Politics at the University of East Anglia. He has previously taught at Huddersfield Polytechnic and the State University of New York at Albany. His publications include *Foreign Policy Adaptation* (Gower, 1981) and a number of articles on foreign policy analysis and nuclear strategy. His current research interests concern the American hostages in Iran, foreign policy implementation, and aspects of nuclear strategy.

William Stafford is a senior lecturer in Politics at Huddersfield Polytechnic. His publications include articles on Godwin, Disraeli and eighteenth-century nationalism. His current research interest is British Socialist thought.

John Street is lecturer in Politics at the University of East Anglia. He has been a lecturer in Politics at Merton College, Oxford, and a Heyworth Research Fellow at Nuffield College, Oxford. His research interests include trade union attitudes to workers' control, politics and technology, and democratic theory.

George T. Sulzner is Professor of Political Science and Director of the Masters in Public Administration Program at the University of Massachusetts at Amherst. His publications include *Campaigning for the Massachusetts Senate: Electioneering Outside the Political Limelight, Perspectives on the Presidency: A Collection, The Impact of Labor-Management Relations Upon Selected Federal Personnel Policies and Practices,* and numerous articles about public sector labour relations and personnel administration in the United States. His current research interests include the implementation of civil service in the United States and the impact of governmental reorganization on public sector labour relations.

INDEX